SUFFRAGE
RECONSTRUCTED

SUFFRAGE RECONSTRUCTED

GENDER, RACE, AND VOTING RIGHTS IN THE CIVIL WAR ERA

LAURA E. FREE

CORNELL UNIVERSITY PRESS

Ithaca and London

First published 2015 by Cornell University Press
First paperback printing 2020

Library of Congress Cataloging-in-Publication Data

Free, Laura E., 1971– author.
   Suffrage reconstructed : gender, race, and voting rights in
the Civil War era / Laura E. Free.
   pages cm
   Includes bibliographical references and
   index. ISBN 978-0-8014-5086-0 (cloth)
   1. Women—Suffrage—United States—History—19th
century. 2. African Americans—Suffrage—History—19th
century. 3. Suffrage—United States—History—19th century.
4. Women's rights—United States—History—19th century.
5. United States. Constitution. 14th Amendment. 6. United
States—Politics and government—19th century. I. Title.
   JK1896.F74 2015
   324.6'2097309034—dc23   2015010883

ISBN 978-1-5017-4846-2 (pbk.)

For Arthur and Lucy

CONTENTS

SUFFRAGE
RECONSTRUCTED

Introduction
We, the People

The United States Constitution begins with an assumption of shared national identity, a recognition that government derives its power from those who consent to it, and a declaration of unity: "We, the people."[1] Since those words were written, however, exactly *which* people were allowed to have their political voices heard has been the central problem of American participatory government. From property restrictions to grandfather clauses, from poll taxes to identification requirements, Americans throughout the nation's history have continually grappled with determining the precise limits of the preamble's "we" and have struggled to define who ideally constituted the nation's political "people."

In 1787, when the Constitution was written, the only people believed to be capable of participating in the political system were property-owning men over the age of twenty-one.[2] Given this, and given the colonies' near-complete exclusion of poor men, women, African Americans, Native Americans, and other ethnic groups from most governmental processes, it is rather remarkable that the word "people" was used in the preamble at all.[3] One might reasonably expect the preamble to have stated instead that the Constitution was endorsed by "we, the wealthy adult white men of the United States," or even an easy shorthand for this group—"men." But it did not. In the preamble, as in the full text of the Constitution, there was no gender-specific language to refer to the population of the newly forged nation.

Accustomed as we are today to gender-neutral terms, this word choice may seem unremarkable. However, in 1789, the term "men" was, in proper context, commonly understood as a reference for "humanity" rather than exclusively its male portion.[4] Yet despite this common usage, the words "men" or "man" did not appear anywhere in the Constitution. In fact, the only gender-specific words in its text were a few male pronouns used to identify members of Congress and the president. Aside from these specific references, for the Constitution's first seventy-nine years, its language remained genderless.

In 1866, however, the gender neutrality of the Constitution was eliminated when congressional authors of the Fourteenth Amendment opted to use the term "male" three times in the amendment's second section.[5] It stated:

> Representatives shall be apportioned among the several States according to their respective numbers, counting the whole number of persons in each State, excluding Indians not taxed. But when the right to vote at any election of the choice of Electors for President and Vice-President of the United States, Representatives in Congress, the executive and judicial officers of a State, or the members of the Legislature thereof, is denied to any of the *male* inhabitants of such State, being twenty-one years of age and citizens of the United States, or in any way abridged, except for participation in rebellion, or other crime, the basis of representation therein shall be reduced in the proportion which the number of such *male* citizens shall bear to the whole number of *male* citizens twenty-one years of age in such state.[6]

By encouraging southern states to enfranchise black men, the Fourteenth Amendment's second section passively sought to expand the newly reforming nation's electorate. But there were distinct limits to this expansion. The amendment's language plainly indicated that women were not understood to be legitimate voters. It explicitly outlined in the nation's most fundamental political text its authors' assumptions about the connection between manhood and political privilege.[7] Thus, the Fourteenth Amendment declared that although women had the right to be counted as full persons for purposes of representation, they were to be deliberately excluded from "we," the political "people."

That gendered language was introduced to the United States Constitution with the ratification of the Fourteenth Amendment is well known to historians.[8] But well known does not necessarily mean well understood. To date, no historian has closely examined the political decision-making process that resulted in the use of gendered language in the Fourteenth Amendment or carefully explored how women's rights activists, those nineteenth-century Americans most attuned to the gender inequalities of the times, fought to oppose it.[9] This book seeks to remedy this oversight. I ask why, in 1866, the authors of the Fourteenth Amendment deemed it necessary to specify with explicit language that the ideal, normative voter was "male." The answer, I suggest, is found in the way Americans in the nineteenth century understood the connections between identity—specifically gender and race—and political action, and how that understanding adapted to the unique political circumstances of the post–Civil War Reconstruction.

From the nation's founding until the late eighteenth century, the question of who "the people" were was handled by the states, most of which determined that possession of property was the best indicator of a person's commitment to the democratic republic, of his or her stake in community, and of his or her ability to make responsible political decisions. But starting in 1790, states began to reassess the limits of the political community and redefine the qualities required by their voters.[10] One by one, they abandoned property as a measure of voting fitness and instead deemed race and gender to be the best identifiers of a legitimate political participant. In the process, most states disfranchised the women and African Americans who had been able to vote, albeit in low numbers, under earlier laws. By 1855, few states still required their voters to possess property. Most permitted all adult white men to vote—but only adult white men.

The creation of the "white man's government," as contemporaries called it, did not go uncontested by those it excluded. Northern African American activists and leaders organized, petitioned, campaigned, wrote letters, and held conventions to protest their disfranchisement. Starting in the 1840s, women's rights activists began to protest the laws that held women legally and socially subordinate and fully excluded them politically. They also engaged in letter writing, public speaking, petitioning, and convention organizing. For at least twenty years, the two activist groups challenged the political system that excluded them because of their identities. They had little success.

In the wake of the Civil War, however, Americans faced anew the question of how to define "we, the people." With half of the nation's states returned from open, violent revolt, and with four million formerly enslaved people's legal status suddenly transformed by the Thirteenth Amendment, redefining the polity's membership took on an urgency it had never had before. Emancipation called into question the antebellum laws, politics, cultures, and habits that had rendered African Americans either enslaved nonlegal persons in the South or free noncitizens in the North. It also raised vital legal questions that required a reassessment of the polity's boundaries. Two issues in particular required immediate congressional attention: the problem of African American citizenship and the issue of congressional representation.

In 1857, the United States Supreme Court, led by Andrew Jackson's appointee, Roger Taney, ruled in *Dred Scott v. Sanford* that African Americans in the United States were not citizens. Taney argued that the enslaved Missourian Dred Scott did not have a right to sue because African Americans had not formed a part of the original social compact of the Constitution. Therefore, Taney wrote, they could not share in the benefits of that Constitution, nor were they entitled to the basic rights of citizenship it guaranteed. With the *Dred Scott* ruling, the nation's highest court had declared black Americans to be permanent outsiders in their own country.[11]

However, emancipation after the Civil War made the *Dred Scott* decision untenable. Furthermore, changing postwar public opinion about the status of African Americans made it increasingly unpalatable. To overturn Taney's ruling and acknowledge African American citizenship, Congress passed the Civil Rights Act of 1866. It declared that all African Americans were citizens of the United States with the same civil rights and immunities as any other citizen: the rights to own property, to sue and testify in court, to make and enforce contracts, and to benefit from the equal protection of the laws.[12] It did not include the right to vote.[13] Nevertheless, conservative president Andrew Johnson vetoed the act, prompting Congress to incorporate its provisions into the first section of the Fourteenth Amendment.

The second major legal problem caused by emancipation was the issue of congressional representation. During the Constitutional Convention of 1789, southern and northern states had clashed over questions of both taxation and congressional representation, trying to determine whether or not the enslaved should be included in states' population totals as persons or exempted from them as property. The solution the convention delegates arrived at was the Constitution's infamous "Three-Fifths Compromise." It declared that for both taxation and representation, only three-fifths of the enslaved populations would be counted.[14] But the Thirteenth Amendment eliminated all enslaved populations in the United States, rendering the compromise null and void. This raised the very real possibility that when southern states returned to Congress, with the addition of four million newly freed people to their population totals, they could gain representatives. If they aligned with northern conservatives, the defeated Confederates could possibly even achieve a congressional majority. To prevent this, congressional Republicans needed to replace the three-fifths provision with an alternate model for apportioning representation.

For the Radical Republicans, who favored full and equal citizenship for African Americans and severe consequences for southern rebels, voting rights offered a tidy solution to the representation problem. If southern states returning from rebellion gained representation, they reasoned, letting the freed African American men vote would ensure that at least some of those new representatives would be Republican. As the party of Abraham Lincoln and emancipation, Republicans were fairly certain they would capture black voters' loyalties. But the Radicals were in a minority. Moreover, even they were unsure in 1865 and '66 that the national government should override the traditional bounds of federalism, which granted states the power to determine voter qualifications. Compromising all around, Moderates and Radicals arrived at the Fourteenth Amendment's second section—which did not tell states who to enfranchise but merely offered penalties, in the form of reduced representation, for those states that did not include all "male citizens" in their voting populations.

Whereas the Fourteenth Amendment's first section, as the foundation of all modern rights-based jurisprudence, has received intense scholarly and legal scrutiny, its second section has been mostly neglected. And perhaps rightly so. After the amendment's passage, the second section went no further. Its main purpose, to push the enfranchisement of African American men, was supplanted in 1869 by the Fifteenth Amendment, which prohibited states from restricting voters on the basis of race, color, or previous condition of servitude.[15] Consequently, the Fourteenth Amendment's second section was never enforced. However, in 1866 the authors of the amendment could not have anticipated that section's lackluster future; they spent far more time and energy on its language than they did on the language of the more enduring first section. More critically, the gender-specific language that they chose to define legitimate voters was unprecedented in American constitutional history.

Although the second section ultimately proved inconsequential, it was not without immediate consequences. For women's rights activists, in particular, its timing could not have been worse. Just as the amendment was being drafted, advocates of gender equality were moving into national politics for the first time, narrowing the movement's focus to prioritize the franchise. Throughout the winter of 1865–1866, women's rights advocates petitioned Congress for women's voting rights. But the amendment's authors were focused on protecting the emancipated and so saw little connection between black men's need for the ballot and women's demands.

Elizabeth Cady Stanton and Susan B. Anthony, two of the nation's most prominent women's rights activists, were especially disturbed by the amendment's gendered language.[16] Blaming their ostensible allies—Republicans and abolitionists—for this deliberate rejection of women's rights, they began to seek new political alliances and new constituencies.[17] In the process Stanton and Anthony began to make arguments for white women's enfranchisement that relied heavily on racist rhetoric, themes, and imagery. Particularly in their 1868 newspaper campaign against the Fifteenth Amendment, which implicitly permitted discriminating against voters on the basis of sex, the two activists wielded racist arguments based on the ugliest stereotypes their culture had to offer.[18]

The two central questions of this book—why the word "male" was used in the Fourteenth Amendment and why some key woman suffrage activists embraced racism as a political tool—inevitably lead to broader questions about race, gender, and American democracy. How did nineteenth-century Americans understand the limits of their political community, and how did they justify expanding or contracting it? Why did Americans at certain moments expand the franchise to include some people but not others? How did identity, particularly race and gender, become the central determinant of one's voting status in the antebellum period, and why was race then abandoned (however temporarily) as a marker of voting citizenship in the postwar period? Why, in the political, social, and cultural upheaval after the Civil War, were some outsiders' claims to the ballot understood as legitimate whereas others' were not? In other words, how and why did Americans reconstruct their suffrage?

To address these questions, I examine six decades of franchise-related debates that took place in public forums—in constitutional conventions, in state legislatures, in Congress, and in activists' public conventions and meetings. The public debate reveals much about what politically engaged Americans believed about their franchise and how they shared those beliefs with each other. Politicians' public statements were consciously and deliberately designed to resonate with particular constituencies and so reflected specific regional, religious, political, and partisan cultures.[19] Likewise, activists' public statements were carefully crafted to appeal to their audiences and to those politicians controlling access to the state. Thus public forums where the franchise's boundaries were discussed openly, debated passionately, and decided legally offer a fascinating window into the process by which ideas about democracy were transformed into real restrictions imposed on some American citizens.

Drawing on these public debates, in the first third of *Suffrage Reconstructed* I consider how Americans both defined and contested their democracy in the decades between the American Revolution and the Civil War. In chapter 1

I ask why, as states transitioned from property-based franchises to "universal" white male suffrage, African Americans and women who had previously voted under earlier laws were deemed unsafe voters. Examining key states' public legislative and constitutional convention debates in the decades before the Civil War, I argue that gender and race became rhetorical and ideological substitutes for property in antebellum suffrage expansions. But legislators and politicians were not working in isolation, nor did their actions go uncontested. In chapter 2 I consider the multiple ways that northern African Americans and women's rights activists opposed their own disfranchisement. I focus on how those groups sought access to the rights granted to white American men, aligned their claims for rights with mainstream political rhetoric, and re-imagined the legal relationship between gender, race, and suffrage.

In the next third of the book I explore how Congress, influenced by abolitionists, African American activists, and women's rights advocates, redefined antebellum suffrage restrictions in the postwar period. In chapter 3 I examine how congressional politicians envisioned the political community as a collection of male family members—fathers, sons, brothers—using gender to define postwar political actors. I argue that Republican congressmen used this familial metaphor to explain their right to alter the Constitution and justify expanding rights to the newly emancipated, claiming themselves as worthy sons of the founding fathers and black southern men as legitimate political brothers. In chapter 4 I investigate how congressmen recast black men as legitimate voting citizens only decades after they had been deemed too dangerous to permit safely into the polity. I argue that gender was the key to reconstructing black men's political identities and depicting them as proper voting citizens.

In the last third of the book I focus on the Fourteenth Amendment and the woman suffrage movement. In chapter 5 I offer a close reading of the legislative processes by which the word "male" became a part of the Fourteenth Amendment's text and argue that as the amendment's language evolved, congressmen deliberately added gender-specific language in order to prevent the inadvertent enfranchisement of women. In the book's final chapter I consider how Elizabeth Cady Stanton and Susan B. Anthony reacted to the failure of their congressional petition campaign. I argue that partisan politics, and the linguistic culture it created, constrained both the political choices and the political rhetoric of the postwar moment, making partisan racist speech seem like a viable strategic choice to these two activists.

In *Suffrage Reconstructed* I offer four key contributions to the history of voting rights in the United States. First, I show that from the early Republic through the antebellum period, Americans, through deliberate expansions and contractions of the franchise, situated gender and race as the primary foundation of suffrage rights. Second, I describe how that foundation shifted in the postwar period as some politicians and activists sought to limit suffrage exclusions to gender alone.[20] For advocates of women's enfranchisement, this effort proved extremely difficult to counter. Third, I demonstrate the significant impact that both African American activists and supporters of woman suffrage had on mainstream partisan politics during Reconstruction, despite their legal exclusion from the polity. Finally, I uncover the political rhetoric crafted by partisan elites and political outsiders in both ante- and postbellum America.[21] Tracing public suffrage rhetoric, I reveal Americans' evolving assumptions as they reconstructed their suffrage to define exactly who they meant by "we, the people."

CHAPTER 1

The White Man's Government

On August 18, 1818, Hartford, Connecticut's Democratic-Republican newspaper, the *Times,* published an opinion piece on "who shall possess and exercise the right of constituting the authorities of government" in Connecticut.[1] Its author, "Judd," hoped to persuade delegates to the state's upcoming constitutional convention to expand the state's franchise.[2] "For," he said, "wherever a considerable proportion of the people are deprived . . . of all political rights, the principle of democracy is destroyed." Yet, Judd acknowledged, some limits had to be placed on suffrage rights to protect society from "dangerous individuals."[3] For most of Connecticut's history, as well as that of the United States as a whole, those individuals deemed too dangerous to vote were those without property. However, by the time Judd wrote his article in 1818 this perception was starting to change. Increasingly, Americans like Judd were coming to view a property-based ballot as antiquated, antidemocratic, and fundamentally unjust.

But without property restrictions, how could potentially dangerous voters be excluded from the polity? Judd offered an answer: the franchise, he said, "ought . . . to depend *wholly upon personal considerations*" such as "age, residence, and character."[4] These qualities, he argued, were far better measures of a voter's fitness than anything as arbitrary as economic status. "It would be a juster rule than that of property," he said, "to adopt the principle of a man's height or complexion."[5] His sarcasm, however, failed to acknowledge that "complexion" in the early Republic was not a politically meaningless trait like height.[6] Rather, Judd profoundly misjudged both the degree to which his fellow Americans were coming to equate what he called complexion with character, and the extent to which they would over the next thirty-two years deliberately base the franchise on the arbitrary personal considerations of complexion and sex.

In 1818 Judd and his fellow Americans were engaging in an experiment with the limits of self-governance that was shaped by two conflicting political philosophies: the constrained republican ideology of the founders and the more expansive democratic impulse that developed in the nation's first few decades.[7] The founders had envisioned their government as a representative republic led by a learned, meritocratic elite elected to office by virtuous, propertied citizens.[8] Yet the American Revolution introduced a democratic logic that challenged elites' control of the state. Thus, almost as soon as the war ended, states began relaxing their suffrage provisions and eliminating property requirements for the ballot. By 1855, only three of the nation's thirty-one states retained any kind of property restriction on the franchise; only eight required a tax payment of any portion of their voters.[9]

Even as states rejected property restrictions, most Americans continued to retain the founders' faith that safe government depended on a limited franchise. Thus states had to find a new way to measure voters' stake in the community, their independence from external influence, and their capability for reasoned political action. Between 1790 and 1855, most states adopted a variation on Judd's "personal considerations" to serve as this measure.[10] In particular, two physical markers of identity—whiteness and manhood—became the political and legal shorthand connoting voters' autonomy, responsibility, and commitment to the state.[11] In 1790, only three of the fourteen states had identified their voters explicitly by race, only seven by gender.[12] By 1855, twenty-five of thirty-one states defined voters explicitly as white, and twenty-seven defined them explicitly as male.[13]

The parallel timing of these two changes in suffrage law was not coincidental.[14] As the historian Rosemarie Zagarri notes, in this period "universal male suffrage was increasingly defined against—and even predicated on—women's and blacks' exclusion from governance."[15] By deeming African Americans unsafe voters because of their race and women unsafe voters because of their gender, states were able for the first time to define all white men as safe voters, regardless of the extent of their possessions.[16] Grounding the franchise in gender and race rather than property had three important consequences. First, it enabled states to expand their voting populations significantly. In New York State alone between 1821 and 1846 the number of voters eligible to cast ballots tripled for the senate and doubled for the assembly.[17] Second, eliminating property as a measure of voting fitness disfranchised some wealthy women and African American men who had voted under the old rules. Third, eliminating black and female voters entrenched in both American law and political ideology a vision of the normative voter as white and as male.[18] Ante- and postbellum politicians would ultimately call this system "the white man's government."[19]

Tracking constitutional development between 1790 and 1850 shows how the white man's government was created. During this sixty-year period, almost every state held a constitutional convention either to draft new or revise existing constitutions.[20] In the process eight states simultaneously removed or altered their original property restrictions and added gender or racial restrictions, or both, to their suffrage provisions.[21] Suffrage-related debates in these eight states demonstrate exactly how whiteness and manhood came to mark political citizenship. First, between 1790 and 1825 in the earliest state conventions and legislatures defining suffrage rights, faith that property marked a good citizen waned. As it did, some politicians began to argue that acts of service to the state were what truly made people safe voters. They contended that the actions people took, whether through paying taxes, serving in the militia, or working on road crews, indicated both their stake in the community and their right to decide its leadership. Then, between 1825 and 1850 these service-based suffrage arguments began to be replaced by identity-based claims as delegates instead argued that all white men, simply by virtue of their being white men, were entitled to the franchise. They claimed that black men were automatically disqualified from unrestricted voting, regardless of what actions they took, simply because of their race.[22] Women, on the other hand, were so far removed from the polity by this time that they did not even warrant consideration as voters. Their exclusion, these delegates contended, was so natural and necessary as to be self-evident.[23] Ultimately, as property restrictions were eliminated for all white men in the early Republic, suffrage rights shifted from being grounded in what one had to being based on what one did to ultimately being tied to who one was.

Property Enfranchised and Disfranchised

At the start of the American experiment, governments were almost exclusively elected by those who possessed landed property. Property-based suffrage laws reflected both the colonial economic system, under which most colonists were subsistence farmers, and English and American legal traditions, which dictated that voters with property were those members of society most connected to the state.[24] Only property holders, colonial Americans believed, were independent enough to act politically without being unduly influenced by others; only they had "a will of their own."[25] By the time the thirteen colonies revolted against England, eleven required a voter to possess a quantity of personal or landed property in order to participate in local, state, and federal elections.[26]

Because property was considered the most relevant determinant of voting fitness, after the Revolution many Americans who were neither white nor male but who possessed sufficient property were able to cast ballots. Before the mid-1800s in Maryland, Massachusetts, New York, North Carolina, Pennsylvania, and Vermont, free African American men were "tacitly enfranchised."[27] However, local prejudice may also have served tacitly to *disfranchise* any African American who sought to vote.[28] Thus it is hard to know the extent to which free African Americans actively voted in these states, but given the amount of property required and the constrained economic position of many northern free blacks, it is likely that the number of black voters was fairly low. African Americans certainly cast ballots in areas of New York and in at least seven counties in Pennsylvania, evidence of which comes from sources occasionally blaming them for partisan losses.[29] In these cases, African American voters were probably convenient political scapegoats rather than a swelling tide overtaking the polls. Regardless of how many or few African Americans voted, it is important to note that at least some northern states acknowledged their right to do so.

Although women's voting was significantly less widespread, it was similarly permitted under the property-based franchise. In the colonial period some women voted locally in Massachusetts and New York, but after the Revolution only New Jersey permitted propertied women to vote.[30] The state's first constitution used distinctly gender-neutral terms outlining its suffrage provisions, declaring that "all inhabitants of this Colony, of full age, who are worth fifty pounds in proclamation money, clear estate in the same . . . shall be entitled to vote."[31] In 1790, the state's election law made it clear that the phrase "all inhabitants" really did mean *all* inhabitants. Explicitly acknowledging that women with sufficient property were voters, it declared:

> All free inhabitants of this state of full Age, and who are worth Fifty Pounds Proclamation Money clear Estate in the same, and have resided within the County in which they claim a Vote, for twelve Months immediately preceding the election, shall be entitled to vote for all public Officers . . . and no Person shall be entitled to vote in any other Township or Precinct, than that in which *he or she* doth actually reside at the Time of the Election.[32]

Whether it was the commitment to the principle of the propertied ballot, the logic of American revolutionary political theory, or parties' need for voters, until 1807 New Jersey's politicians actively supported women's enfranchisement, deeming wealthy single women sufficiently independent and capable.[33] Although it is difficult to know precisely how many of New Jersey's female citizens voted, enough did so that they drew complaints from defeated partisans. One Democratic-Republican newspaper estimated in 1802 that women "in some townships . . . made up almost a fourth of the total votes."[34] Although this number seems high, it is clear that some of the state's women were sufficiently politicized and politically engaged to routinely cast ballots in the early Republic.[35]

Despite these opportunities for women and African American men to vote, in the first few decades of America's independence the franchise remained fairly restricted. Alexander Keyssar estimates that by the Revolution the "proportion of adult white males who were eligible to vote was probably less than 60 percent."[36] During the early Republic, however, American ideas about the link between property and voting began to shift. Reflecting the war's rallying cry of "no taxation without representation," as well as the demands of the landless for the ballot, in the late 1700s some states expanded the franchise to taxpayers and to poor men who had served in the military.[37] But in the early nineteenth century, as America expanded and began to modernize and as many middle-class men moved away from land accumulation and toward commerce, industry, and professions, the link between property and the franchise weakened.[38]

First, economic, demographic, and political changes altered the meaning of land in the American imagination. In the first few decades of the nineteenth century, in the shift from subsistence agriculture to capitalist production, farmers increasingly began to rent land. Hence land ownership lost a degree of political significance.[39] At the same time, America's northern cities grew into commercial centers of industrial production and domestic economic exchange populated by growing numbers of American migrants and European immigrants—none of whom owned enough land to qualify for the franchise.[40] Cheap western land also disrupted the connection between property ownership and voting rights. In the fifty years after the Revolution, as European Americans displaced and decimated the West's Native American populations, they opened up wide swaths of land for settlement and speculative purchase. Speculation transformed the land that once had been a "source of independence and authority," Gordon Wood argues, into a "commodity to be exchanged . . . fluctuat[ing] and chang[ing] hands so frequently" that it offered "no basis for the right to vote."[41] Reflecting this sentiment, the new western states adopted suffrage laws that were more liberal than those of the older eastern states.[42] None of the fifteen states added to the Union after 1800 required voters to own property, and only four adopted a tax-based restriction to the franchise.[43]

Southern states were also in the process of rethinking the relationship of property to the ballot in the years after the Revolution. As northern states gradually eliminated slavery, it expanded in the South, becoming increasingly interpreted as essential to the southern way of life.[44] For slaveholders, therefore, enlisting propertyless southern whites in defense of slavery offered a powerful motivation for expanding the franchise.[45] Between 1790 and 1850, the five original slaveholding colonies dropped or reduced their property and/or taxation requirements to permit poorer whites to vote.[46]

At the same time that slavery was becoming more entrenched in the South, white Americans in all regions increasingly championed their own equality and independence.[47] In the first half of the nineteenth century, Americans, particularly northerners, celebrated their own perceived equality and social mobility, revering the "self-made man" as the paragon of autonomous, political manhood.[48] In light of these shifts, many Americans began to view independence not as an artifact of property possession but rather as a reflection of how successfully a man contracted his skills in exchange for wages. As the historian Eric Foner put it, "Every man had a property in his own labor."[49] If the most critical property men owned was their labor power, which alone identified them as autonomous individuals, it seemed excessively restrictive to identify either real estate holdings or personal wealth as the mark of an independent voter.[50]

But perhaps the most significant factor weakening the link between property and voting rights was the development of competitive partisan politics. Infrastructural improvements such as roads, bridges, canals, railroads, and eventually the telegraph all facilitated the rapid movement of political ideas in the early nineteenth century.[51] Further, a new sense of transparency in American political procedure also fostered the growth of popular politics; for the first time many legislatures began to offer gallery seating space for observers. Some states even mandated open legislative deliberations in their new constitutions.[52] These policies enabled newspapers between 1810 and 1830 to begin routinely carrying transcriptions of legislative debates.[53] When the policies were combined with improved printing and papermaking that led to the rise of the partisan press, Americans in the early nineteenth century had greater, and faster, access to information about their communities, states, nation, and world than ever before.[54] These changes increased Americans' interest in politics and encouraged their political engagement regardless of their economic status.[55]

This interest found an outlet in the emerging competitive partisan system that was organized around dual-party competition, relied on popular appeals, and cultivated individuals' ideological commitments to their preferred party.[56] Fostered by urban artisans' activism and organization, the popular politics of partisan competition was codified during the presidency of Andrew Jackson with the professionalization of the Democratic Party and the emergence of the opposition Whigs.[57] Both parties' appeals to the "egalitarian" public resulted in the development of an extraordinarily vibrant public political culture; backroom negotiations and influence wielding were replaced by democratic expressions of political fervor in the streets, taverns, and parade grounds.[58] Because this new politics of popular engagement was fundamentally incompatible with property restrictions, states began changing their suffrage laws. Of the thirty-one states present in the union, between 1790 and 1855 seventeen eliminated the possession of property as a qualification for voting.[59]

Although the parties needed voters to win elections, they were interested only in certain *kinds* of voters: those who were white and male. In the fifteen new states added after 1800 and before 1850, all but Maine and Texas used the word "white" to define voters.[60] By 1850, only in Maine, Massachusetts, New Hampshire, Rhode Island, Georgia, and Vermont could free African Americans vote without restriction.[61] Scientific racism, the general rise in hostility toward free African Americans, and increasing social marginalization of free black communities before the Civil War all fueled this trend.[62] Contemporary science and emerging political practice combined to disfranchise women as well. Though women had once been able to engage in politics by exerting personal influence, as politics shifted to distinctly gendered spaces such as taverns, women's political actions were interpreted as untimely, unwelcome intrusions from creatures whose biological roles precluded logical political thought and action.[63] State laws reflected this attitude. In 1807, New Jersey's legislature passed a restrictive suffrage law that essentially disfranchised any but white, adult male citizens who paid taxes.[64] And it was not alone. Every state added between 1800 and 1850 explicitly defined voters as "male" in their constitutions.[65]

Whereas the newer states entered the Union in the early nineteenth century with gender- and race-based franchises instead of property restrictions in their new constitutions, the oldest states had to adapt their existing suffrage provisions to the new politics. In the process, they also altered the language of their suffrage rules to specify a voter's race and gender.[66] Of the seventeen states that changed suffrage provisions between 1800 and 1850 to reduce or eliminate property restrictions, eight added a racial qualification, and six added a gender restriction. (See table 1.) The remaining nine states that did not add a racial requirement either included the word "white" in their original constitutions (Louisiana, Mississippi, Ohio, South Carolina, and Virginia) or were New England states with both small black populations and a tradition of liberality toward African Americans (Maine, New Hampshire, Rhode Island, and Massachusetts).[67] Regardless of their action on race, all states altering their constitutions in this period either added or retained a gender restriction.

As members of these eight state legislatures and constitutional conventions contemplated why the franchise should not be restricted by economic factors, they also discussed very explicitly why it should be restricted by race.[68] They did not, however, discuss why it should be restricted by gender. Apparently this fact was so obvious that it did not warrant debate. In New York, North Carolina, and Pennsylvania, constitutional convention debates about eliminating property in favor of race (and gender) were particularly interesting because each of these states either adopted or considered adopting a property qualification for African American male voters only while either reducing or eliminating one for white men.[69] Further, in each of these states,

Table 1   State Franchise Restrictions 1790–1840

States that altered property qualifications and race/gender provisions for voters	Year property qualifications first scaled back or eliminated or alternative offered in constitution (C) or statute (S)	Year racial qualification first altered in constitution (C) or statute (S)	Year gender qualification first altered in constitution (C) or statute (S)
PA	1790 (C)	1838 (C)	No change; gendered language ("freeman") already present
DE	1792 (C)	1792 (C)	1831
MD	1801 (S)	1801 (S)	1801
NJ	1807 (S)	1807 (S)	1807
CT	1817 (S) / 1818 (C)	1818 (C)	1817
NY	1821 (C)	1821 (C)	1821
TN	1834 (C)	1834 (C)	No change; gendered language ("man") already present
NC	1835 (C)	1835 (C)	1835

Sources: Benjamin P. Poore, *The Federal and State Constitutions, Colonial Charters, and Other Organic Laws of the United States*, 2 vols. (Washington, D.C.: U.S. Government Printing Office, 1878); Alexander Keyssar, *The Right to Vote: The Contested History of Democracy in the United States* (New York: Basic Books, 2000), app. A.1–15; Horst Dippel, ed., *Constitutions of the World from the Late 18th Century to the Middle of the 19th Century* (Munich: K.G. Saur Verlag GmbH, 2010).

reporters' accounts of convention debates were published to supplement the convention's journal of proceedings, indicating that the conventions' information was being disseminated to the public.[70] These debates clearly show the link being forged between voting, whiteness, and manhood.

Constitutional Conventions: From Property to Service

In early debates, when delegates to the states' constitutional revision conventions began to consider eliminating property qualifications, their central concern was that only qualified people be permitted to vote.[71] Supporters of property restrictions argued that enfranchising the propertied did exactly that, eliminating those dangerous persons who were both subject to undue influence and inherently incapable of making good political decisions. For example, in 1817 the Federalist "Mentor" argued in the *Connecticut Journal* that universal suffrage would enable "every beggar in the streets . . . to decide the most important political questions, and the most interesting Elections, by their worthless votes."[72] Yet even as early as 1818, the influence of Federalists with these views was waning as property requirements came increasingly under fire. By 1821, when New York's first constitutional convention took up the question, the lawyer and delegate John Cramer articulated the growing national sentiment, calling property restrictions "odious . . . aristocratical, [and] . . . worse than useless. . . ."[73] But states still needed to ensure that only the qualified continued to vote. To do so, many states adopted a middle ground between the expanded suffrage Mentor feared and the landed property provisions Cramer abhorred, replacing property with a taxation or military service requirement.[74] These provisions indicated that people's actions could entitle them to the franchise.

Taxation had an advantage as a means of regulating the franchise both because it was a simple measure of a voter's active support of the community and because it seemed to be sanctioned by the nation's founders, whose declaration of no taxation without representation was echoed in many suffrage debates. New Haven, Connecticut's Democratic *Columbian Register* argued in November of 1818 that requiring voters to pay taxes was grounded in "the doctrine that 'taxation and representation should go together'" and would prevent corrupt Federalist rivals from secretly smuggling into the polls "the very dregs of society,—men who never paid a tax or shouldered a musket in their lives."[75] In Pennsylvania's 1837 convention, the future congressman and Pennsylvania convention delegate Thaddeus Stevens likewise defended a taxation requirement as an important means of preventing those "victims of vice, intemperance, and folly" from casting ballots.[76] Aside from keeping the undesirable poor from voting, some delegates argued that tax payment was the best indication of a person's stake in the community. Stevens's fellow Pennsylvania delegate Andrew J. Cline argued that the state, like other collective "associations," should require any voting member to "divide . . . with his fellows the responsibility and the expense" should he desire to "exercise an equal influence with the rest."[77]

By turning to taxation as a measure of political commitment, delegates determined that it was what men did or did not do that qualified or disqualified them to vote. But was this action enough? If a poor white man without property could pay taxes to demonstrate his support for the polity, and hence his voting fitness, were other Americans who paid taxes, such as unmarried women and African American men, likewise entitled to the ballot? Some delegates, such as North Carolina's Weldon Edwards, argued yes. Edwards claimed that because North Carolina's bill of rights explicitly linked taxation and representation in its 1835 constitutional convention, "colored freemen equally with the whites" were entitled to vote. "It would appear wrong," he said, "while we continue to tax them, to deny them a vote for members of the Assembly."[78]

But Weldon was in a minority. Most convention delegates felt that tax payment was insufficient to transform African Americans into desirable voters. Even Judge Joseph Daniel, the author and advocate of a proposed property provision considered for black voters in 1835, claimed that North Carolina's "Bill of Rights did not apply to men of colour. . . . It embraced only free white men."[79] Many Democratic Pennsylvania convention delegates agreed with Daniel's principle two years later. But instead of denying the link between taxation and voting for black citizens, they claimed that black Pennsylvanians lacked any connection to the state, and thus no actions they could take would enable them safely to vote. For example, George W. Woodward, a delegate from Luzerne County, argued that African Americans in Pennsylvania were "exempted from the payment of such taxes as are assessed on the person," and therefore were likewise exempted "from the performance of those duties which attend the right of suffrage."[80] Not only were they not taxed, but, these delegates claimed, African American men did not engage in any kind of civic action. John Cummin of Juniata County queried, "If the negroes were citizens . . . were they ever permitted to come into your legislative halls? Were they ever permitted to enter a jury box? Were they ever allowed to hold any office, civil or military, in the commonwealth of Pennsylvania? . . . No. Sir . . . in no way did they ever enjoy equal privileges with white citizens."[81]

Claiming that the legal restrictions that prevented African Americans from fully participating in public life were evidence that they lacked a connection to the state seems like particularly faulty circular logic, but it was a strategy that many opponents of African Americans' enfranchisement adopted. For example, the North Carolina delegate Jesse Wilson noted that state courts would not accept the testimony of African American men against whites, even though a "white man may go to the house of a free black, mal-treat and abuse him, and commit any outrage upon his family." Why, therefore, should the state trust a free African American man "with the more important rights of a *freeman*—the high privilege of exercising the function of a voter?"[82] That free African Americans lacked both a legal voice within the court system and the right to protect their families from violence did not seem to disturb Wilson. According to these delegates, free African Americans could take no action that would demonstrate a connection to the state. As Hugh McQueen of Chatham County, North Carolina, declared in convention on June 13, 1835, "The white portion of the population of this country constitutes the proper depository of political power. They bled for it, they wrote for it, they spoke for it, they expended their treasure for it." Thus "there is no sort of polish which education or circumstance can give him, which ever will reconcile the whites to an extension of the right of suffrage to the free negro."[83]

Bleeding for the state was becoming increasingly central to how Americans defined legitimate voters in this period. After the War of 1812, poor veterans began to agitate for enfranchisement, asserting that their military service, and not their lack of property, entitled them to the ballot.[84] Opponents of any taxation requirements, most frequently Democrats in the 1830s, also adopted arguments like these to claim that military service, not taxation, forged the most powerful link between the individual and the state.[85] For example, the Pennsylvania delegate John Fuller claimed that poor soldiers had a greater right to the ballot than wealthy taxpayers: "The poor man alone was called to do military duty in time of war, while the rich man provided a substitute instead of going in person." While "the rich man . . . discharged his duty," Fuller "considered the mere payment of fines as very inferior in merit to personal service."[86]

If poor white men had proved their commitment to the state with their military service, could African American men show the same commitment? As with the question of taxation, opponents of a race-neutral franchise denied that this was a possibility. Primarily they argued that African Americans had never served in the military. For example, in New York's 1821 convention the former congressman Erastus Root argued that African American men should be disfranchised because they did not serve as soldiers: "In case of an invasion or insurrection, neither the alien nor black man is bound to defend your country. They are not called on, because it is supposed . . . they might desert the standard and join your enemy—they have not any anchorage in your country which the government is willing to trust." In view of this exclusion from military duty, Root declared that black men "cannot complain at being excluded from voting, inasmuch as they are not bound to assist in the defense of the country. It would be improper that they should . . . vote for the election of a commander in chief, whom they were not bound to obey."[87] Root's fellow delegate John Ross agreed. "But why," he said, "it will probably be asked, are blacks to be excluded? I answer because they are seldom, if ever, required to share in the common burthens or defense of the state."[88]

On the other hand, supporters of black men's continued enfranchisement in New York, North Carolina, and Pennsylvania pointed to many historical examples of African Americans' military service. For example, in New York in 1821 the Delaware County physician Robert Clarke argued that "in the war of the Revolution, [African Americans] helped to fight your battles by land and by sea. . . . In [the War of 1812] they contributed largely toward some of your most splendid victories." More significant, Clarke argued, was the fact that this service was entirely voluntary and in defense of a nation that treated them poorly. In North Carolina's 1835 convention, the Halifax judge Joseph Daniel also noted that during the Revolutionary War, "a number of free persons of color rendered effectual service in the ranks of the army."[89] This service, if supplemented with a property provision, Daniel argued, legitimized free African Americans' right to participate in the states' governance. The Pennsylvania delegate William Darlington of Chester County turned to the former president and Democratic party hero Andrew Jackson to support black men's claim of service to the state. Jackson's proclamation of September 1, 1814, addressed to the "free coloured inhabitants of Louisiana," identified free black soldiers as "noble-hearted freemen," "sons of freedom" who would receive bounties equal to those of "the white soldiers of the United States" for their voluntary participation in the Battle of New Orleans.[90] Darlington's fellow Pennsylvanian James Montgomery was more direct: "I do not know of a single instance, where the blacks have been called upon to perform military duty, where they have refused to do it. . . . It strikes me that it would be a poor way to pay them for fighting the battles of their country, to deprive them of their votes."[91]

Faced with incontrovertible evidence of African American men's satisfactory military service, opponents of their voting rights were then forced to argue that military service did *not* mean one had a legitimate stake in the state.

For example, in North Carolina in 1835, the convention delegate James W. Bryan of Carteret County, although conceding that free African Americans had fought during the Revolution, noted that "this argument would apply with equal force and pertinency to our slaves, many of whom . . . 'did the State great and important services,' in that trying and momentous period, and fought manfully and bravely in the embattled ranks of our Revolutionary armies."[92] Yet no North Carolinian was willing to enfranchise the enslaved. Further, Bryan claimed, the meaning of black men's military service was significantly "diminished" after the Revolution when Congress prohibited free African Americans from serving in the militia. This exclusion, he insisted, was tantamount to a public declaration that African Americans did not constitute part of the body politic. Like Bryan, the Pennsylvania delegate E. W. Sturdevant of Luzerne County also noted legal restrictions on black men's military service. Since Pennsylvania's 1790 constitution required that the "freemen" of the commonwealth "shall be armed and disciplined for its defense," but its militia laws prevented "negroes . . . from doing militia duty," then black men were not full members of the polity. Otherwise, "why exclude them if they are *freemen*?"[93] The North Carolina convention president Nathaniel Macon articulated this point more concisely: "[Black men] have been employed to fight, but were never made citizens—they made no part of the political family."[94] If contesting the meaning of African American men's service was too oblique, simple denial was also an option, as the Pennsylvania delegate John Sterigere demonstrated: "No Pennsylvania negro," he said, "periled his life or shed his blood to acquire the glorious privileges secured by the Revolutionary War."[95]

Although paying taxes and serving in the military were ways for some men to demonstrate their commitment to the state, these were not politically meaningful choices available to women. In the early conventions, women were simply not considered persons who could, with their actions, demonstrate their commitment to the state and thereby their legitimacy as voters. In New York in 1821 and North Carolina in 1835, women were hardly even mentioned in convention debates.[96] When their connection to the state was raised, it was usually to defend a constrained franchise. For example, in New York's 1821 convention, the lawyer and Columbia County delegate Elisha Williams argued that suffrage was not universally given to all people in any political community, particularly those "who are helpless and dependent," and incapable of "expressing their wills independently and intelligently."[97] This arrangement, Williams argued, was natural because "all are entitled to civil and religious liberty . . . yet they have not all a voice in choosing their rulers; many female, as well as many a legal infant, is in possession of large estates, but they cannot vote."[98] As a defender of the link between property and the franchise, Williams used property-owning women as a rhetorical foil to demonstrate that neither land ownership nor membership in the state directly conveyed political rights.

Discussions about taxpaying women's legal disfranchisement was more prevalent in later conventions, particularly after the 1820s when delegates started to use women's status as a way to oppose enfranchising African American men. To reject the idea that tax payment conferred a right to the ballot, opponents of black men's voting rights noted that although white women also paid taxes, by common consent they did not vote. For example, the Philadelphian John McCahen asked if "taxation and representation . . . should go together," then what about white women? Did not "the white women of this commonwealth . . . pay taxes on their real estate, and on the food they ate?" In light of this, McCahen challenged his rivals to declare "whether [they] did not think it good and sound policy, too, that although these women and minors pay taxes, they should be excluded from participating in the right of suffrage?"[99]

Opponents of enfranchising black men also used women to refute the link between military service and the state, noting that despite many women's military sacrifices for the state, they remained disfranchised. In New York's 1821 convention delegate Williams opposed removing the property restriction in favor of a service requirement because, he argued, if such a connection existed, then the widowed mother of a dead soldier would be entitled to vote on the basis of both her own sacrifice and her son's military service.[100] Pennsylvania delegate McCahen contended in 1838 that if Pennsylvanians continued to allow African American men to vote because of their military service, then "would [delegates] not be equally justified in asking this convention to confer the same right upon the white women of this commonwealth? . . . We read in history of [women's] heroism . . . in the field, in dressing the wounds of the gallant soldier, or soothing him in his dying moments. Surely this class of our population, were as much entitled to vote as the negroes!" Moreover, McCahen claimed that white women had a greater sense of patriotism, and hence a deeper emotional connection to the state: "What has the negro cared in time of war, whose arms were victorious? His feelings were dead to every joy in the success of the American arms." Women, on the other hand, had prayed "by day and by night . . . that the God of battles would guide our countrymen unto victory." White women's demonstrated commitment to the state rendered them "as well qualified to exercise the right of suffrage as the . . . negro."[101]

Although these delegates argued that the logic of a franchise based on either military or fiscal service to the state could be applied to women as easily as to African American men, women's enfranchisement was not an outcome they sought. Despite his tribute to white women's patriotism, McCahen dismissed their enfranchisement in a sentence: "We, perhaps, ought to give the right of suffrage to every human being, but then, the interest and happiness of the whole people, required [that it] should not be thus given."[102] But what alternative was there? If property was no longer an acceptable model and a service-based franchise opened up complicated questions about whether or not the service of such problematic potential voters as women and African American men counted, then delegates needed to find a different foundation for voting rights. By 1838, as the Pennsylvania delegates were critiquing the service-based franchise, they were already offering an alternative—one based on racial and gender distinctions. As the Philadelphia delegate Charles Brown argued, "We have to look to the colored race, as one marked by God and nature as distinct from that to which we belong. We do not degrade them by acting on this distinction. Did it degrade the females, when the state of New Jersey took from the ladies the right to vote? . . . It is in obedience to the natural order of things, that we make a division between distinct species of men."[103] After 1838, Brown's suggestion that biological distinctions between people serve as a guide for making political distinctions between potential voters would come to dominate convention discourse and, ultimately, suffrage law.[104]

Constitutional Conventions: From Service to Identity

In New York, North Carolina, and Pennsylvania convention delegates who argued that race and gender, rather than service or property, determined voting fitness had a particular problem: in their states African American men already *were* enfranchised and had been so for decades—if they had enough property. Therefore, anti-black suffrage delegates had to explain exactly why black men should be disfranchised. While some delegates did this by arguing that African American men could not take the proper actions to indicate a connection to the state, others claimed that black men's actions—as voters— endangered the state. For example, in North Carolina's 1835 convention, delegate McQueen claimed that if a "foreign power from abroad" were to invade North Carolina, free blacks would "as soon take sides with that power as with the citizens of this State," presumably because they would fare better under a different regime.[105] This threat seemed fairly distant, but the prospect that free African Americans would make bad political decisions (or perhaps bad partisan decisions) seemed fairly likely to some delegates.[106] McQueen's Carteret County colleague, James Bryan, claimed that black men's voting behavior during county elections was sufficient evidence of their inability to handle the franchise:

> Their excitement and interest never extend beyond the temporary gratification of the enjoyments of the muster ground and election, and their patriotism is limited to the little selfish feeling of self-importance, which these occasions give them, together with the sycophancy which the demagogue evinces to them, in the shape of spirituous liquors and congratulations for the welfare of his wife and children![107]

If free African Americans were so easily manipulated at election time in a section of the state where illegal local practice prevented them from actually voting, what damage could these men do, Bryan asked, if given the right to vote without restriction in the whole state? "Long experience, expediency, and good policy," he declared, "have convinced all our southern sister States, that they are dangerous and useless citizens."[108]

Southerners seeking to align their voting laws with the imperatives of slavery were not alone in arguing that African American men's actions would harm the state. In 1837–38, some conservative Pennsylvania delegates also expressed concern that black voters would spell certain doom for democracy. If black men were permitted to vote en masse, these delegates contended, there would be two troubling consequences: a race-neutral franchise would attract hordes of free blacks to Pennsylvania, and whites would react violently. Delegates were particularly worried about potential social unrest, perhaps thinking of Pennsylvania's recent race riots.[109] Charles Brown of Philadelphia County declared that

> we ought not to do anything that was calculated to endanger [African Americans'] safety. In [his] district . . . the coloured population amounted to between three and four thousand, and he entertained not the slightest doubt that the signal for them to attend and give their votes would be the signal for their destruction. Yes! In twenty-four hours from the time that an attempt should be made by the blacks to vote, not a negro house in the city or county would be left standing.[110]

Whereas Brown's interest seemed to be for the safety of Philadelphia's African American population, other delegates were more worried about white Pennsylvanians. The Crawford County delegate George Shellito contended that if Pennsylvania were to "give these negroes the right of suffrage . . . they will overthrow the government. . . . The time will come," he said, "when every white, except the abolitionists, will be compelled to shoulder his musket, in order to defend his wife and children from the ruffian assaults and violence of the blacks." A race-neutral franchise was not a step in the creation of equality for peoples of the state, he argued, but a dangerous inversion of the currently accepted social hierarchy: "The moment that the right of suffrage was conferred on the black man, that moment would he raise his head above the white, and . . . shed his blood [when] the first favorable opportunity should occur."[111] The scene of rioting black voters that Shellito imagined seemed more consistent with southerners' fear of slave uprisings than with northerners' experiences with race-based violence directed at African Americans. But connection to and concern for the South dominated many Pennsylvania Democratic delegates' approach to the suffrage question in the 1830s.[112] Conservative delegates particularly argued that the Union's safety, as well as that of Pennsylvania's citizens, depended on black men's disfranchisement.[113]

Even as some delegates were arguing that black men either did not take the right actions to justify their enfranchisement or would act dangerously when enfranchised, other delegates actively supported their right to access the ballot.[114] They argued that denying African American men the ballot was unjust and undemocratic. They bypassed the question of African American men's actions by rejecting the idea that voting rights were defined by either property or behavior. Instead, they capitalized on the emerging claim that only men's identity as men determined their voting rights. For example, the Pennsylvania delegate James Clarke argued on June 19, "The time has come when the tax qualification should be dispensed with, for a man should vote because he is a man."[115] Like Clarke, the Philadelphia county abolitionist delegate Thomas Earle claimed that manhood was sufficient to measure anyone's voting fitness: "A man should be entitled to vote because he is a man; and, as such, interested in all that concerns the community in which he resides, and the laws under which he lives."[116] Supporters of African Americans' voting rights applied this principle fully to black men. For example, Pennsylvania's John Montgomery declared that he was "utterly opposed to a skin qualification for voters, as I am fully persuaded that it is oppressive, as well as unjust."[117] Walter Forward of Allegheny County, agreed, declaring, "I will not, by word or action of mine, here or elsewhere, exclude a man from the exercise of the right of suffrage, simply upon the ground that he has a dark complexion."[118]

Similar arguments were made in 1846 by New York convention delegates, who, after twenty-five years of property restrictions for African Americans, revisited the link between action, identity, and voting. The Delaware County representative Isaac Burr declared that the suffrage committee's proposal to include the word "white" in New York's constitution was "a retrograde movement" against the national trend of suffrage expansion. Burr argued that "the standing committee . . . intended, it seems, that the color of a man's skin should be the test of his fitness to approach the ballot-box. [I dissent] from this altogether." His colleague, the Madison County representative Benjamin Bruce, agreed, declaring that "Sir, distinction in the exercise of the elective franchise, on account of color or complexion, is invidious and anti-republican."[119] Burr's fellow Delaware County delegate, David Waterbury, also found race-based suffrage preposterous: "The argument that because a race of men are marked by a peculiarity of color and crooked hair, they were not endowed with a mind equal to another class who had other peculiarities, was unworthy of men of sense."[120] The Onondaga delegate Elijah Rhodes agreed, regretting that anyone "should advocate the deprivation of rights, simply on the ground of a difference in the complexion of the skin, or the curl of the hair."[121] A franchise grounded in something so arbitrarily contingent as the physical markers of racial identity, these delegates argued, was simply and fundamentally unjust. For, as Bruce declared, "If 'colored persons' are *men* then give them the rights and privileges of *men*."[122]

Yet for opponents of African American suffrage rights, the racial identity of black voters, or rather the socially perceived meaning attributed to race, was precisely the problem. In the next few decades, blatantly racist claims for restricting African Americans' rights became increasingly prevalent in suffrage discussions. In the few days that New York's 1846 convention debated suffrage, only a handful of delegates referenced voters' service to the state or their connection to the community. Instead, most relied on racial prejudice to reject removing property restrictions for black voters. These delegates argued that the simple fact of black men's race indicated that they were not universally legitimate voters. For example, the Onondaga County delegate Dr. William Taylor declared that "color constituted a physical characteristic which distinguished a class of persons who for many reasons were not supposed to be well qualified for the exercise of this right [of suffrage]."[123] The New York City delegate John A. Kennedy referenced the science of the time to support the restriction. Because "physiologists" had determined that the "Caucasian" and "Ethiopian" races had the "fewest points of resemblance," the distinction between two kinds of people "was the work of nature, and was not without its object. Let not government dare to counteract and overthrow the distinctions and divisions that nature designed should exist."[124]

At the heart of these delegates' arguments was the belief in the immutability of racial distinctions and their faith that voting rights should rely on this foundation. Although any person might serve the state, pay taxes, own property, be in the military, and hence gain political rights, no person, they believed, could change his or her racial (or gendered) nature. Hence, the polity would be protected because political rights would be forever out of reach of those who lacked the "correct" political identity. The New York City delegate John Hunt articulated these ideas more explicitly than any other member of the convention. Like Kennedy, Hunt also claimed that racial differences disqualified black men from voting, but he contended that the nature of race itself meant that this disfranchisement was impossible to change. African American men, he argued, "were aliens—aliens, not by mere accident of foreign birth—not because they spoke a different language—not from any petty distinction that a few years association might obliterate, but by the broad distinction of race—a distinction that neither education, nor intercourse, nor time could remove—a distinction that must separate our children from their children forever."[125] No actions African Americans could take, Hunt claimed, would transform them into voters: "We might close our eyes in a fit of amiable enthusiasm," he said, "and try to dream their wool out of curl; but our dreams did them no good. They knew and felt all the while, (that is all sane negroes,) that they were negroes and aliens by the act of God, and there was no remedy." Hunt had no doubt that race alone accounted for black men's unequal disfranchisement: "If any good could come of wishing, he could wish as heartily as anyone, that the Ethiopian might change his skin, and become a part of our body politic." But, he supposed, "all such wishes and all efforts to realize them were idle."[126]

Regulating Suffrage, Making Race

For delegates like Kennedy and Hunt, the distinctions of race and gender seemed an essential way to determine voting fitness. Racial and gender identities, as these delegates understood them, were immutable, permanent, and obvious, and already served as a readily patrolled boundary between persons.[127] But not all delegates to the conventions believed race to be so simple. In particular in the northern conventions in New York in 1821 and 1846 and in Pennsylvania in 1838, some supporters of black men's voting rights argued that racial distinctions were neither as easy to identify nor as readily regulated as their opponents seemed to think.[128] Instead, these delegates wrestled with what race meant, exactly how it was defined, and how to determine the racial identity of any individual voter.

Convention delegates were particularly worried about how to identify an individual's racial status to decide whether he was a legitimate voter. In New

York's 1821 convention, supporters of equal suffrage wondered who would decide the limits of each racial category if New York decided to divide its voters racially. And how, exactly, would they decide? For example, the delegate Robert Clarke declared that any racial distinction was "impracticable in its operation," for even among those "who have never been slaves, there are many shades of difference in complexion." Color, Clarke argued, was so widely variable, that using race as a means of determining voting rights was inherently subject to abuse: "Men descended from African ancestors, but who have been pretty well white-washed by their commingling with your white population, may escape your scrutiny" and vote without restriction.[129] A more frightening prospect for Clarke, however, was that reverse discrimination could occur: "Others, whose blood is as pure from any African taint as any member of this Convention, may be called upon to prove his pedigree, or forfeit his right of suffrage, because he happens to have a swarthy complexion."[130] The Pennsylvania delegate John Dickey of Beaver County echoed this argument a few years later, as he worried about who, exactly, would determine a voter's racial identity. Should that decision be "left to the arbitrary decision of the inspectors and assessors[?] [Dickey] imagined not. It might happen that a man might be excluded from the exercise of this right, because he did not happen to have as fair a skin as the inspectors and assessors required at his hands, although his ancestors might have had more pure white blood in their veins than these men."[131] And again, the potential for abuse was high: "What chance would a white man, but of dark complexion, have at the polls," Dickey asked, "in a time of great political and party excitement?"[132]

Although Dickey and Clarke were not particularly enlightened advocates of racial equality, they did seem to grasp that there was a vital link between the definition of the franchise and the creation of race. If, they argued, one could not tell the difference between white and black, and if the political system depends upon that difference, then how could the political system be safely regulated? More troubling for them, how could race even exist? And, the New York delegate David Buel wondered in 1821, what would that mean for whites? "In the West Indies," he noted, "a man became white according to law, when only one sixteenth part of African blood ran in his veins." If New York began asking "these questions," Buel said, it "might lead to unpleasant elucidations of family history, and ought to be avoided."[133] In a state that still counted the enslaved among its occupants in 1821, this concern with the limits and meaning of whiteness was not merely hypothetical. In Pennsylvania seventeen years later, John Dickey offered a solution. Although noting that if the word "white" were introduced into the state's constitution it would "lead to . . . difficulties," Dickey suggested that, as in North

Carolina, in Pennsylvania "it would be necessary to set forth the exact construction that must be given to the term, so that no doubt could arise as to the true meaning of it."[134] These delegates were essentially arguing that race was contingent, not static, and therefore it was difficult, without legal management, to define it with any degree of certainty.[135] Determining the social meanings of "black" and "white" was not a project easily undertaken at the ballot box on election day.

Some delegates emphasized the difficulty of making racial distinctions by pointing to Americans who did not fit easily into a white/black taxonomy. If a racial qualification were enacted, should these "others" be treated as white or as black? The New York delegate James Kent of Albany noted this potential problem in 1821: "What shall [be] the criterion in deciding upon the different shades of colour? The Hindoo and Chinese are called yellow— the Indian *red!* Shall these be excluded should they come to reside among us?" Kent "thought it inexpedient to erect a barrier that should exclude them forever from the enjoyment of this important right."[136] His colleague David Buel seemed to agree, claiming that "philosophers have distinguished the human race by five colours, the white, black, brown, olive, and red. By [including the word "white" in the franchise provisions,] four of the races would be excluded."[137] If different voting standards for African Americans and whites were implemented, the convention opened up questions about ethnic and racial others that New York did not have ready answers for. For example, where in the body was race situated? Was it in the skin? The blood? Or externally in the actions and prejudices of others? If race, and hence political ability, were merely a matter of skin *tone*, the Pennsylvania delegate James Montgomery of Mercer County argued, then white women would be qualified to vote. "If we are to make a white skin the qualification of a voter, then females will have a permanent right to vote, as we have only to open our eyes and look at females to be convinced that their skins are much finer and fairer than men's."[138]

Like the attendees of the previous two northern conventions, some delegates in New York's 1846 convention were also concerned about the meaning of race. In their short debate, the delegate Isaac Burr, arguing that race was a faulty standard for determining voting rights, eloquently summarized the problems of defining a voter's race. He said that implementing a race-based franchise was "beset with difficulties. He did not see how a board of inspectors could, in all cases, determine who were 'white male citizens.'" Burr acknowledged that readily identifiable "Anglo Saxon" and "full-blooded African" men would be permitted or denied the right to cast a ballot with no problems. But, he said, "suppose the next man who offered his vote should be a free native born citizen, whose father was a white man and his mother a black woman, and possessing all other qualifications of a voter; was not he entitled to vote?" Burr acknowledged that this individual would likely be identified as a person of color and therefore also rejected. But, he asked, how far did the principle apply? What about a person who "had but one-sixteenth of African blood"? What about those who "had skins as fair as many who never had any taint of the African"? Or even more problematic, what of someone who by "common fame" within the community was believed to be black, but "denied it. . . . Should the inspectors themselves be permitted to determine the question on the spot? If so, he feared that some-times the color of a man's political coat may be taken into consideration as well as the color of his skin." Getting to the heart of the definitions of race, Burr was asking his fellow delegates what exactly they meant by people of color and how they thought such a people should be identified.[139] Whether partisan or race politics dominated these scenarios, Burr was clearly con-cerned that race was by no means a simple rule easily applied. Rather, he seems to have been grappling with the social and constructed nature of race, both acknowledging that its meanings shifted between communities and recognizing that what defined black and white was either arbitrary law or equally arbitrary social practice. Indeed, his arguments suggest that he was at least in some measure concerned that the legal actions the convention took to make racial distinctions were, in some way, actually making race as well.

Opponents of African Americans' voting rights in the conventions also recognized that race-based suffrage laws were responsible for making racial meaning, and thus they sought to defend the boundaries of whiteness. In particular, conservative delegates argued that racial intermingling at the polls would result in racial intermingling in other spheres of life, which, they con-tended, would "degrade" whiteness. In New York in 1821, Colonel Young declared that a race-neutral franchise would be abhorrent to whites: "No white man will stand shoulder to shoulder with a negro in the train band or jury-room. He will not invite him to a seat at his table, nor in his pew in the church. And yet he must be placed on a footing of equality in the right of voting, and on no other occasion whatever, either civil or social."[140] Other delegates echoed the claim that political mixing would result in other modes of racial mixing. Admitting blacks and whites to the franchise equally, Eras-tus Root declared in 1821, "will disturb our political family."[141] In 1838, the Philadelphia delegate John Scott concurred, declaring that he did "not wish the coloured man to come into our political family."[142] Delegates' depiction of African Americans as members of the political family raised a scenario in which whites and blacks would interact socially, perhaps within a biological family, not just a metaphoric one. Whether it was the virtual mixing of the races in political and social interactions that the delegates feared or the questions that could arise from literal intermingling of the races in sexual interactions, they viewed black men's equal enfranchisement as a challenge to racial distinctions.

Delegates concerned with protecting and patrolling whiteness made no effort to disguise that power lay at the heart of their concerns. The Pennsylvania conservative John Sterigere claimed in 1837 that whites' political power would be diminished by a race-neutral franchise because an "effect of admitting negroes to vote, will be to keep respectable citizens . . . from the elections. Such persons will not go to the polls and jostle with negroes. You will then have, as substitutes for such persons, a posse of shoeblacks."[143] Although it seems unlikely that Sterigere truly feared that whites would surrender their political power rather than submit to political integration, he did seek to arouse other delegates' fear of sharing power. In 1846, the New York delegate John Russell articulated this fear most explicitly, claiming that whites "want no co-partners to share with their elections . . . who comes fresh from an inferior race of men."[144] At the heart of conservatives' fears of race mixing lay just this: the idea that any integration or social interaction between the races would invert current racial hierarchies and deprive white men of their traditionally held power over others. As the Pennsylvania delegate George Shellito argued, "Give these negroes the right of suffrage, and your sons and your daughters will, by and by, become waiters and cooks for them. Yes! For these black gentry—that will be the result of it."[145] Delegates like Shellito patently ignored the fact that propertied African American men had been voting in Pennsylvania and New York for decades without causing such transformations in social hierarchies. This perhaps did not matter as much as their fear that racial boundaries would be transgressed if political rights were defined without reference to race. Grounding voting rights in the fertile ground of racial identity, these delegates contended, was the best way to keep the nation, and whites' political power, safe.

Over the course of the antebellum period Americans such as these convention delegates gradually defined race and participatory citizenship as mutually dependent—so much so that any change to one threatened the other. In earlier decades, when suffrage rights were dependent upon the acquisition of property, they were presumably accessible by anyone able to acquire enough property to meet the requirements. This system was, in theory, fluid—the boundaries of the body politic expanded or contracted given the number of people who qualified to vote. But over the course of the first half of the nineteenth century, as ideas about the meanings of property ownership changed and more people gained access to the ballot, Americans shifted their means of determining the franchise and turned to service as a better marker of voting fitness. This too was a fluid system, for men at least. Ostensibly, if a disfranchised man desired the ballot, he could serve the state in numerous ways to indicate his commitment to the political community and hence acquire the ballot. But even this came to be seen by many antebellum Americans as a restrictive system: taxpaying provisions echoed too directly the idea that economic status conveyed voting privileges. To substitute for property and service, delegates to constitutional conventions like the ones held in New York, North Carolina, and Pennsylvania turned to gender and race to mark voters. To white men making decisions to expand their franchises, permitting all white men to vote seemed to be a move toward greater national equality. Further, identifying voters by their gender and race offered a means of limiting the political community that was seemingly more stable, as these social categories were ostensibly unchanging; individuals could not alter their gender or racial status to acquire the ballot.

However, as the delegates themselves revealed in convention debates, race, at least, was truly not a stable category that was defined the same way everywhere and by all people. But in the process of eliminating or restricting black voters from the polity, these delegates created and emphasized racial distance, defining suffrage by race, and race and gender through suffrage. By exchanging gender and racial position for property as indicators of political independence and hence as makers of legitimate status as political actors, white men created a white male polity across class, ethnic, sectarian, regional, and partisan divides. Through this polity, they forged a collective white male identity that alleviated and diffused tensions among white men that had the potential to threaten the peace and safety of the nation state.[146] This imagined fraternity, what the literary critic Dana Nelson calls "national manhood," tied all white men to each other and to the state through their gender and race.[147] Disfranchising African Americans and women made the national white male voting fraternity possible. But it also fixed in state law and national imagination a connection between Judd's personal considerations—whiteness and manhood—and voting rights, a connection that would persist in the American polity through the end of the Civil War. This connection, which forged the white man's government, would face numerous challenges in the ensuing decades.

CHAPTER 2

Manhood and Citizenship

On Tuesday August 18, 1840, 140 men gathered in Albany for New York's first statewide political convention of African Americans. The geographically diverse delegates, a "large majority" of whom were young men, assembled to "devise means and deliberately to act . . . that we may remove that proscriptive clause in our State Constitution" requiring black men to possess $250 worth of property to vote. On the convention's first day, the delegates declared that New York's complexion-based property clause violated the principles of equality laid out by the founding fathers, deprived black New Yorkers of the rights of citizenship, ignored their service to the state as soldiers, and "unwarrantably [withheld] rights inherent to us as men."[1] After three days of debate, the convention issued two public statements, one addressed to "their colored fellow citizens" that called upon readers to "redeem" themselves through "united, vigorous, and judicious and manly effort" to gain the franchise.[2] In the other statement, addressed to "the people of the state," delegates argued that their "claim [to the ballot rested] upon the possession of those common and yet exalted faculties of manhood." Black men required the ballot, they declared, because "WE ARE MEN."[3]

Six years later, six upstate New York women also gathered to protest the white man's government. But they did so by asking the 1846 constitutional convention to enfranchise women. Their petition, one of four similar appeals presented to the constitutional convention, requested that the delegates "extend to women equal, and civil and political rights with men."[4] The petitioners based their claim to the ballot on three central tenets of the American political tradition: first, that "all governments must derive their just powers from the consent of the governed"; second, that it was unjust to "impos[e] upon [women] the burdens of taxation . . . without admitting them to the right of representation"; and finally, that "as citizens of the state of New York [women] may reasonably and rightfully claim" this right. The "present government," the petitioners argued, "has widely departed from the true democratic principles upon which all governments must be based" by depriving women of rights that were "originally inherited" yet now "ungenerously . . . withheld."[5]

These public statements reflect the two primary ways that northern free African Americans and women's rights activists protested their disfranchisement in the antebellum white man's government: with gender and traditional American political rhetoric.[6] The advocates of free African Americans' political rights initially asserted in conventions and petitions that American democratic ideals and black men's actions, particularly their military service, entitled them to membership in the American political community. But as the movement evolved, activists argued more and more that black men's gender identity *as men* alone legitimated their political rights. Particularly in wake of the Civil War, both black and white activists claimed that military service transformed black men into men in the eyes of all Americans, and it was as men that they required the ballot.[7] For black men seeking the ballot, gender-based suffrage rhetoric was a readily available, politically relevant, and particularly potent tool for empowerment.[8] If, as advocates of the white man's government insisted, manhood was essential for political rights, then in the postwar period African American men appropriated that manhood and its accompanying political privileges for themselves.[9] As Frederick Douglass declared in 1864, "We . . . claim our rights as men among men."[10]

When women began to hold conventions in 1848, they necessarily adopted a different rhetorical approach for protesting their political exclusion. Unable to rely on manhood to stake their claim to political rights, women's rights activists protested their disfranchisement by turning to democratic principles and rhetoric. The quintessential example is the "Declaration of Sentiments," the founding text of the first formal women's rights convention in Seneca Falls, New York, in 1848.[11] Adopting both the format and the language of the Declaration of Independence, the Declaration of Sentiments did not so much directly challenge the white man's government as simply refuse to accept the premise of a gender-based state, declaring that "we hold these truths to be self-evident: that all men and women are created equal."[12] But women's rights activists also used gender to declare women's equality, relying on ideas about gender, morality, and motherhood rather than manhood to claim political rights.

For a time, particularly in the 1840s, activists seeking African Americans' and women's rights worked, if not necessarily together, certainly in mutual recognition of the political oppression that both groups shared. But in the wake of the Thirteenth Amendment's passage, both the black convention and the antislavery movements transitioned away from the goal of emancipation, focusing instead on enfranchisement. Some women's rights activists, convinced of the logic of seeking suffrage for all adult citizens, expected abolitionists and African American rights' activists to support voting rights for all men and women. Instead they were told that women's rights were inopportune because, as Wendell Phillips said in his address to the thirty-second annual meeting of the American Anti-Slavery Society, "This hour belongs to the negro."[13] But merging the two equal rights movements would not simply have burdened black men's postwar cause with an unpopular radical rider. More than that, woman suffrage fundamentally challenged the association between manhood and the franchise.

African Americans' Conventions

Drawing on a long heritage of organized black resistance, in the antebellum period northern African Americans engaged in varied forms of public political action to protest their disfranchisement.[14] Some community organizations sent petitions and memorials to legislatures and constitutional conventions, particularly in the later decades of the antebellum period. For example, of three petitions sent to New York's 1821 constitutional convention, one requested a provision to prevent the legislature from passing discriminatory legislation. In 1846, of sixty-some petitions sent to the convention, at least two requested the equal enfranchisement of African Americans. Pennsylvania's 1837–38 convention likewise received suffrage petitions and memorials from African Americans.[15]

Although petitions were essential means of protest, conventions were the most visible public actions free blacks took in the antebellum period.[16] In local, state, and national meetings activists protested the American Colonization Society's (ACS) plan to forcibly "return" free African Americans to Africa; advocated education, moral reform, and temperance as effective means of self-improvement and community uplift; considered voluntary emigration to Canada; agitated against slavery; and claimed equal civil and political rights for African Americans.[17] Led by some of the most prominent northern African American activists—James Forten, Rev. Richard Allen, Junius C. Morel, James Pennington, and Benjamin Paschal—conventions offered a forum for black activists separate from, although generally allied with, the abolition movement. At a point when some white abolitionists supported the ACS or demonstrated a racist perspective that neglected northern black communities' needs, this separate forum provided African American activists an essential "base for social protest."[18] Between 1830 and 1835, six consecutive national meetings were held in Philadelphia and New York. By 1836, however, the convention movement had split on issues of strategy. New Yorkers and Pennsylvanians and older and younger activists disagreed primarily about connections to white organizations and the efficacy of moral reform.[19]

In part because of these disagreements, between 1836 and 1843 no national conventions were held. But African Americans in New York, Pennsylvania, Indiana, and Michigan held five statewide conventions, where younger activists such as Robert Purvis, Frederick Douglass, Charles L. Remond, and Henry Highland Garnett moved into leadership positions.[20] These leaders helped reenergize the national convention movement in 1843, holding twelve annual meetings before the Civil War. These conventions shifted their focus from improving the black community to changing African Americans' legal and social status.[21] This reflected alterations in national political culture: by 1840 tensions around slavery and race in the United States were increasing, and black voters had been disfranchised in most states. In response, delegates to black conventions became more radicalized, demanding immediate emancipation and political and legal rights for African Americans.

Delegates to the state and national conventions held in the 1830s and 1840s spent a significant portion of their time making recommendations for improving northern African Americans' social condition in hopes that social "elevation" would lead whites to view them as legitimate political actors. The conventions pointed to three key modes by which northern free blacks could become elevated: temperance, education, and occupational improvement. By regulating what they did in northern society, delegates to these conventions argued, African Americans could advance socially and claim political rights. For example, at the first national convention in Philadelphia in 1830, the African Methodist Episcopal senior bishop and convention organizer Richard Allen declared to the "Free People of these United States" that "we have been led to the following conclusions: that our forlorn and deplorable situation earnestly and loudly demand [sic.] of us to devise and pursue all legal means for the speedy elevation of ourselves and brethren to the scale and standing of men."[22]

Many conventions in the 1830s contended that temperance was a key means of this elevation to manhood. For example, at the second national convention in Philadelphia in 1831, the committee on the "condition of the free people of colour of the United States" reported that *"Education, Temperance,* and *Economy,* are best calculated to promote the elevation of mankind to a proper rank and standing among men, as they enable him to discharge all those duties enjoined on him by his Creator."[23] The delegates to the 1843 Michigan state convention argued that it would "promote . . . Education, Temperance, Industry, and Morality among our people; and by our correct, upright and manly stand in the defense of our liberties, prove to our oppressors, and the world, that we are determined to be free."[24]

Although temperance was one thing that activists claimed northern African Americans could do to gain equality, most antebellum conventions argued that the surest path to equality was education.[25] For example, New York's 1851 convention members contended that although education was important for African Americans' own enlightenment and rights, it could also enable black northerners to uplift all of humanity: "In order that the general welfare of the *colored* people be improved . . . it's all important that they become educated; without education we cannot hope to be emancipated from . . . the cruel and malicious system of prejudice and caste. By education . . . all members of the great human family shall have accorded to them their full and complete rank . . . regardless of any outward circumstances as denote birth or country."[26] With education, particularly in schools "where manhood is acknowledged as an equal inheritance," African Americans could achieve their political goals.[27] For as Illinois convention delegates declared in 1856, *"knowledge* is *power."*[28]

But knowledge and education would not be enough, convention delegates recognized, if African Americans did not achieve economic independence. Echoing the Jeffersonian-era romanticization of the yeoman farmer, the delegates in the 1840s conventions viewed the acquisition and cultivation of landed property as the best way for African Americans to become autonomous freemen. At the national convention in Troy, New York, in 1847, the committee on agriculture argued that farming was the best way that a man could achieve the respect of others. For, it claimed, "the farmer is an *independent man.* . . . He may do without what men of trade and traffic have to dispose of . . . but they cannot do without what he produces. . . . Without him, they have neither house, home, food, nor clothing.[29] To African Americans defined by their white northern neighbors as powerless dependents, the idea not only of being free from reliance on others but of being relied on was plainly appealing. Agricultural independence, the delegates to the convention

in Philadelphia in 1841 argued, also offered a means for battling racial prejudice, which, they contended in their address, resulted from whites' distaste
for blacks' urban dependence: "By settling in the country, and becoming
independent farmers, we would escape almost entirely that prejudice which
operates so injuriously against us in the cities. . . . A full suit of black is universally considered the most rich and magnificent that can possibly be worn.
Hence prejudice is not against *color*, but against *condition*; therefore improve
the condition, and you destroy the prejudice."[30]

Throughout all the conventions in this period, northern African American activists argued that they were entitled to equality not only because they
pledged to abandon alcohol, pursue education, or become productive farmers, but because they had already taken action that reflected their citizenship.
They argued that African Americans both belonged to and had served the
state as founders, as taxpayers, and most critically, as members of the military.
At New York's earliest black state convention in 1840, the delegates claimed
membership in the northern political community because *"We are the descen-*
dants of some of the earliest settlers of the State. . . . Our fathers were among those,
who, with sinewy frame and muscular arm, went forth to humble that wil-
derness in its native pride. Since that time, our fathers, and we ourselves, have
lent our best strength in cultivating the soil, in developing its vast resources,
and contributing to its wealth and importance."[31] The delegates also claimed
they had served the state by protecting it during the American Revolution
and the War of 1812.

> When the whole country . . . arose as one man, for the maintenance
> of the natural and unprescriptable rights; the dark browed man stood
> side by side with his fairer fellow citizen, with firm determination and
> indomitable spirit. . . . Their blood is mingled with the soil of every
> battle field, made glorious by revolutionary resistance; and their bones
> have enriched the most productive lands of the country. In the late war
> of 1812, our people were again called upon to defend their country.
> The splendid naval achievements on Lakes Erie and Champlain, were
> owing mostly to the skill and prowess of colored men.[32]

By ignoring this service and requiring black voters to own property, the
delegates argued, New York's state constitution made black men "aliens and
strangers . . . a disfranchised class in the very land where lie the bones of our
fathers—the land whose liberties they helped achieve by patriotic services
and whose soil is enriched by their purest and noblest blood."[33] Other state
and national conventions also noted black men's military service as a justification for their enfranchisement. Like black New Yorkers in 1840, the delegates

to Michigan's convention in 1843 highlighted service in the American Revolution and the War of 1812: "During the Revolution, the white and black
soldiers fought and messed together without hesitation. The records of that
period clearly prove that the blacks rushed forth to the conflict, and poured
out their blood with as much bravery as their white fellow soldiers." Black
soldiers, they argued, "under the command of General Jackson in the Southern Army, and especially at the battle of New Orleans, distinguished themselves as valiant soldiers, fighting in defense of their country's honor."[34] Black
men's defense of the nation-state, the delegates claimed, entitled them to the
rights and blessings of citizenship.

The American Revolution pointed to another way that black men served
the state: financially. Convention delegates such as those in Cleveland in 1848
often referenced the rallying cry of the Revolution: "we firmly believe with
the Fathers of '76 that 'taxation and representation ought to go together.'"
Therefore, the Cleveland delegates argued, "we are very much in doubt as to
the propriety of our paying any tax upon which representation is based, until
we are permitted to be represented."[35] This idea was echoed in later conventions as well. The address written at the 1853 Rochester national convention
also suggested that the financial service African Americans had offered the
state justified their enfranchisement: "We ask that (in as much as we are, in
common with other American citizens, supporters of the State, subject to its
laws, interested in its welfare, eligible to be called upon to defend it in time
of war, contributors to its wealth in time of peace) the complete and unrestricted right of suffrage, which is essential to the dignity even of the white
man, be extended to the Free Colored man also."[36] Black men served the
state and paid its taxes; therefore, they were entitled to all the rights of men.

But over the course of the 1840s and '50s, states increasingly based suffrage rights on who a citizen *was* rather than on what he *did*. African American convention delegates adapted their arguments accordingly. For example,
the 1848 Pennsylvania convention's "Appeal to the Colored Citizens of
Pennsylvania" urged activists to abandon moral and social uplift because it
did not matter what actions black men took since it was not their "impiety,
. . . ignorance, . . . immorality, or [their] wicked customs and habits that
place[d them] without the pale of constitutional landmarks." It was instead,
their "*complexion alone.*"[37] The "Appeal" continued:

If we could by a single "feat" of nature change our complexion, every
objection to our full exercise of constitutional privileges would be ban-
ished before tomorrow's sun. We must therefore hope that our friends
will cease to place any faith in the doctrine, that our religious, literary,

and moral improvement will be the means of enfranchising us. . . . The people of Pennsylvania, in their conventional capacity, did not set up such a test on which to base the rights of elective franchise. To have carried out such a principle would have disfranchised a portion of the whites, while it would have clothed thousands of our people with those very privileges of which they are now denied.[38]

Unlike earlier convention delegates who denied that color had political meaning, these authors recognized that white Americans' ideas about race alone accounted for the political oppression of African Americans. Black men's actions mattered far less than their identities, and only by improving the "white man's heart" and not the "black man's mind" could suffrage rights be achieved and political manhood restored to African American men.[39]

As the conventions' suffrage language evolved in the late 1840s, the delegates increasingly adopted arguments that either combined calls for virtuous action with arguments based on identity or rejected the notion that any actions African Americans could take, aside from political agitation, would lead to enfranchisement. With this change, the delegates started to focus more on gender. Conventions in the 1830s had used gendered language occasionally—the 1830 and 1831 national conventions adopted the term "freemen" to identify the possessors of rights—but these early conventions typically used this gendered language to refer to all people.[40] For example, the 1832 "Address to the Free Colored Inhabitants of these United States" used the term "manhood," but only to refer to the black community's growth: "How beautiful must the prospect be of the philanthropist, to view us, the children of persecution, grown to manhood, associating . . . to devise plans and means for our moral elevation."[41] Here "manhood" connoted maturity, or adulthood. Moreover, as a rule, these early conventions also used more neutral terms when discussing rights, referring to the rights of "people" and "citizens" rather than "men."

But by the later 1840s and '50s, the African Americans that activists depicted in conventions as having served the state as soldiers and taxpayers, those fathers whose "sinewy frame" and "muscular arms" helped "penetrate" the virginal forests of New York and whose "bravery," "honor," and "valor" served the fledgling new nation to fight the British in the Revolution and in the War of 1812, were all clearly imagined as men. The default agriculturalist who would pursue independence through professional development, and hence equality through personal uplift, was likewise envisioned by the convention delegates as male. In addition to making these implicit assumptions, when activists at the state and national conventions discussed voting rights explicitly, they conformed to nineteenth-century social practice and identified suffrage as an exclusive right of men. For example, in the 1845 "Address to the People of New York" delegates argued that "when you have taken away an individual's right to vote . . . when a distinct class of the community . . . are wholly and forever disfranchised and excluded . . . they have lost . . . their panoply of manhood."[42] Pennsylvania's 1848 state convention delegates wrote to their fellow disfranchised African Americans that the state's "constitution, by disfranchising us, while it claims to be republican, has stricken a blow at our manhood, and not only ours, but a majority of those who people this globe. We intend suing for our rights as *men.*"[43] The address urged black Pennsylvanians to "be careful to present a manly bearing by the exercise of politeness and good manners" in order to appear as reliable voters to whites. But more affirmatively, it urged its readers to "reject every attempt to dethrone the dignity of our manhood so long as the spirits of freedom runs [*sic*] in our veins."[44]

Black men's convention delegates often characterized their own actions in gendered terms, identifying as manly the work to pursue their rights. New York's first state convention in 1840 addressed its fellow "colored citizens" and urged them to "put forth our own exertions" and to "redeem" themselves through "manly effort."[45] Whereas they contended that the only way rights would be achieved was if the whole black community, young and old, men and women, worked together, the primary message conveyed was gendered: "We invoke the entire people, in their strength and manliness, to put forth intelligent, and well directed effort in this matter."[46] The delegates to Illinois's first state convention in 1853 declared that though they had long endured the oppression whites imposed on African Americans, "we have now resolved to come forward; and, like *men, speak* and *act* for ourselves."[47] Social protest was defined by delegates as a way for African American men to claim their own political manhood. When that status was finally recognized by whites, the abolitionist orator Charles Remond argued at the 1858 Massachusetts convention, "a more manly set of men than we are cannot be found."[48] Defining their own political actions as gendered allowed African American activists to claim an identity that carried with it political privilege in the antebellum white man's government.

Every Woman's Rights

African American activists' claim to the ballot as a gendered political right left little room for women. However, African American women were dedicated and active partners in the antebellum work of "racial uplift."[49] Although many black women engaged in behind-the-scenes activist work through churches and sex-segregated ladies' auxiliary organizations, others—such as the abolitionists Margaretta and Charlotte Forten, Sarah M. Douglass, Maria Stewart, Frances Ellen Watkins Harper, and Sojourner Truth—helped to bring the question of women's rights to the fore of racial justice organizations.[50] They were aided by many individual black male activists, including Robert Purvis, Charles Langston, William Howard Day, Martin Delaney, and Frederick Douglass, who all actively pursued women's rights. Moreover, in the 1830s and '40s, women were often present as observers at African Americans' national and state conventions.[51] A few women were also permitted to address the early conventions. In 1848, the National Convention of Colored Freedmen voted to admit women as delegates and included women's rights in their activist agendas.[52] Women also formed both a core constituency and an activist cohort in antebellum abolition organizations, as well as serving as effective fundraisers.[53] William Lloyd Garrison and his followers in the mostly white-led abolition organization, the American Anti-Slavery Society, advocated for women's equal participation and leadership in the society in the 1840s, and subsequently some women were admitted as delegates to its conventions and as full members of the organization.[54]

Despite significant overlap in constituency and personnel and the inclusion of some women in reform organizations, women's equality was not welcomed by all activists. In 1840 the American Anti-Slavery Society split in part because of disagreements among the members about women's role in the movement.[55] But the historian Bruce Dorsey argues that this schism was not precisely about women but was more about how abolitionists defined manhood in relation to their own public political life. For those white reformers who left the society, such as the brothers Lewis and Arthur Tappan, women's leadership in the abolition movement threatened their understanding of their own manhood and challenged men's exclusive access to the power of the ballot.[56] Some antebellum African American rights activists also rejected women's rights as they declared their own manhood. To many northern black activists it felt essential to claim for themselves the distinctions between men and women that white society denied to the enslaved and failed to recognize among the free.[57] Although women were often welcome at black men's conventions—such as the ladies who had "arranged, in an adjoining hall, a table loaded with the most palatable refreshments" at New York's 1858 Troy convention—increasingly women's claims for equality were not.[58] Three years earlier, the Troy delegates had struck "the name of Miss Barbary Anna Stewart . . . from the roll" because "several gentleman object[ed] to it on the ground that this is not a Woman's Rights Convention."[59] By the late 1850s, as sectional and racial tensions flared, women's rights, as the historian Martha Jones argues, "were put out of the realm of black politics."[60]

Over the course of the 1850s, increasingly confined by the communities and movements that had brought them to activism—whether abolition, African American rights, partisan politics, temperance, radical Quakerism, legal reform, or protests against Indian removal—women's rights advocates developed their own movement for equality.[61] As was the case for African American activists, conventions formed the core of the early women's movement. After the first local meeting in Seneca Falls in 1848, there were numerous other local and state women's rights meetings, as well as ten annual national conventions, held in various northern cities between 1850 and 1860.[62] These conventions grappled with a wide range of issues that the delegates felt reinforced gender-based oppression, from divorce to education to dress reform. The convention delegates sought ways for women to empower themselves and seek autonomy. Alongside calls for open education, equal wages, and married women's property rights, the convention delegates routinely objected to women's disfranchisement. But voting rights were not central to the antebellum women's rights movement; women's enfranchisement was an idea so radical that many felt that pursuing it could damage the broader cause of women's equality. As they were organizing the Seneca Falls convention, the Quaker abolitionist Lucretia Mott told Elizabeth Cady Stanton that asking for the ballot would make their nascent movement seem "ridiculous." Stanton's abolitionist husband, Henry, agreed and refused to attend the convention because he felt the call for suffrage would "turn the proceedings into a farce."[63] Stanton persisted, but at the convention itself although most delegates willingly conceded that women's disfranchisement was a fundamental cause of their legal and social inequality, many felt that claiming the ballot would be too scandalous.[64] Only when Frederick Douglass spoke in its favor did the convention narrowly agree to include the ballot in the list of women's demands.[65] Despite the controversy, within the next few years some women's rights groups began to pursue enfranchisement actively. In the 1840s and '50s, activists organized major petition drives for suffrage in Indiana, Massachusetts, New York, Ohio, and Vermont. Ohio's activists sent eight thousand signatures to the 1850 state constitutional convention requesting that the delegates remove the word "male" from the constitution's suffrage provision. Other petitions were sent to state legislatures. None of these efforts were particularly successful; Ohio's convention voted seventy-two to two to keep the word "male."[66]

Despite these setbacks, the delegates to almost every antebellum national women's rights convention raised the issue of the ballot. But unlike the activists at African Americans' conventions, women's rights advocates could not fully appropriate current mainstream suffrage rhetoric to make their claims.

Consequently, their speeches did not echo the service- and manhood-based political arguments being made in state constitutional revision and African American conventions.[67] Instead, some delegates, particularly in the earlier years, argued that qualities attributed to women's gender identity—their morality and their "civilizing" natures—would be beneficial to both politics and the state. More frequently, though, delegates appealed to gender-neutral principles of equality consistent with the American political tradition.

This rhetoric served a few critical purposes: it included women in the national political heritage and adapted the malleable democratic political constructs of the framers for women's purposes. Further, it facilitated alliances with other reformers because claims of universal equality were more likely to resonate with abolitionists and African American activists than were claims derived specifically from women's identities, particularly given how controversial the "woman question" was in reforming circles.[68] In addition, because political connections to abolitionists and African American activists were essential to the development of the antebellum women's movement, creating rhetorical space for all disfranchised Americans in women's rights arguments was an important strategic choice, even if it had limited success in the pre–Civil War years.[69]

Like the delegates to African American conventions, the women's rights convention delegates argued that women's actions were essential for their own empowerment. Women must claim the ballot, they asserted, directly through political engagement or indirectly through employment and education. For example, in her 1850 presidential address to the first national women's rights convention, Paulina Wright Davis said that "equality before the law, and the right of the governed to choose their governors are [benefits] . . . enjoyed exclusively by the sex that in the battlefield and the public forum has wrenched them from the old time tyrannies. They are yet denied to Woman, because she has not yet *so* asserted or won them for herself."[70] At the following year's national meeting, the renowned orator Lucy Stone also suggested that women's actions could result in their empowerment, if not enfranchisement. "I want every one of you to feel that this work rests upon us," she said. "Instead of asking, 'give us this, or give us that,' let us just get up and take it." Her audience responded with "loud cheers."[71] These women, while certainly seeking to energize their activist community, were also articulating a theory of rights acquisition that was consistent with that of other activists and politicians in the period. Just as the constitutional convention delegates and African American activists had argued for an expanded franchise based on the actions of the disfranchised, so too did women's rights activists. As the call for the third national convention in Syracuse in 1852 said,

"Let woman no longer supinely endure the evils she may escape, but with her own right hand carve out for herself a higher, nobler destiny than has heretofore been hers."[72]

Although women's actions might result in their empowerment, antebellum women's rights activists knew they had to address contemporary arguments that defined women as unsafe and inappropriate voters. To do so, the convention speakers argued primarily that the fundamental principles of the American democracy entitled female citizens to vote. By adopting this argument, they connected women to the broader political community and insisted that the category "citizen" was gender-neutral. For example, in her 1850 address to the Worcester convention, Davis argued that among the many ways to ask for the ballot, women "could plead our common humanity, and claim an equal justice. We might say that the natural right of self-government is so clearly due to every human being alike, that it needs no argument to prove it."[73] Her fellow convention delegate, Mrs. Abby H. Price, of Hopedale, Massachusetts, made a similar argument, claiming that men and women

> are absolutely equal in their rights to *life, liberty* and the *pursuit of happiness*—in their rights to *do*, and *to be, individually* and *socially*, all they are capable of. . . . These are every *man's* rights, of whatever race or nation, ability or situation, in life. These are equally every *woman's rights,* whatever her comparative *capabilities* may be—whatever her relations may be. These are human rights, equally inherent in male and female. To repress them in *any* degree is in the same degree usurpation, tyranny, and oppression. We hold these to be self-evident truths, and shall not now discuss them.[74]

Price's adoption of the language of the Declaration of Independence was surely no accident. And it was echoed throughout the conventions. Wendell Phillips's 1851 speech offered a resolution explicitly quoting the Declaration's fundamental principle that all men are created equal but yet critiquing Americans for their heretofore biased interpretation of the term "men": "We charge that man with gross dishonesty or ignorance who shall contend that 'men,' in the memorable document from which we quote, does not stand for the human race; that 'life, liberty, and the pursuit of happiness' are the 'inalienable rights' of *half* only of the human species."[75] The following year Ernestine Rose, a Polish-Jewish immigrant and one of the staunchest antebellum advocates of women's enfranchisement, echoed this language, arguing,

> It is in accordance with the principles of republicanism that, as woman has to pay taxes to maintain government, she has a right to participate

in the formation and administration of it. That as she is amenable to the laws of her country, she is entitled to a voice in their enactment, and to all the protective advantages they can bestow; and as she is as liable as man to all the vicissitudes of life, she ought to enjoy the same social rights and privileges. And any difference, therefore, in political, civil and social rights, on account of sex, is in direct violation of the principles of justice and humanity.[76]

The traditional American political principle that delegates relied on most to contend for women's enfranchisement was the link between taxation and representation. Like African American activists and advocates of universal white male suffrage, delegates to the antebellum women's rights conventions pointed out the fundamental injustice of denying any taxpayer the right to elect her representatives. This argument was particularly wielded at the 1852 third national convention in Syracuse, after the convention's business committee reported a resolution declaring "the right of every woman holding property, and as a citizen also of this Republic, to resist taxation, till such time as she is fully represented at the Ballot Box."[77] Lucy Stone defended this resolution fervently. "Resist," she said, "let the case be tried in the courts; be your own lawyers; base your cause on the admitted, self-evident truth, that 'taxation and representation are inseparable.' . . . We want, that our men friends, who are so justly proud of their 'Declaration of Independence,' should make their practice consistent with it."[78] Even Elizabeth Cady Stanton, at home in Seneca Falls pregnant with her fourth son, sent a letter for Susan B. Anthony to read in support of the resolution.[79] Stanton urged women to have courage and act to defend this principle:

> Shall we fear to suffer for the maintenance of the same glorious principles, for which our fore-fathers fought, and bled, and died. Shall we deny the faith of the old revolutionary heroes, and purchase for ourselves a false peace, and ignoble ease, by declaring in action, that taxation without representation is just! . . . Let us suffer our property to be seized and sold—but let us never pay another tax, until our existence as citizens, our civil and political rights, be fully recognized.[80]

This push for women to protest taxation never gained much ground, most likely because in 1851 only three states permitted married women to own property: New York, Pennsylvania, and Wisconsin.[81] But regardless of how effective tax protest was as a plan of action, linking taxation and the ballot for women was a useful and frequently adopted rhetorical strategy. In contending that women paid taxes to the state and hence required a say in the selection of their representation, delegates laid claim to women's service to the state. Although they did not adopt the service argument as explicitly as did constitutional convention delegates and African American activists, the claim that women served the state as taxpayers let activists make an explicit connection between women's public service and their political rights. For example, the Ohio delegate J. Elizabeth Jones declared in her 1852 speech to the Syracuse convention that she "wanted what the men were most unwilling to grant—the right to vote. . . . This we claim on the ground of humanity; and on the ground that taxation and representation go together."[82]

But this was not the only way women's rights activists addressed the link between service and suffrage. Recognizing that state lawmakers in the 1820s had justified expanding the ballot on the basis of poor white men's military service, women's rights activists could not ignore this variation of American democratic theory. Opponents of women's enfranchisement claimed that because women did not perform military service, they should not vote. Some women's rights activists rebutted this argument by countering that some women *did* serve in the military. For example, in his 1852 letter to the Syracuse convention, John Neal of Portland, Maine, addressed this issue. "What are the duties," he asked, "which a woman, admitted to all the rights of citizenship, would not be able to discharge?" Some might suggest that "'she could not enter the militia.' I deny this; for women are found in all the armies of the earth—shamefully disguised, to be sure, and acting as men; not only in the ranks, but as leaders."[83] But Neal did not stop there. He also dissociated military service from the ballot, arguing that because not all men served in the military, there was an imperfect correlation between martial commitment and political rights. "The aged, the wealthy, the learned, and the weak and sickly, among men, are all excused from serving in the militia," he noted, "and, if not within certain ages, and *able bodied*, they are not even required to furnish a substitute. If men may escape themselves, why not exempt women, for correspondent reasons?"[84]

Military service was not the only way women acted as citizens. Many convention delegates argued that republican motherhood already linked women to the state.[85] The "heaviest burthens of citizenship," Neal noted, women "already bear. Being the mothers of all who claim to be citizens, from the mightiest to the lowliest."[86] Other convention speakers argued that women's domestic duties were also patriotic service essential to the America democracy. At the 1851 national convention, Clarina Howard Nichols contended that motherhood was the primary ground for women's claim to equality.[87] "As a mother I may speak to you, freemen, *fathers*, of the rights of my sons. . . . It is in behalf of our sons, the future men of the Republic, as well as for our daughters, its future mothers that we claim the full development of our energies by education and legal protection in the control of all the issues and profits of ourselves, called *property*."[88] As for suffrage, Nichols claimed that these sons of good mothers would share their power, and so she "looked forward" to offering "greater admiration [to] sons who, in the good time coming, will have won for themselves the unappropriated glory of having given justice to the physically weak."[89] Good republican sons, raised by empowered and equal republican mothers, these delegates asserted, would grant equality to women and align the nation's government with its unfulfilled democratic ideology.

Although motherhood was valuable to the state, some convention delegates argued that women's greater duty to the nation was to bring women's special morality to the unruly world of nineteenth-century American politics.[90] Unable to claim that manhood entitled women to the ballot, these delegates argued instead that the particular morality attributed to women would bring domestic order and ethical values to politics. This reflected one of antebellum women's rights advocates' central theories—that by separating men's and women's activities and responsibilities, Americans had created an imbalance in human affairs that could be remedied only by women's equality. For example, in her letter to the 1852 Syracuse convention, Elizabeth Cady Stanton argued that America's "isolation of the sexes, in all departments, in the business and pleasure of life, is an evil greatly to be deplored."[91] Ernestine Rose put it best in 1852, arguing that "'the benefit of society,' calls for woman's 'purifying influence'. . . . Let woman then be with him wherever duty calls her, and she will soon cleanse the Legislative Halls."[92]

Womanhood may not have had the political clout that manhood had in American political rhetoric, but it nonetheless offered women's rights advocates a way to give women's unique gendered social roles political value and to protest the white man's government. Delegates to women's conventions understood clearly that state constitutional conventions had deliberately chosen to exclude women from politics. In the 1852 Syracuse convention, Paulina Wright Davis argued that the purpose of gender-based language in state constitutions was to create a male polity: "When the Rhode Island Convention to alter the Constitution, was sitting, in the draft they said, 'all citizens'; but they discovered afterwards that the word male, was not inserted, and they immediately put it in, intending of course, to exclude women."[93] Despite activists' resolve to ensure that "the word 'male' . . . be stricken from every State Constitution," they were not successful in any state before the Civil War.[94] After 1860, they stopped trying; women's rights activists ceased annual conventions to devote their collective energies to the antislavery cause. This, and the all-consuming and more urgent nature of civil war, pushed the cause of women's equality from national consciousness, if not from the minds and hearts of women's rights activists.

Our Rights as Men

Although the Civil War put an obstacle in the path toward women's political equality, it offered new opportunities for African American men. In addition to ending slavery and bringing African American rights to the forefront of the national political agenda, the war enabled a new generation of African Americans to serve the state. The Union's initial reluctance to arm black men only heightened the significance of their service when the federal government finally overturned the 1792 Militia Act and enlisted African Americans in 1862–63.[95] This enlistment forged a new connection between African American men and the nation.[96] By inducting black men into the military, the United States government legitimated and sanctioned their services, acknowledged their status as citizens with duties to the state, and thus rendered service-based arguments for enfranchisement more potent.

Throughout the war years, in at least five separate political conventions, African American activists expressed their faith that a key outcome of the war would be legal and political equality for all races.[97] In these conventions, the speakers, resolutions, and official public statements often focused on black men's military service, which, they argued, explicitly entitled them to equal rights at the war's end. Linking this service to that of their Revolutionary forefathers, the Bostonian John Rock, a delegate to the 1864 national convention, declared that "everywhere where our men have faced the foe, they have nobly written with their blood the declaration of their right to have their names recorded on the pages of history among the true patriots of this American Revolution for Liberty."[98] The convention's public statement, the "Declaration of Wrongs and Rights," extolled the military service of black soldiers who, it noted, had faced greater challenges than white servicemen. "When the nation in her trial hour called her sable sons to arms, we gladly went to fight her battles: but were denied the pay accorded to others, until public opinion demanded it; and then it was tardily granted. . . . We have fought where victory gave us no glory, and where captivity meant cool murder on the field, by fire, sword, and halter; and yet no black man ever flinched."[99]

Through their unflinching service, wartime convention delegates argued, black soldiers refuted the *Dred Scott v. Sanford* decision, which held that African Americans were not citizens.[100] By serving the state and shedding blood for its sake, black soldiers had earned full and equal citizenship in the national political community. As John Q. Allen, a Philadelphia delegate to Pennsylvania's 1865 state equal rights convention, put it, he "hoped that the blood of the Negro, shed upon the fields of this rebellion, would prove sufficient to wash away the obstacles which prevent us from the enjoyment of our political rights."[101] One of the national convention's resolutions made the link between service and citizenship quite explicit: "As citizens of the Republic, we claim the rights of other citizens. We claim . . . that proper rewards should be given to our services, and that the immunities and privileges of all other citizens and defenders of the nation's honor should be conceded to us. . . . These . . . we deem to be our rights as men, as patriots, as citizens, and as children of the common Father."[102]

Military service had also shattered the prewar link between race and the franchise. In light of black men's participation in the Civil War, the 1865 Pennsylvania convention delegates collectively declared that "it cannot be true that color renders us ineligible to bear arms and to exercise the right of suffrage."[103] Since the Union had overlooked race during enlistment, it must now surely overlook race for enfranchisement. National delegates in 1864 put this point very explicitly:

> Are we good enough to use bullets, and not good enough to use ballots? May we defend rights in time of war, and yet be denied the exercise of those rights in time of peace? Are we citizens when the nation is in peril, and aliens when the nation is in safety? May we shed our blood under the star-spangled banner on the battle-field, and yet be debarred from marching under it to the ballot-box? . . . May we give our lives, but not our votes, for the good of the republic? Shall we toil with you to win the prize of free government, while you alone shall monopolize all its allied privileges? Against such a conclusion, every sentiment of honor and manly fraternity utters an indignant protest.[104]

John Rock argued that black soldiers had exhibited "moral heroics" when they rejected unequal pay for their military service; they "bore [the insult] manfully, [living] to see the right triumph."[105] Through military valor in the face of danger and resistance to racist policy, black soldiers had, delegates contended, "vindicate[d] our manhood."[106] And so after the war they "fully expected that [black men would] remain in the full enjoyment of enfranchised manhood, and its dignities."[107] Although black men had served the state in its time of need, it was finally their gender—their manhood—that fully entitled them to all of the rights of men in the postwar American democracy. The right to vote was theirs, African American activists declared, because "we are men and want to be as free in our native country as other men."[108]

The Educator of the Race

As black men fought in the war and agitated for their manhood and the ballot, northern women activists also engaged in political action to support the war.[109] Although they could not serve the state as soldiers, women's rights activists joined many northern white women to form "loyalty" organizations designed to combat conservative northerners' calls for peace without abolition.[110] In April 1863, Elizabeth Cady Stanton and Susan B. Anthony issued a call for a new loyalty group that emphasized "patriotism over partisanship, unqualified condemnation of northern traitors and . . . unconditional support of the Union."[111] Although early in the war they had eschewed women's rights agitation in favor of abolition, the two activists hoped that this group would offer a new forum for advocating women's political engagement and rights.[112] As Anthony wrote to her fellow abolitionist Amy Kirby Post, the Women's Loyal National League would provide "an opportunity for Woman to speak her thought on the War."[113] Anthony later said, "The hour is fully come when woman shall . . . assume her God-given responsibilities, and make herself what she is clearly designed to be, the educator of the race."[114]

Although some members, with Anthony, saw women's political action as the organization's most critical responsibility, it soon became clear that the league would instead use women's energies primarily to advance abolition; five of the seven resolutions proposed at the league's first meeting on May 14, 1863, dealt with slavery in some form. In light of this, William Lloyd Garrison's description of the meeting to his wife as "a dead failure . . . in fact . . . a woman's rights convention," seems exaggerated.[115] By the May 14 business meeting, women's rights had been sidelined and abolition codified as the league's primary goal. To achieve this goal, the league's executive committee decided the best course of action was to petition Congress for a constitutional amendment emancipating all enslaved persons.[116] Petitioning was not a new strategy for activists. Throughout the antebellum period women had sent numerous petitions to national and state governments for many purposes, from opposition to Indian removal and slavery to women's property rights and temperance laws. Through this direct relationship to the state, women defined themselves as legitimate political actors.[117] Drawing on their experience in these campaigns, throughout the summer of 1863 Loyal League members circulated the antislavery petition, gathering signatures and cultivating connections with both national and local antislavery and women's rights reform organizations.[118]

The Loyal League's petition campaign was by any measure quite successful. The league managed to collect over four hundred thousand signatures by the end of the Thirty-Eighth Congress's first session in July 1864. And unlike some antebellum antislavery petitions, the women's petitions were referred to committee rather than tabled, ensuring a degree of influence on congressional deliberations.[119] The league's petitions were so critical that the Massachusetts senator Charles Sumner later credited the organization with having had a significant impact on the passage of the Thirteenth Amendment ending slavery.[120]

While this petition drive aided the antislavery effort and sustained the shaky connection between abolitionists and women's rights activists, one of its most critical results was to pull Stanton, who was elected president of the Loyal League, and Anthony, its secretary, into the realm of congressional politics.[121] Though both women had been long engaged in political agitation and counted the nation's premier radicals and abolitionists among their friends and correspondents, with the Loyal League Stanton and Anthony began to interact with national politicians in a sustained and formal way, especially as antislavery congressmen aided and accepted the Loyal League's petitions.[122] Sumner, in particular, became an important ally of the league, using his franking privilege to help distribute its petitions via mail and presenting the petitions to the Senate starting on February 9, 1864.[123] In this way the Loyal League and Radical Republicans crafted a mutually beneficial relationship: the league received financial assistance and in return produced a massive number of petitions that could be presented at critical moments in policy debates. Most important for the later movement, however, the Loyal League's leadership gained valuable national political experience. Stanton privately acknowledged this, proclaiming the league to be "the first and only organization of women for the declared purpose of influencing politics. In petitioning Congress for an act of emancipation . . . [we] have thus made ourselves a power for freedom with the people and with their representatives."[124] Stanton had high hopes for how women would use that power in the future.

The Negro's Hour

Just as African American activists saw hope for a race-neutral franchise after the war and turned their activist energies toward this goal, Anthony and Stanton hoped both that a gender-neutral franchise would result from the postwar political reconstruction and that their promising new political relationships would help facilitate this change. As early as 1863, Stanton demonstrated her faith that women's wartime work would be rewarded in the new government: "By our earnestness and zeal in the exercise of this one right," Stanton declared of the right to petition, "let us prove ourselves worthy to make larger demands in the readjustment of the new government."[125] As the war ended and Reconstruction began, Stanton began advocating for a postwar government based on a united, equal power of all men and women that would eliminate what she called the "class legislation" that had restricted suffrage to white men.[126] Many of her radical colleagues were starting to agree—but only when it came to the political participation of all men.

Throughout the summer of 1865, abolitionists, radicals, and politicians were seriously discussing enfranchising African American men. This seemed to Stanton and Anthony to be a positive sign for the cause of women's rights.[127] The Republicans they had worked with so successfully in the Loyal League petition campaign had swept the northern elections in 1864, raising hopes that the party would remake the government along egalitarian lines.[128] However, woman suffrage was simply not the central concern of abolitionists, politicians, or the American public. Not even all the activists who had supported antebellum women's rights were willing to take up the cause of woman suffrage after the war. Many actively rejected associating woman's enfranchisement with the enfranchisement of African American men, fearing that linking the two would ensure that black men would be denied the ballot. The white man's government, it seemed to them, could be challenged on only one front at a time.

The most publicized rejection of women's rights occurred at the thirty-second annual meeting of the American Anti-Slavery Society on May 10, 1865, when Wendell Phillips, the newly elected president of the society, denounced outright any connection between woman suffrage and black male suffrage. Though he had been an active participant in the antebellum women's rights movement, in his inaugural address Phillips directly rejected women's enfranchisement. As he declared his support for a constitutional amendment prohibiting states from making "any distinction in the civil privileges . . . on account of race color or condition," Phillips rejected women's voting rights as inopportune: "I hope in time to . . . add to that clause 'sex.' But this hour belongs to the negroes. As Abraham Lincoln said: 'One war at a time.' So I say one question at a time. This hour belongs to the negro."[129]

Throughout the winter of 1865–66, Stanton and Anthony privately pushed Phillips to change his position, but he remained adamant. He told Stanton in a January 14 letter, "I'm fully willing to ask for women's vote now & will never so ask for negro voting as to put one single obstacle in the way of her getting it. But, I shall not do much or go out of my way or spend money or time on it [woman suffrage] largely, deeming the old rule of 'one thing at a time' wise—& this time is the negro's."[130] That Philips, who only fourteen years earlier had declared that women had a definitive right to access the ballot, offered this rejection was a substantial blow to Stanton's and Anthony's hopes of a common radical movement for a truly universal suffrage.[131]

Phillips was not alone in thinking that a movement for women's voting rights was less than ideal. The abolitionist Lucy McKim Garrison declared it "out of time."[132] Even the women's rights pioneer Lucretia Mott felt the same, writing to her sister, Martha Coffin Wright, that woman suffrage "as a general move . . . would be in vain, while the all-absorbing negro question is up."[133] Radicals such as Phillips, Garrison, and Mott, who viewed expanding the southern franchise as the best way both to preserve the peace and protect the civil rights of the newly emancipated, felt that associating universal male suffrage with such a controversial issue as woman suffrage would doom both issues to defeat. Most African American activists, who had already focused their movement on black men's rights, likewise demonstrated little interest in merging their cause with women's rights.

Because ideas about manhood had become so central to the way African American activists designed their own suffrage activism during the war, abolitionist organizations transitioning into equal rights advocacy after the war could not advocate women's enfranchisement without undermining their primary rhetorical tool. Moreover, women's wartime activism, unlike black men's military efforts, did not resonate with long-standing democratic theory that grounded men's connections to the state in their performance of military duty. Women could not claim that they had died for the state; they could not claim they had earned their manhood in battle. Women simply could not argue that their gender identity entitled them to the franchise. This would have significant consequences for the postwar polity. As Reconstruction commenced and members of Congress started to build a new American voting polity, they likewise viewed it as the negro's hour, eschewing a broad expansion of the franchise based on democratic principles in favor of an identity-based ballot tied explicitly to the rights of men.

CHAPTER 3

The Family Politic

On December 18, 1865, the Thirteenth Amend-
ment to the Constitution was ratified. As the end product of decades of African
American activism, abolitionist agitation, and women's petitioning, as well as the
official legal acknowledgment of African Americans' wartime self-liberation,
the amendment was a triumph for advocates of American freedom. However,
its ratification also generated a profound political crisis that required further
constitutional amending to remedy. As the Thirteenth Amendment outlawed
slavery, it overturned the Constitution's organization of congressional representation. Article I, Section 2 had permitted southern states to count three-fifths
of their enslaved populations toward their representation in the House. As part
of the Great Compromise of 1787, this three-fifths clause kept southerners
from gaining national political power through the representation of people they
defined as property. It stated, "Representatives and direct taxes shall be apportioned among the several States which may be included within this Union,
according to their respective numbers, which shall be determined by adding
to the whole number of free persons, including those bound to service for a
term of years and excluding Indians not taxed, three-fifths of all other persons."[1]
By eliminating the category of unfree "other persons" in the United States,
the Thirteenth Amendment added four million free persons to southern states'
representation totals and created a situation whereby the South stood to benefit
politically from the emancipation it had fought a long and bloody war to prevent.

The newly convened Republican-dominated Thirty-Ninth Congress put replacing the three-fifths clause at the top of its policy agenda. Although the prospect that the South could gain a significant political victory in the face of its military defeat was galling, more disturbing for Republicans was that a conservative alliance could result if the House's representation were not adjusted. If the South returned to Congress able to count its whole population, southern representatives could ally with northern conservatives and gain a congressional majority for the Democrats. Radical Republicans feared that they would then use this majority to overthrow the northern victory and re-enslave the newly emancipated. More moderate Republicans feared the partisan losses that could occur. Regardless of their political alignment, most Republicans found it simply unthinkable that white southerners could gain power by the liberation of the very persons they had been so determined to keep enslaved. To prevent this, the Republican members of the Thirty-Ninth Congress understood that they would have to further amend the Constitution.

Yet this was not a proposition to take lightly. Since its ratification, excluding the Bill of Rights, the Constitution had been amended only three times. Two of those previous amendments made no alterations to the original founders' text: the Eleventh Amendment supplemented and clarified existing constitutional provisions, and the Thirteenth Amendment introduced a new national policy (emancipation). Only one constitutional amendment since the document's creation had changed any of the founders' original provisions: the Twelfth Amendment modified the procedure for electing the president and vice president. But this amendment, ratified in 1804, had been drafted and passed by some of the founders themselves. Thus, in 1865 the members of the Thirty-Ninth Congress were poised to become the first new group of American politicians actually to change the founders' Constitution.

To justify this action, postwar congressmen sought to persuade themselves and their colleagues of two things: first, that they had a legitimate right to modify the founders' constitutional arrangements, and second, that the changes they sought were consistent with the ideals of those founders. But for many Republican politicians after the Civil War, America's founders were problematic models to turn to for guidance in rebuilding the postbellum polity. Many Republicans viewed the founders as partially responsible for the recent war because of the concessions they had made with slave interests. But they were also aware that these compromises had created the very representation problems they were now facing. This produced a distinct sense of anxiety among congressmen about the founders' flawed political legacy, about themselves as the heirs of that legacy, and about their own abilities to alter the nation's fundamental text. As New York representative Roscoe

Conkling put it, "Did the framers of the Constitution ever dream of this? Never, very clearly. Our fathers trusted to gradual and voluntary emancipation, which would go hand in hand with education and enfranchisement. They never peered into the bloody epoch when four million fetters would be at once melted off in the fires of war. They never saw such a vision as we see."[2] Members of the Thirty-Ninth Congress frequently expressed similar anxiety in congressional debate as they reassessed the founders' original intentions, assigned new meanings to their behavior, and interpreted the founders' residual texts in a manner consistent with their own current political theories. At the very least, congressmen had to overcome this anxiety and redefine their national paternal legacy in a way that was consistent with their own policy goals. Ultimately, however the members of the Thirty-Ninth Congress reconstructed the founders' ideological and political legacy as they reconstructed the nation.[3]

Republican Reconstruction

When the Thirty-Ninth Congress began to meet in December of 1865, Reconstruction policy was its primary task. Because of the timing of nineteenth-century elections, Congress was not in session in April of 1865 when Robert E. Lee surrendered at Appomattox on the ninth, when President Abraham Lincoln was assassinated five days later, or when Vice President Andrew Johnson inherited the nation's highest office on the fifteenth. Although elected in 1864, the Congress did not convene until December 1865.[4] Therefore, in the months immediately following the war's end, the task of reconstructing the nation fell to the new president. Refusing to call a special legislative session, Johnson preferred to believe that he could rapidly and simply reunite the warring sections before Congress resumed.

Shut out of the earliest days of Reconstruction, Republican congressmen kept a close watch on the new president. Frustrated with Lincoln's cautious conservatism, radicals hoped that Johnson's well-known dislike of the southern aristocracy, combined with his interest in an expedited national reunification, would translate into justice for the emancipated.[5] But by the early summer of 1865, it was becoming increasingly apparent that Johnson was more interested in restoring political citizenship to white southern aristocrats than in extending it to southern freedmen. He rapidly reconstituted state governments and tacitly approved the restrictive labor and social "black codes" that they passed. These actions signaled to northerners and southerners alike that the Johnson administration welcomed both a resumption of white planter power and a resurgence of the antebellum race-based system of oppressive labor—everything that radical Republicans had feared from a conservative Reconstruction.[6] Charles Sumner met with the president when he arrived in Washington for the congressional session and reported that Johnson "does not understand the case. Much that he said was painful, from its prejudice, ignorance, and perversity."[7]

Although forced to the sidelines by the intersession break in Congress, many Republicans in addition to Sumner were developing their own Reconstruction plans as the congressional session approached.[8] In a vital presession caucus meeting on December 2, a seven-member group, including the leading radical Pennsylvanian Thaddeus Stevens, the Illinois moderate Elihu B. Washburne, and the Missouri abolitionist Henry Blow, proposed that Congress organize a special joint committee on Reconstruction. This committee would investigate southern conditions to determine whether the states were ready to return to Congress and would evaluate the condition of the emancipated.[9] This committee, the *New York Times* reported hopefully, "is indicative that the matter will be promptly and speedily disposed of."[10] Despite the *Times*'s optimism, a speedy resolution to the myriad of Reconstruction's problems seemed unlikely. However, the Republicans' plan to form this committee certainly indicated the new Congress's intent to promptly and speedily replace, or at the very least supplement, Johnson's policies. When it convened two days later, before any other regular business had begun, Stevens proposed the caucus's Joint Committee on Reconstruction.[11] The resolution passed immediately, and Stevens was appointed to chair the nine-member House delegation. On December 9, the Senate passed a similar resolution and appointed the moderate William Pitt Fessenden of Maine to lead the committee's six senators. Over the next six months, these two congressmen would preside over a diverse group that would formulate Congress's early Reconstruction plan, define the civil rights of all Americans, debate the legitimate boundaries of the American political community, and determine a new means for apportioning representation in postwar nation.

Although the Joint Committee on Reconstruction was primarily responsible for addressing the critical questions of reunification, in the first few months of the Thirty-Ninth Congress, other members of the House and Senate also debated how to redefine both the rights and duties of individuals and postbellum political relationships. In particular, questions of political participation, individual rights, and the obligations of citizens were at the heart of the debate on four key legislative proposals: the Civil Rights Act (Senate Bill 61), the bills in both House and Senate to enfranchise black men in Washington, D.C. (House Bill 1 and Senate Bill 1), and the Joint Committee of Fifteen's first representation amendment (House Resolution 51). In debating these bills senators and representatives sought to clarify exactly which rights accompanied membership in the reconstructed American political community.

The Civil Rights Act (Senate Bill 61) was one of Congress's earliest attempts to define the legal, civil, and political status of the emancipated. Primarily, the act sought to overturn the black codes that reconstructed southern legislatures passed to keep African Americans in de facto enslavement. Interpreting these laws as signs of southern resistance to northern military victory, even moderate congressional Republicans sought to overrule them by using federal power to enforce the Bill of Rights.[12] To do this, a number of civil rights measures were proposed in the early weeks of the Thirty-Ninth Congress.[13] But the proposal Congress pursued was that proposed by the powerful moderate and chair of the Judiciary Committee, the Illinois Republican Lyman Trumbull.[14]

Like other congressional efforts to legislate equality, Senate Bill 61 did not address social changes, focusing instead on legal and political privileges. Civil rights, Trumbull said, were the rights of all "inhabitants" of the United States to "have the same right to make, and enforce contracts, to sue, be parties and give evidence, to inherit, purchase, lease, sell, hold, and convey real and personal property, and to full and equal benefit of all laws and proceedings for the security of person and property, and shall be subject to like punishment, pains, and penalties."[15] The bill's language precisely mirrored that of the Fugitive Slave Act of 1850, a deliberate attempt to underscore the bill's constitutionality.[16] Trumbull believed the bill to be fairly moderate and thought it would appease both President Johnson and conservative Republicans. His belief was not unfounded. He had discussed the bill with the president and supplied him with drafts as the bill evolved in committee. With no indication of executive disapproval, Trumbull brought the bill to the floor convinced that Johnson approved of both its language and its goals.[17]

Senate Bill 61 passed the Senate on February 2, 1866. In the House, it was referred to the Judiciary Committee for consideration.[18] After some deliberation, the committee changed the bill's language to apply its provisions to "citizens" rather than "inhabitants." This was a critical change. Because the 1857 *Dred Scott* decision denied all African Americans citizenship, "changing the Civil Rights Act's language required the House to explicitly determine who was a citizen in postwar America. With the bill's passage on March 13, the House defined citizenship as belonging to all native-born Americans regardless of race or color, and identified the rights adhering to that citizenship as those historically possessed by white male Americans.[19]

Two days later, the Senate agreed to the House's amendments and sent the bill to President Johnson for his signature.[20] Reflecting the increasing distrust between the executive and Congress, Johnson vetoed it on March 27. This veto surprised Trumbull, further alienated radical Republicans, and drove many moderates such as Fessenden to oppose Johnson's policies.[21] Although both chambers overrode Johnson's veto in early April, Republicans remained concerned that the conservative courts would not uphold the act's provisions.[22] To sidestep any potential judicial opposition, in late April the Joint Committee on Reconstruction incorporated the Civil Rights Act's provisions into the first section of its omnibus bill House Resolution 127, which would ultimately become the Fourteenth Amendment.

Whereas extending civil rights to African Americans was an almost universal goal among Republicans, extending political rights was a far more controversial proposition. Despite the controversy, the political needs of the Republicans, the views of the radicals, and the goals of African Americans themselves drove the issue to the center of congressional conversations and ultimately into the second section of House Resolution 127. As early as 1864, Congress began receiving petitions, hearing outside speakers, and fielding proposals for how to enfranchise African Americans in the District of Columbia.[23] Although the traditions of federalism dictated that the states controlled the franchise, because the Constitution gave Congress exclusive jurisdiction over Washington, D.C., and the territories, the District had long been considered as an ideal place for implementing policies that would be more difficult to actualize in the states.[24] This theory was tested during the Civil War when, in April of 1862, Congress emancipated the District's enslaved people nine months before Lincoln's Emancipation Proclamation and three years before the Thirteenth Amendment ended American slavery permanently in all U.S. territory.[25] During early Reconstruction, some black suffrage advocates and Radical Republicans argued that a similar trajectory could be applied to universal manhood suffrage, claiming Washington as a good site for this political "experiment."[26]

Public sentiment about universal manhood suffrage in D.C. was mixed. Black Washingtonians mobilized in the months between emancipation and the congressional session to support enfranchisement efforts. In addition to a July 4, 1865, rally at the White House, the African American community in D.C. formed the United Franchise League and First Ward Civil Rights Association to petition Congress for the ballot.[27] These groups sent seven petitions in the first five weeks of the Thirty-Ninth Congress supporting black men's suffrage in the District, one of which was signed by 2,500 of the city's African American citizens.[28] Support among the white community was less enthusiastic. In July of 1866 the Democratic National Association of the District of Columbia issued a public proclamation declaring that African Americans lacked sufficient intelligence to vote in the District and warning that racial amalgamation would result if they were enfranchised.[29] In December, the District's city council officially declared that "the white man, being the superior race, must . . . rule the black." That same month, 6,591 people in D.C. and Georgetown agreed and defeated a black suffrage referendum. Only 35 Washingtonians voted in favor of enfranchising the District's black male citizens.[30] Congressional radicals dismissed these results, blaming the referendum's defeat on abolitionists who had abstained from voting to protest African Americans' exclusion from the polls. Others argued that the skewed election results indicated the extent to which Washington's population was disloyal to the Union, and thus it was even more urgent to fill the capital's voting rolls with loyal African American voters.[31]

But voters in Washington, D.C., were not alone. In most states suffrage referenda met the same fate as the one in Washington did.[32] Voters rejected universal manhood suffrage in New York in 1846 and 1860, in Connecticut and Wisconsin in 1847, in Michigan in 1850, and in Iowa in 1857. The only black suffrage referendum to pass before the war was in Wisconsin in 1857.[33] During and immediately after the war, this trend did not change: voters in New York (1860), Illinois (1862), Colorado Territory, Connecticut, Wisconsin, and Minnesota (1865) all defeated referenda to enfranchise African American men.[34] Radical congressmen were undeterred by these election results. The very first bills introduced in the Thirty-Ninth Congress were to enfranchise African Americans in the District (House Bill 1 and Senate Bill 1).[35] After five days of consideration in December, the Judiciary Committee advised the House to pass the bill, and it did so on January 18, 166 to 54.[36] It then sent the measure to the Senate for consideration.[37] Despite the bill's rapid early momentum, enthusiasm lagged in the more conservative Senate, where many moderates remained ambivalent about the implications of federalism. Even with the right to control the franchise in Washington, moderates were concerned that without a constitutional amendment, Congress could not justify interfering with suffrage rights in the states. Thus the Senate only briefly considered Senate Bill 1 in January and House Bill 1 in February before postponing them until June.[38] On June 27, it further postponed Senate Bill 1 until the next congressional session.[39]

The Senate's inaction reflected an emerging approach to the franchise that preserved traditional state sovereignty over suffrage by linking voting rights to congressional representation. This enabled Congress to tackle both of its most pressing problems at once: how to replace the Three-Fifths

Compromise and how to protect the rights of the freedmen without over-extending federal power.[40] Logically, supporters argued, if the southern states were permitted to count their full populations toward their congressional representation, but the African Americans in these states were empowered to vote (and by implication voted Republican), then those Republican voters could prevent a Confederate resurgence. But to implement this plan for protecting the Union and the freedmen, the Constitution had to be amended.

The first significant proposal for a suffrage/representation constitutional amendment came from the Joint Committee on Reconstruction. Thaddeus Stevens's initial proposal was to base a state's congressional representation on its voting population. Regional objections from eastern states with high numbers of women and children rendered this proposal untenable. So the committee agreed instead on House Resolution 51, which declared that if states did not enfranchise African Americans, they would lose the right to represent that portion of their population. But if the states did enfranchise their black citizens, they could count fully toward representation. The committee believed that Resolution 51 was a fairly moderate proposal with a good chance of passing both House and Senate.[41] Thus it sent the measure to the House for consideration on January 22.[42]

Debating the resolution brought members of the Thirty-Ninth Congress face-to-face with their own political legacy. When these men were elected during the war, they knew that they would have a profound responsibility for continuing the national struggle. With the war's end, they surely realized that the responsibility for reconstructing the war-torn nation had become theirs. But the problem of suffrage and representation created by the Thirteenth Amendment put them in the position of having to alter the nation's fundamental founding text. The members of the Thirty-Ninth Congress had to become the founders of the new postwar America.

To grapple with this responsibility, congressmen sought to understand, in debates about representation and suffrage, the values and goals of the founders. Primarily, they had to decide whether the Constitution was fundamentally a proslavery or an antislavery document. From this assessment, it seemed that they could then extrapolate what the founders might have intended for a postslavery nation and evaluate the extent to which their own policy proposals were consistent with the founders' ideals.[43] Not surprisingly, congressmen's interpretations of the Constitution and the founders' legacy divided along party lines. The Democrats, who sought to maintain both partisan power and white supremacy, claimed that the intent of the founders was best reflected in their behavior, which indicated that they had not intended for African Americans to join the body politic. Many Republicans, on the other hand, were familiar with antebellum abolitionists' attacks on the founders and the Constitution as proslavery. Even if they disagreed with these attacks, Republicans were nevertheless acutely uncomfortable with the compromises the founders had made with the slave interests. To grapple with these compromises, they turned to the founders' own words. They argued that the founders' real perspective on equality was reflected in the text of the Declaration of Independence, a document free from any problematic concessions to slavery. Thus both parties, to a certain extent, acknowledged the Constitution's complicity in perpetuating inequality among the races in the antebellum United States.

However, a problem remained. Neither the founders' behavior nor their constitutional language offered a definitive record of what they had thought about slavery, let alone presented some sort of plan for a postslavery nation. So how could the Union be reconstituted in a manner consistent with the wishes of the founding fathers? Gender offered a means by which this problem could be resolved. By appropriating gendered familial relationships as the central metaphor for arrangements of institutional power, congressmen based their reconstruction of the political nation on the connections between men: past, present, and future.[44] In debates, both Democrats and Republicans repeatedly referenced the founders as "fathers" and sought to justify their own policies as legitimate filial legacies.[45] Both parties adopted fraternal language to reunite the sections, and both used ideas about masculinity to distribute power within their imagined national political families. Positing the founders as benevolent fathers, themselves as legitimate and worthy sons, and either southern white or African American men as brothers, the members of the Thirty-Ninth Congress were able to disregard the founders' problematic slaveholding legacy, celebrate either their language or their behavior as their partisan interests deemed proper, and thus reconstruct both the founders and the political union. In this manner, gender became central to congressional rights-based rhetoric, particularly in discussions about Senate Bill 61, House Resolution 51, and House Bill 1, as both parties mobilized masculinity to structure their ideal vision of the community politic.[46]

The Constitution of Our Fathers

The Joint Committee's proposal to amend the Constitution (House Resolution 51) was immediately controversial. Congressional conservatives, most often Democrats, particularly opposed any amendment that dealt with voting rights because they viewed it as improper federal interference with the states' right to determine their franchises. But more fundamentally, they contended that any alteration to the Constitution violated the founding fathers' original intent. To reject constitutional amendment and black suffrage, both congressional Democrats and some conservative Republicans structured political relationships as familial connections existing exclusively between white males, claiming that to properly maintain the founders' legacy, this imagined white male political family must be preserved without intrusion from outsiders.

Situating the founders as infallible white fathers whose legacy conservative sons sought to preserve and protect, Democrats rejected the inclusion of African Americans in this political family as incompatible with the fathers' vision of an ideal republic. Using a familial metaphor for the political community enabled Democrats to gender political belonging, draw analogies between political and gendered interactions, and capitalize on the power of gendered racialized rhetoric to identify the legitimate political family as white. These rhetorical maneuvers upheld Democrats' leniency toward the white South and antipathy toward African Americans but also emphasized the importance of gender in the reconstruction of political rights.

Democrats first expressed their opposition to constitutional amendment by claiming that the Constitution simply did not need revision. Emphasizing that the constitutional words of the founders were clear reflections of their true intent, congressional Democrats argued that in the Constitution itself the founders had sanctioned racial inequality.[47] Further, the Constitution's text was such a sacred legacy that it could not be changed without desecrating the fathers' original plans. For example, Reverdy Johnson, a minority member of the Reconstruction Committee, opposed House Resolution 51 on the grounds that it violated the fathers' intentions for the separation of powers. On February 9, he asked, "The question is, what did our fathers design? Where was the regulation of suffrage to be left? Until . . . the last three or four years—no man was so wild as to imagine that the suffrage was not exclusively for State jurisdiction."[48] The "wild" idea that Congress could influence how states regulated their suffrage, Johnson argued, violated both the founders' arrangements of power and their federalist ideals. Some Democrats took this argument a step further and claimed that the Constitution made by the fathers was so sacred that any attempt to amend it in any way imperiled the fundamental principles of the American democracy. Andrew Rogers, a conservative Democratic representative from New Jersey, declared on January 22, 1866, that the resolution was particularly dangerous because it associated voting rights with representation. It was

a proposition to change the organic law of the land . . . which was laid down by our fathers at the formation of the Constitution. . . . Our fathers, in pursuance of the object of the Revolution, and in the exercise of their wisdom, embodied in it the doctrine that representation should not be based upon the voting population of the country. . . . This joint resolution . . . saps the very foundation and principles upon which the genius and institutions of this country have rested from the commencement of its political existence.[49]

Rodgers's fellow New Jersey representative Edwin Wright agreed, declaring that "this continued tinkering with the Constitution is pregnant with danger in the last degree."[50] The danger, the Kentucky senator Garrett Davis claimed, came from allowing the passions of the present moment to overshadow the ideals of the revolutionary generation. Congress's attempts to legislate civil and political rights, he argued, would "be a development of our system of government of which the fathers never spoke or wrote, or which their sons never dreamed until the acme of the present great national frenzy."[51]

Any proposed change to the Constitution in the midst of the national frenzy of early Reconstruction, Democrats such as these declared, was not only a dangerous threat to the ideals of the fathers but also a dangerous usurpation of their paternal role. For example, Representative Wright attacked Thaddeus Stevens, claiming that his advocacy of constitutional amendment was an illegitimate use of power that rightly belonged to the fathers: "Sir, this is a question that calls for our most mature reflection. Yet the patriarchal chairman of the committee, who brought forth this amendment . . . seemed inclined to treat it as an ordinary resolution of the passing hour."[52] Using "patriarchal" here pejoratively, Wright critiqued Stevens for attempting to "father" the Constitution in a manner he deemed inconsistent with the founders' original ideals. Such casual treatment of their legacy, as well as an improper appropriation of their role as the fathers of the government, Democrats argued, indicated how poorly prepared the current generation was for making constitutional changes. Representative Lawrence Trimble of Kentucky declared, "While I have some confidence in the ability and capacity of some of the friends on the opposite side [of the House] to make a constitution, yet I prefer the Constitution as made by our fathers eighty years ago."[53] Illinois Representative Samuel Marshall disapproved of the Republican effort to amend the Constitution even more vehemently than Trimble: "I believe, notwithstanding the conceded wisdom, ability, and virtue of this House, that the fathers who framed our glorious Constitution were wiser, better, and nobler than we are. . . . There seems to be no more regard here for the Constitution and its guarantees, as our fathers made it, than there would be for resolutions in a common caucus or in a town meeting. It is monstrous; it is absurd."[54] Reverdy Johnson even extended the argument to apply to the Thirteenth Amendment, which he considered the first Republican "tinkering" with the fathers' Constitution. He stated, "I think and have ever thought that slavery is wrong . . . but am I to quarrel with the men who have thought otherwise, with the Washingtons, with the Jeffersons, and the Madisons who must have entertained a different opinion practically, or at least an opinion that it was not advantageous to have instantaneous emancipation."[55] Contending that the founders had actively supported slavery and, by implication, racial inequality, Johnson both construed the ideologies of the founders as consistent with his partisan interests and reaffirmed their role as national fathers. Who were the mere members of the Thirty-Ninth Congress, Johnson asked, to attempt to change the principles and policies of the nation's founding fathers?

In fact, congressional Democrats argued, any worthy inheritors of the founders' legacy would not attempt to tinker with their sacred ideals and texts. True sons of the fathers, Democrats implied, would uphold their political legacy by opposing constitutional change. Representative Trimble declared that he was "opposed to this amendment, and to all kindred amendments, and I have no hesitation in saying . . . that I expect, while I remain true to myself and to the Constitution of my fathers, which I have so often sworn to support, to continue to oppose the submission of all such amendments to the people."[56] The only true way to protect the national paternal legacy, Democrats such as Trimble declared, was to preserve the original text of the Constitution intact. New Jersey's Andrew Rogers also declared his love for and commitment to maintaining the fathers' ideals unchanged.

> Sir, it is because I love my country, because I love these States, because I love the grand foundations of liberty which were cemented by the blood of our fathers. . . . It is because this joint resolution saps the foundations of the principles which induced our fathers to spill their blood upon the battle-fields of the Revolution that I, in my humble capacity . . . as a Representative . . . use my voice and my power in behalf of that great constitutional Government . . . whose foundations were laid broad, strong, and deep in the beginning by George Washington and the other patriots and heroes of the Revolution.[57]

Although this statement can be read as an example of rhetorical bombast wielded by a minority-party congressman, many other conservative Democrats repeatedly declared in early 1866 that it was the duty of congressmen, as political sons, to preserve, protect, and maintain, and absolutely refrain from innovating or changing the fathers' institutional legacy.

Occasionally, in defense of their role as conservative sons protecting the fathers' legacy, Democrats adopted an overtly gendered rhetoric that capitalized on the gendered meaning notably embedded within the rhetorical familial metaphors they were using. For example, Representative Wright lauded those who sought to uphold the Constitution of the fathers, regardless of their party, by complimenting their manhood: "Thanks to the conservative members upon the other side of the House for their manly resistance against . . . stifling debate upon so momentous a question [the constitutional amendment]."[58] Also using the idea of manly virtues to describe his actions and those of his colleagues, Senator Thomas Hendricks of Indiana asserted that those who sought constitutional changes were less manly than the founders and were therefore essentially illegitimate heirs of the fathers: "The men of 1866 are not the men of 1776."[59] Although Democrats declared that Republican attempts to tamper with the original text of the fathers' Constitution were unmanly and illegitimate, they were even more disturbed by any attempt to legislate racial equality.

Nineteenth-century Democrats had for decades been creating and wielding racist distinctions between whiteness and blackness to define themselves as a political party, determine partisan ideology, and attract constituencies.[60] Consistent with their party's racist ideology, in the Thirty-Ninth Congress many Democrats adopted race-based language both to interpret the founders' ideologies and to assign fraternal roles in the rhetorical political family. Primarily, they ignored the history of suffrage contraction in the antebellum period, claiming instead that the founders had from the nation's start deliberately restricted African Americans' political participation to create a white man's government. For example, on February 1, 1866, the Kentucky senator Garrett Davis said that African Americans and Native Americans had never been a part of the national polity.

> The first or revolutionary Confederation among the colonies, then their Articles of Confederation, then their Declaration of Independence, and then the present Constitution of the United States, were all acts of the white people of the colonies, undertaken and performed by them exclusively for no object or benefit but their own. The negroes or Indians were not parties to them or either of them. . . . Those results were intended to be and were limited to white people alone.[61]

Just as conservatives in antebellum constitutional conventions had done, postwar congressional Democrats denied that African Americans had ever, in any degree, participated in electoral politics in America. Davis continued, asserting "that the fundamental, original, and universal principle upon which our government rests, is that it was founded by and for white men; that it has always belonged to and been managed by white men; and that to preserve and administer it now and forever is the right and mission of the white man."[62] The Pennsylvania representative Benjamin Boyer agreed: "The truth is too plain for discussion. . . . Our fathers . . . fortified by the bulwarks of the Constitution itself the subjection of the inferior race. No man can read with open eyes and candid mind the Constitution of the United States, as made by our fathers, and fail to see that this Government was intended by its founders to be a white man's Government."[63]

These Democrats insinuated that true sons of the fathers upheld and were loyal to the white political family created by the fathers, and they seemed indignant that Republicans would even think of altering the composition of this family. This indignation was evident in Ohio representative William Finck's speech on December 21, 1866:

> Are the principles of the old Constitution to be abandoned, and the whole character of our system of government changed in order that the white men of eleven States may be disfranchised, and the negro clothed with political rights? Is it possible, sir, that within the limits of our Republic white men will combine to degrade their own race and kindred in order to confer political power into the hands of black men?[64]

Finck conveniently ignored the fact that the white men of those eleven states had recently made war on the Union explicitly to deny the rights of black men. Furthermore, in proclaiming that white men would lose the franchise if African American men gained the ballot, Finck disregarded the antebellum history indicating that precisely the opposite had occurred. Democrats such as Finck declared that the connections between all white men transcended both history and the recent national schism; whiteness alone forged their political bonds. Therefore the white man's government must be protected from any incursions by others. As Thomas Hendricks asserted, "I am not in favor of giving the colored man a vote, because I think we should remain a political community of white people. . . . I want to see the white race kept a white race, and the power in this country without mixture and without an attempt at mixture."[65] Here, Hendricks played the Democrat's ultimate trump card: miscegenation. Any mingling of voters in the political family, Hendricks insinuated, would lead to the sexual mingling of persons in the literal family.

Postwar congressional Democrats frequently adopted the race-mixing argument, most likely to stir up white Americans' racial prejudice for partisan gain.[66] In so doing, they explicitly conflated sexual activity and political activity. But this argument was not the only way Democrats tied the body to the state. Many also identified gender, rather than race, as the central axis of government. For example, Kentucky representative Aaron Harding swore that the government "was a 'white man's Government' once, I know, and as a 'white man's Government' it had my first love—a love even stronger than a woman's love."[67] It is unclear what Harding was implying about his own relationship to the state, but by sexualizing loyalty, Harding drew upon his peers' understandings of masculinity to situate himself, and those committed to a white polity, as men willing to profess their full devotion to the state. Furthermore, within a broader American culture concerned with domesticity, Harding's declaration that he had rejected woman's love for love of his country's racial order was, perhaps, the definitive expression of a masculine commitment to the white political family.

As Democrats used whiteness and gender to patrol the borders of the political family, they used gender and race to reintegrate its straying white members. To reconnect the northern and southern political communities, they adopted a fraternal rhetoric that reconstructed southern white men as the true, if errant, national brothers. As Andrew Rogers of New Jersey argued, now that the war was over, the white men of the two sections should "bind [them]selves together as a band of brothers."[68] Reverdy Johnson declared that "the time had passed when we [the North and the South] were to esteem ourselves as different peoples. Our fathers esteemed us as one. The Constitution deals with us as one."[69] Therefore, he asserted, the best way to deal with the consequences of the rebellion was to treat southern whites as "prodigal sons," returning to the fraternal Union of their fathers, saying to them, "'You have wandered away from the household of your fathers; you have seen the error of your ways; . . . we receive you with open arms and with warm and gushing hearts." This would be possible because of the common bond between white soldiers: "Look at the conduct of their military men and our military men. How do they meet? . . . They meet . . . as brothers."[70] A shared masculine military culture, Johnson asserted, could overcome political or ideological differences between estranged brothers.

Johnson was not the only congressman to invoke the military. As with African American activists, in the wake of the very recent and transformative Civil War, the military experience loomed large in American national political rhetoric. Although many Democrats appropriated this rhetoric to re-create the white male political brotherhood, most preferred not to bring up the recent conflict and so instead turned to the military experience of the American Revolution to reconnect the men of the South and the North. For example, in the February debate, Reverdy Johnson again articulated the martial connection between sections: "We want to be what our fathers were, . . . going shoulder to shoulder through the perilous conflict of the revolutionary struggle, moistening every field of battle in which they were engaged with their joint blood. . . . We came out of that struggle as we went in, brothers, animated by an equal love of country."[71] These Democrats undoubtedly did wish they had just lived through a uniting American revolution rather than a divisive civil war. But for them, the joint spilling of blood and the intimate connections between men created by the nation's founding permanently cemented the fraternal relationship between the sections regardless of any subsequent schism. The Indiana senator Thomas Hendricks demonstrated this, relying on the bonds of revolutionary-era homosocial martial connections to overcome sectionalism. He argued that during the Revolution "the men of every section had mingled . . . they had dwelt under the same tent together; they had shared the hardships of the field, the dangers upon the rough edge of the battle; their comrades had fallen together and slept in a common grave."[72] Therefore, white southerners and white northerners should return to their original, common political connection. Throughout Congress's debates on civil and political rights, evoking the masculine military connections between white men in a distant, sanitized Revolution enabled Democrats to avoid uncomfortable references to the more immediate war the brothers had made on each other. It enabled them to reconstruct political relationships on the grounds of common gender identity and rendered southern white brothers safe members of the family politic.

While arguing for a reunification of the white political brotherhood, Democrats also occasionally used gender to challenge Republican visions of the fathers' legacy. In particular, they contended that any attempt to restrict southerners' rights was an unmanly violation of fraternal bonds unworthy of political sons. For example, in February 1866, Reverdy Johnson queried his peers: If the southerners were essentially emasculated by their defeat in the Civil War, then why were northern Republicans reluctant to reunite with those impotent brothers? "You have proved yourselves adequate to the duty of defeating them in their mad and . . . traitorous purpose. And now, having proved your physical manhood, do you doubt your intellectual manhood?"[73] If northern Republicans were men enough to defeat their southern brethren in the war, then they were certainly capable of managing them politically when they returned to the Union without resorting to unmanly and illegitimate expansions of fraternity. Like Johnson, Representative John Nicholson of Delaware also challenged the masculinity of his partisan opponents, arguing that if the Republicans desired an immediate enfranchisement of African American men, they should express that purpose openly rather than linking it to congressional representation: "If this be your real object, come out like men and avow it." Furthermore, he asserted that if Republicans attempted to amend the Constitution without the presence in Congress of the southern brethren, "their conduct must at least be pronounced unmanly and ungenerous."[74] Ultimately, using metaphors of male family connections and gendered critiques of their opponents' behavior enabled Democrats to justify their conservative policies toward African Americans, to legitimate their liberal stance toward the white South, to appropriate the founders as their ideological and political fathers, and to validate their opposition to amending the Constitution.

We Are Coming Back to the Doctrine of Our Fathers

Like the Democrats in the Thirty-Ninth Congress, Republicans, and occasionally African American petitioners, also used the metaphor of male familial roles to reconstruct political relationships damaged by civil war. Like Democrats, Republicans posited the founders as the fathers, presented themselves as worthy sons, and argued for the return of the nation to political brotherhood. Unlike their colleagues, however, Republicans portrayed the founders as fallible patriarchs who, by their compromises with slavery, had undermined their own egalitarian political ideals and consequently sacrificed a true political brotherhood among all men. Good Republican sons, they argued, would become political fathers themselves and create an equal political family among all men, thereby redeeming the founders' tainted legacy. To define African American men as equal brothers in this new idealized political community, Republicans appropriated gender to obscure the racial differences antebellum Americans had used to exclude African Americans from the polity.

As they considered amending the Constitution, Republicans could not ignore the fact that they were seeking to rewrite a portion of it by replacing its provision for congressional representation. To justify their right to make such a significant change, they argued that the fathers themselves had been so tainted by slavery they were unable to fully implement their own egalitarian ideals. Although no Republican, save perhaps Charles Sumner, went as far as the radical abolitionist William Lloyd Garrison did when he proclaimed the Constitution "a covenant with death," many Republicans had nonetheless rejected the founders' compromises with slavery.[75] For example, in January 1866, Illinois representative John Farnsworth placed the blame for the Civil War squarely on the founders' shoulders: "We have learned by sad experience, that what have been called in these days 'the compromises of the Constitution' have proved a Pandora's box, out of which have come all manner of evils to afflict this country. They have brought on this war. They have produced all of this bloodshed in the struggle through which we have passed for the last four years."[76] Daniel Clark, the senator from New Hampshire, agreed, calling the founders' compromise with slavery "the sad, the wretched mistake."[77]

Despite critiques like this, most Republicans were reluctant to be too critical of the founders. Instead, they solved the problem of the founders' imperfection by separating the men themselves from their actions. Republicans argued that although the mistaken compromises with slavery were shameful, they did not reflect the fathers' real intentions, which were for a nation in which "all men were created equal." For example, although Kansas senator Samuel Pomeroy bemoaned the fathers' compromises with slavery, he took solace in the fact that they did not explicitly use the word "slavery" in the Constitution's text: "Slavery . . . got a recognition, I am sorry to say, in the Constitution itself. The fathers gave it a place there, but thank God, they left it without a name."[78] Even though they had not explicitly named slavery in the text of the Constitution, the founders had nevertheless failed their descendants, Republicans asserted. Republican sons, Charles Sumner said, should, "while confessing sorrowfully [the founders'] inconsistency in recognizing slavery, and throwing over their shame the mantle which the son of Noah threw over his father . . . reject every argument or inference on this account against the true idea of a Republic, which is none other than where all citizens have an equal voice in the Government."[79] The Constitution, these politicians claimed, was a flawed text badly in need of revision because it did not represent the fathers' real ideals.

The founders' true legacy, Republicans argued, was most clearly expressed in one of their earlier political treatises—the Declaration of Independence. Congressional Republicans used the Declaration as evidence that in the Constitution the fathers not only had compromised with slavery but had compromised their own original intentions. In the House, Thaddeus Stevens argued, "Our fathers made the Declaration of Independence . . . [that] they intended to be the foundation of our Government. If they had been able to base their Constitution on the principles of that Declaration it would have needed no amendment during all time . . . [but] an institution hot from hell appeared among them. . . . It obstructed their movements and all their actions, and precluded them from carrying out their own principles in the organic law of this Union."[80] In this argument, Republicans were supported by African American activists. For example, one group of "colored petitioners, residing in the State of Georgia," petitioned for the right of suffrage by declaring their faith in that "ever-memorable sentiment contained in the 'Declaration of Independence,' viz. 'that all men are created equal; that they are endowed by their Creator with certain inalienable rights; among these are life, liberty, and the pursuit of happiness."[81] Looking to the Declaration rather than the Constitution not only relieved the Republicans of the fathers' uncomfortable compromises with slavery but also allowed them to refute the Democratic claim that the founders had deliberately created a political community bounded by whiteness. In this, Pennsylvania representative Glenni Scofield declared, "We are coming back to the doctrine of our fathers. . . . In the Continental Congress they asserted that 'all men are created free and equal.' . . . Both the precept and practice of our fathers refute the allegation that this is exclusively a white man's Government."[82]

In fact, some Republicans argued, it was not the founders' connections to slavery itself that made the Constitution suspect; rather, the problem lay with the way that people in subsequent generations had used the document to support slavery. This Republican version of history allowed representatives to separate interpretations of the Constitution from the document itself. For example, Charles Sumner shifted the blame for the current constitutional crisis to a disjuncture between antebellum constitutional interpretation and the fathers' true ideals: "For generations the Constitution has been interpreted for Slavery. From this time forward it must be interpreted, in harmony with the Declaration of Independence, so that Human Rights shall always prevail. The promises of the Fathers must be sacredly fulfilled. . . . It is nothing less than the Emancipation of the Constitution itself."[83] African American petitioners also adopted this argument. When William Nesbit, Joseph C. Bustill, and William D. Forten—prominent African American activists representing the Pennsylvania State Equal Rights League—sent a memorial to Congress, they noted that the Constitution did not contain any reference to race. They argued that Congress, by enfranchising and protecting African Americans' civil rights, would do "justice to the Constitution which the Fathers of the Republic steadily refused to disgrace by incorporating into it the word *white*, or any other distinctive feature which would deprive any portion of civilized humanity of finding protection under its broad and ample aegis."[84] By depicting the founders as well-intentioned, yet fallible, egalitarian idealists, African American activists and Republicans sanctified their own policies with the fathers' approval. This Republican emancipation of the Constitution would fulfill the founders' original ideals and serve as a redemptive mission for their sons, who would essentially save the fathers from themselves.

Republicans argued that as political sons they had a duty to emancipate the Constitution by realigning it with the Declaration of Independence. Thaddeus Stevens articulated this explicitly in the February debate: "The time has come when we can make the Constitution what our fathers desired to make it. . . . Now . . . when the rebels have lifted their parricidal hands against the country . . . shall we so recall this desire of our fathers as to place [the Constitution] upon the broad foundation of human rights?"[85] His radical colleague Sumner agreed, reiterating his conviction that it was the duty of the congressional sons to redeem the principles of the Declaration from the failure of the fathers. "Our fathers solemnly announced the Equal Rights of all men," he said. "Looking at their Declaration now, it is chiefly memorable for the promises it then made. . . . And now the moment has come when these vows must be fulfilled to the letter. In securing Equal Rights of the freedman . . . we shall perform these early promises of the Fathers."[86] Congressmen, Sumner claimed, must adopt the "masculine sense and exalted love of liberty" to complete the work of the fathers and create a polity where all men would be equal.[87]

Through this explicitly gendered argument, Sumner implicitly challenged Republicans to stand up and be men. And he was not alone in issuing this challenge. Nesbit, Bustill, and Forten's memorial also asked congressmen to look to their "calm and honest judgement, and the warm and manly feelings of [their] hearts" and do justice to the nation's African American population.[88] Some Republicans responded to these challenges by defining themselves as the next generation of political fathers, rather than taking the subordinate role of sons of the fallible founders. They drew direct parallels between the early days of Reconstruction and the nation's founding. Illinois Representative Henry Bromwell declared that "this Congress sits, for all practical purposes, as a convention revising the Constitution."[89] If the Congress was a constitutional convention, then its members were surely the new founding fathers. Senator Samuel Pomeroy made the connection directly, appropriating political fatherhood for himself and his colleagues: "I think I know and feel somewhat of the responsibilities of this hour. These responsibilities are upon us. They cannot be laid aside or transferred to another. The fathers have gone to their rewards, and posterity sleeps. We, the men of to-day, must make our triumph secure or lose all, and plant the path of coming generations with thorns. We must do it!"[90] Arguing even more explicitly that Republicans needed to become political fathers, Sumner asserted that "you cannot consent that the child Emancipation, born of your breath, shall be surrendered to the custody of the enemies. Take it in your arms, I entreat you, and nurse it into strength."[91] As political fathers themselves,

Republicans would integrate the nation's African American brothers into what the Nevada Republican James Nye called "the family of American citizenship."[92]

In their roles as redeeming sons and as Reconstruction's political fathers, Republicans used gendered language to construct African American men as political brothers. Like Democrats, they referenced the military fraternity to construct this brotherhood, but unlike Democrats they construed the Civil War as the site where fraternal bonds were forged.[93] When African American men offered their lives for the Union, Radical Republicans argued, they earned both their manhood and the ballot—the dual badges of membership in the political family.[94] As the Massachusetts radical George S. Boutwell asserted, African American soldiers had "stood in the place of our sons and brothers and friends. They have fallen in defense of this country. They have earned the right to share in the Government."[95] As brothers in arms fighting battles in place of white sons, brothers, and friends, African American men had in war performed the martial role of those male family members, and thereby, Boutwell implied, joined the political family of American men. Emphasizing black men's military service in this way enabled Republicans to distinguish loyal black men from white southern traitors who had both attempted parricide and rejected their fraternal duty to the Union. For example, Representative George Julian of Indiana argued that African American men "have done their full share in saving the nation's life. Many of them went into the Army as the substitutes of white ruffians and vagabonds who daily 'damn the nigger,' and whose unprofitable lives were saved by the black column which stood between them and the bullets of the rebels. . . . It would be a very mean mockery of justice to withhold the ballot from loyal negroes who . . . furnished the Government with their full share of men."[96] Like Julian, James Wilson of Iowa asserted that African American men "took the risks which justly belonged to the white residents," and consequently "many of them are buried with their white comrades on scores of battle-fields."[97] Battle rendered African American men substitute brothers and members of the military community, but it was in death that a permanent fraternal bond was forged between men in shared soldiers' graves. Thus, in the reconstructed political family shaped by the fathers' fundamental texts and implemented by loyal Republican sons, African American men's service for the family, service that Charles Sumner called "a filial throb for the Republic," transformed black men from political and social outsiders to honored brothers.[98]

African American petitioners also emphasized their military service to claim fraternal membership in the family politic. A suffrage petition from a group of "colored citizens of the District of Columbia" also noted that African Americans served the state as soldiers when their white brethren did not. The petition reminded Congress "that out of a population [in Washington, D.C.] of less than 15,000, we have contributed three full regiments, over 3500 enlisted men, while the white citizens . . . of a population of upwards of 60,000 sent only about 1500 enlisted men for the support of the Union." Thus, the "loyal" black men in the District had earned "the political rights enjoyed by every other man."[99] Petitioners from Georgia likewise emphasized African American men's Civil War service in their request for the franchise. "As many of our people of color," the petitioners said, "have been willing at the point of the Bayonet—and at the cannon's mouth, to defend the blessed Government under which we live," therefore, congressmen should "if it is not incompatible with your sense of justice" grant African American men the "right of the elective franchise."[100] Of all the petitions from African Americans to the Thirty-Ninth Congress, that sent by Nesbit, Bustill, and Forten expressed the link between military service, the duplicity of white Confederates, and the ballot most directly:

> Go to Port Hudson and count the slaughtered of our race and bid them tell you if they, whose arms are now palsied in death, ever drew a sword, sped a bullet or thrust a bayonet at the nation's life. Call back the spirits of the murdered heroes of Milliken's Bend, Olustee and Fort Wagner and the affirmation that they went to the presence of their God in defence of liberty, equality, the Constitution and the Union, and perfect enfranchisement of their race, will challenge a denial. . . . Gentlemen, the voice of God invites you to do justice to the brave black men, who have so nobly proven their fitness to exercise the franchise.[101]

For God, these activists declared, had "render[ed] every child of His creation conscious of his right to liberty, and equality with his brother."[102] Identifying African American men as soldiers serving in defense of liberty and using the language of family to define the political relationship between men, African American petitioners, like congressional Republicans, wielded gender to claim their own political rights and to demand that Congress recognize those rights. For without the ballot, the Washington petitioners argued, African Americans would remain enslaved. This "possession of only a partial liberty, makes us the more keenly sensible to the injustice of withholding those other rights which belong to a perfect manhood."[103]

As they considered Senate Bill 1, House Bill 1, Senate Bill 61, and most particularly House Resolution 51, the first proposal to amend the Constitution's representation provision and the basis of what would ultimately become section 2 of the Fourteenth Amendment, members of the Thirty-Ninth Congress outlined the terms of representation debate for the remainder of the session. Deprived of a clear precedent by the inconsistencies between the behavior of the founders and their foundational texts in relation to slavery, partisans in Congress had to develop their own ideological principles upon which to base a new formula for representation. Not surprisingly, each party advocated a solution to the representation problem that would benefit its own particular interests. Republicans, fearful that losing a congressional majority would diminish their party's power and derail Reconstruction, posited black men's enfranchisement as the solution, envisioning them as brothers in arms, literally and figuratively. Democrats, frustrated with the subordinate minority role they had been relegated to by the war and seeing potential electoral gains if the South returned to Congress with full representation, preached compassion for the white southern brethren. To legitimate these conflicting policies and cloak them with an aura of power, each party turned to the fathers, claiming that its own particular approach best represented the true legacy of the revolutionary paternity. Interpreting the fathers as supportive of their policies enabled partisans not only to lend historical legitimacy to their own ideas but also to rescue the founders from themselves. If the true legacy of the founders was not the problematic Three-Fifths Compromise but rather the policies advocated by either Republicans or Democrats, then the founding fathers themselves could be reconstructed and cleansed of the taint of the failure that had contributed to the Civil War.

By appropriating familial metaphors for political organization and emphasizing the fraternal connection between men in the political community, partisans in Congress also introduced gender into the debate on representation, used masculinity to redefine political relationships among states and peoples in the postwar nation, and identified the public as a male political family. At a moment when national political relationships were in flux, Congress adopted what it understood to be a natural category of social organization, the family, to reconstruct those relationships. Thus, ultimately, within the family politic—defined by African American petitioners, Republicans, and Democrats alike as a masculine political community—there could be no room for mothers, daughters, or sisters.

CHAPTER 4

The Rights of Men

Thursday evening, June 14, 1866, Iowa congressman Josiah B. Grinnell stepped out of the House of Representatives into a sudden deluge.[1] Accustomed to Washington's brief summer showers, Grinnell ducked under the portico between the House and the east side of the Capitol building to wait out the downpour. As he looked for a break in the rain, a group of four men approached and then surrounded the stocky Congregational minister and first-term representative. Grinnell knew only one of the group—his congressional colleague from Kentucky, Union Party member Lovell H. Rousseau.[2] Rousseau, a tall, physically imposing former Union Army general, cornered Grinnell and demanded that the Iowan apologize for insulting him in House debate a few days earlier. Undaunted by Rousseau's demand, Grinnell refused to apologize. Rousseau then raised his cane and began to strike Grinnell, thrashing him about the face and head. Grinnell covered his head with his arms to protect himself, but it was hardly necessary. After about six to ten weak blows, Rousseau's narrow, iron-ended rattan walking stick broke, leaving Grinnell relatively unharmed. After this brief physical exchange, the two congressmen argued for a few more minutes before going their separate ways.[3]

Echoing the infamous attack on Senator Charles Sumner ten years earlier, this brief violent incident also involved the assault of an unarmed and non-resistant northern antislavery Republican by a southerner with a cane.[4] Like the attack on Sumner, Lovell Rousseau's caning of Josiah Grinnell stemmed from a question of personal honor raised in congressional debate. Unlike Preston Brooks's attack on Sumner, however, this dispute was not about race or slavery. It was exclusively about gender.[5] Three days before their violent encounter Grinnell had declared on the floor of the House that Rousseau was a coward who, during the Civil War, had shirked his manly duty to the state as a soldier and instead had "whine[d] off with a woman's plea, taking refuge under feminine skirts."[6]

This was not the first time Grinnell and Rousseau had expressed their political differences in personal terms. For months the two congressmen had intermittently skirmished in House debates, earning an occasional informal censure from their colleagues. Whereas in earlier exchanges Rousseau had seemed satisfied with verbally responding to Grinnell's various jibes at his politics, his ideology, his beliefs about race, and the virtue and honor of his home state, this particular comment was too much to bear. Rousseau simply could not stand being called a woman.

Enacting the ritual forms of a duel, Rousseau sought to deal with Grinnell as a good southern man should. He waited a set period of time for an apology after a serious insult, and when he did not receive one, he called out his opponent in the presence of carefully selected witnesses. But rather than demanding an equal exchange of blows or pistols, Rousseau attacked Grinnell with his cane—a procedure southern men reserved for subordinates unworthy of dueling. In this way Rousseau contemptuously denied the Iowan equal rank as a man.[7]

On any other day, Rousseau might have let Grinnell's comment about his manhood go unchallenged. But on June 14, he and his conservative allies had suffered a serious political defeat. Before the House had adjourned that summer evening, the Speaker had announced that House Resolution 127 had successfully completed its journey through Congress.[8] The resolution's five sections granted civil rights to all persons in the United States, redesigned congressional representation, repudiated all Confederate debt, prevented former Confederate officials from holding office, and empowered Congress to enforce its terms. This omnibus resolution was one of Congress's first steps toward clarifying the status of the emancipated and defining the rights of the freedmen. When ratified by the states, it would become the Fourteenth Amendment to the Constitution.

It was no accident that a bitter dispute about manhood broke out between political rivals on the same day that Congress officially completed the Fourteenth Amendment. During the seven-month period between December 1865 and June 1866, as Congress debated the provisions of the amendment,

Rousseau and Grinnell enacted at a personal level larger partisan disagreements about emancipated African Americans' and former Confederates' relationships to the state. At the heart of these disputes lay different interpretations of the proper rights of men—what those rights were, how they were best protected and enacted, and most critically, who should have them.

In the early days of congressional Reconstruction, between December of 1865 and June of 1866, Republican congressmen seeking to redefine African Americans' position within the postbellum civil and political community used the core rights and responsibilities of nineteenth-century white manhood—the possession of property, control over home and family, and access to the state—as a template for integrating black men into the body politic. Many of these Republicans, such as Grinnell, echoed African American activists in arguing that the right to securely head a household, to contract one's skills, to safely possess the fruits of one's labor, and to contribute to, participate in, and benefit from the political community, were essential rights owed to African American men both as a tool for their future protection and as payment for their past military service. But more fundamentally, they claimed that these rights of manhood could not legitimately be denied to free male African Americans simply because they were men. In this way, congressional Republicans redefined African American men as full members of the political community, deeming them legitimate citizens and voters.

Democrats and conservatives like Lovell Rousseau also proved adept at interpreting the rights of manhood to support their partisan views. Unlike Republicans, who focused on the political and economic power attributed to men in the nineteenth century, conservative congressmen instead emphasized the legal and social power of manhood. In particular, they focused on men's social and sexual control over women in nineteenth-century America. They argued that the most important prerogatives white men possessed were the right to sexually access white women, to contract marriages with white women, and to rule those women within a family. In linking the social and political power of manhood to white women, Democrats posited dominance over white women as the ultimate expression of male power. They claimed that if all the rights of white manhood were extended to African American men, then the right to control, access, and rule white women would have to be extended to them as well. Capitalizing on Americans' racist fears of miscegenation, Democrats took this claim one step further and argued that if given political power, black men would seek sexual control over white women through violence. Refuting many Republicans' assertions that political and economic rights did not necessarily convey social and sexual rights, Democrats contended that the rights of manhood were not divisible—that men's right to control women could not be distinguished from their right to control property, labor, or politics. Like their antebellum political predecessors, these conservatives claimed that white men were the only safe repository of those rights.

As Democrats and Republicans had used the rights of manhood to defend their respective visions of the proper body politic, the members of the Thirty-Ninth Congress situated gender as central to the way that they understood the connection between citizens and the state. Their use of gendered language created a rhetorical context that shaped individual congressional interactions, such as the conflict between Grinnell and Rousseau, and partisan debates such as those between Democrats and Republicans about the rights of African Americans. But, most critically, emphasizing gender profoundly shaped postbellum understandings of political citizenship. Associating the rights of manhood so closely with the rights of citizens ensured that in early Reconstruction debate and policy, the default imagined citizen remained male—a vision that was made official in the language of the Fourteenth Amendment.

Manhood—Private and Public

Members of the Thirty-Ninth Congress drew upon common cultural definitions of American manhood to determine who should possess the rights of men. Although Americans had long associated independence, economic and political autonomy, and virtue with men's gender identity, by the mid-nineteenth century the rights of men were codified by the emerging market economy and its subsequent development of the "separate spheres," which identified the private world of the home with women and the public worlds of politics and the market with men.[9] The definition of manhood promoted by this ideology was racially determined, class-based, and regionally focused, but some common elements held true across race, class, and regional lines. All free men, many nineteenth-century Americans believed, possessed the right to head a household, to exchange their labor for remuneration, and to make contracts. Free white men, in addition, had the right (and duty) to protect and defend the country and to benefit from and participate in government. At the opposite end of the spectrum were enslaved African American men, who could not access any of these rights and thus inhabited a unique gender position as male dependents. Regardless of the degree to which individuals or groups could access the full spectrum of the rights of men, male gender identity in the nineteenth century was commonly defined in relation to three related and interconnected social institutions: family, property, and the state.[10]

Although separate-spheres ideology dictated that nineteenth-century adult manhood was displayed in the public worlds of the market and politics, the domestic sphere was also a critical source of power and authority for men. Early in the century the removal of middle-class men's primary remunerative work from the home farm to the public market dictated that most fathers were less intimately engaged with day-to-day family activities. However, this cultural change did not necessarily mean that men had less power within their families. While fathers shifted their responsibility for children's moral education and routine punishment to mothers, they were still the ultimate authority within the household and meted out discipline when at home.[11] Further, as heads of their households, nineteenth-century men were legally and socially entitled to control family members, to benefit from their labor, and to possess their earnings.[12] The eighteenth-century ideal of coverture, the subsuming of a married woman's legal identity into her husband's, was somewhat mitigated by the mid-1800s, but it still persisted as the foundation of marriage law.[13] In most antebellum states until the 1850s, a married woman had neither an official identity that the government recognized nor the right to possess property in her own name. Although within individual relationships men and women negotiated differing degrees of power and autonomy, as one nineteenth-century analyst of the family wrote, "In the domestic constitution the superiority vests in the husband; he is the head, the lawgiver, the ruler."[14]

As the lawgivers and rulers of families, married white men were also deemed the best lawgivers and rulers of the state. Eighteenth-century American political culture had equated marriage and fatherhood with a man's political fitness and worth and viewed with suspicion any man who was not head of a family.[15] Nineteenth-century Americans also recognized the public power that married men gained from private life and legitimized their head-of-household status by granting them the right to represent politically that household's interests.[16] In 1854, the *Southern Quarterly* journal reported that "the husband acquires from the union increased capacity and power. He represents the wife in the political and civil order."[17] The acquisition of political power from a wife and family definitively determined one's status as a man and admitted one into an imagined fraternity of white men who ruled both the home and the state.[18] As a correspondent for the *Charleston Mercury* put it in 1830, "We are equally interested [in politics] as citizens—as owners of the soil—as the fathers of families."[19] Although this editorialist's primary focus was in the protection of slavery, the clear connection he drew between citizenship, property possession, and head-of-household status indicated how intertwined those ideas were for antebellum men.

While head-of-household status conveyed a degree of power to American men, both within the home and in public politics, it also carried a heavy burden to protect and support the subordinate and dependent members of their households. Nineteenth-century men met this responsibility by acquiring and successfully managing property, which, in the antebellum period, increasingly relied on the acquisition of cash income from outside the home as subsistence farming gave way to market exchanges.[20] As men navigated this new public world as wage earners, providers, property owners, and economic agents, those most successful—the most manly—were understood to be independent and self-made men.[21] This cultural ideal's prominence can be readily seen in antebellum political campaigns capitalizing on a candidate's mythic rise from "log cabin" origins to political prominence. These campaigns deemed that the most admirable (and presumably the most electable) men were those who had managed to sell their labor power the most profitably, permitting social advancement, economic success, and, consequently, political power. Although many presidential candidates throughout the antebellum period successfully wielded this cultural myth, it was best manipulated by Abraham Lincoln, who capitalized on his rise from humble origins to capture the nation's highest office.[22] The process of becoming successfully self-made, even for those less ambitious than Lincoln, was a source of great anxiety for nineteenth-century men. They were aware not only that their livelihood, economic prosperity, and family's class status depended on their abilities to achieve and provide but that their very identity as men was at stake.[23]

If in nineteenth-century America financial success in the market and personal dominion within a family defined a free white man's economic and personal identities, participatory citizenship formed the foundation of his public, civic identity. Along with possessing a family and developing profitable skills in the workplace, voting on election day marked white men as adults, as citizens, and as full members of the political community. The primary act of participatory citizenship allowed antebellum white men both to enact and to publicly display their manhood.[24]

Those who most benefited from the gendered ritual of voting, officeholders, also engaged in public displays of political manhood. As the members of the Thirty-Ninth Congress used male family metaphors for the state and defined themselves as worthy sons of the nation's founding fathers, they assessed their own and their colleagues' political actions in gendered terms. Just as Democrats had decried the manhood of their political opponents and lauded that of their allies in equality-related debates, Republicans likewise used masculinity to define collegial relationships.[25] The Illinois Republican Jehu Baker, arguing on January 27, 1866, that a constitutional amendment was necessary for the nation's safety, claimed that if congressmen "would assert [their] manhood," they would pass such a measure.[26] The Wisconsin Republican Ithamar Sloan used manhood to argue for amending the Constitution's representation provision: "Let us adopt [the resolution] like men."[27] Congressmen such as Baker and Sloan who used manhood to prod fellow members into supporting their policy goals wielded gender as a coded language for political cowardice and legislative courage. This language indicated to the members of Congress that not only was martial bravery required of men within the reforming national community, but political bravery was needed as well. The Republican senator Samuel Pomeroy of Kansas made this connection best when he declared that "when the soldier was mustered out Congress was mustered in."[28] By defining political action and manhood as synonymous for themselves, antebellum white men such as the members of the Thirty-Ninth Congress created, maintained, and exercised their political and social power—power they were not likely to surrender lightly. But sharing political power with men outside the imagined fraternity of white men was exactly what many Republicans in the Thirty-Ninth Congress contemplated.

The Inevitable Negro

To congressmen faced with reconstructing the political community, precisely how much power—and which rights of manhood—should be shared with the emancipated was both extremely controversial and patently unclear. As Maine senator Lot Morrill declared three days into Senate debate on the Civil Rights Act (Senate Bill 61), "If there is anything [about] which the American statesman is perplexed and vexed, it is what to do with the negro, how to define him, what he is in American law, and to what rights he is entitled. What shall we do with the everlasting, inevitable negro? is the question which puzzles all brains and vexes all statesmanship."[29] In slavery, the legal and political status of enslaved men was clear. They were dependent on those who owned them, members of white men's households akin to women and children and ostensibly both represented and protected by that owner, the head of the plantation household and the sole possessor of the rights of men. Citing the British legal authority *Blackstone's Commentaries*, Charles Sumner acknowledged the male slave's dependent and feminized status. "The slave," he said, "was always regarded legally and politically, as a part of the family of his master. . . . Master and servant were grouped with husband and wife, parent and child, and as in the case of wife and child, the slave was represented by the head of the family, who also paid the taxes on his account."[30]

By tying productive labor, duty to the state, and head-of-household status to white men exclusively, the New York representative Roscoe Conkling argued, slavery had created an anomaly whereby enslaved African American men, whose labor produced the goods that were "the proper subject of taxation," lacked both the political right of participation that was associated with taxation in American political life and the manhood rights that productive labor created. Slavery had created men who were "natural persons," "producers," but who, like women and children, were not political persons.[31] Emancipation disrupted this arrangement. Conkling declared that emancipation created "a new anomaly," whereby "four million people are suddenly among us not bound to any one, and yet not clothed with any political rights. They are not slaves; but they are not, in a political sense, 'persons.'"[32]

Republicans like Conkling wondered what would happen to the power of representation once granted to slave owners on behalf of their human productive property. "Does this fraction of power still survive?" Conkling asked his colleagues, "If it does, what shall become of it? Where is it to go?"[33] He articulated emerging Republican Party policy when he claimed that "there is no place logically for this power to go save to the blacks."[34] If African Americans were to have this power of representation, other Republicans argued, then they must be members of the political community. These congressmen contended that emancipation alone had transformed enslaved people into American citizens, despite the Supreme Court's *Dred Scott* decision. For example, John Bingham of Ohio declared that "every slave the moment he is emancipated becomes a 'free citizen' . . . a 'free person,' [who] . . . becomes equal before the law with every other citizen of the United States."[35] Union Republican Richard Yates asserted that this citizenship meant that "every man made free by the [Thirteenth Amendment] is . . . one of the citizens of the United States, and entitled to the same rights and privileges as . . . myself or any other one of the people of the United States, by force of the Constitutional Amendment abolishing slavery and emancipating that people, as I contend, into the sovereignty, into the body-politic of the United States."[36]

However, all the people in the United States who possessed sovereignty, who were full members of the body politic with the right of participatory citizenship, and who held the status of political persons were white men. Race, as a marker for dependence and property status in the South and political disability in the North, had been used in the antebellum period to eliminate or prevent the full participation of African Americans in the democratic political process in both regions. Despite the Thirteenth Amendment, the racial prejudice that persisted in both the North and the South remained a powerful barrier to congressional efforts to grant free southern

African Americans full participatory citizenship. In the face of this prejudice, gender offered a powerful, alternative way of defining black men as worthy of accessing the state.

As Republicans sought to incorporate the emancipated into the political community and protect their rights to that membership, they turned to gender as a means of overcoming the perceived political disability of race.[37] While enslaved, Conkling acknowledged, a black man was "a man and not a man . . . a native, an inhabitant, a producer, but without recognized political attribute or prerogative . . . he was nowhere."[38] But with emancipation, many Republicans contended, southern African American men were liberated from dependence—they were no longer members of other men's households—and so were now independent men. Every former slave, Henry Lane of Indiana argued, had "become a freeman and is counted for the purposes of taxation as a man—a free man."[39] Lot Morrill, answering his own haunting question about the "inevitable negro," also turned to manhood, arguing that the Civil Rights Act "defines [the freedman] to be a man and only a man in American politics and American laws; it puts him on the plane of manhood."[40] It was as a "citizen and as a man," Lane asserted, that "his rights shall be protected." Lane's fellow Kansan Samuel Pomeroy concurred, arguing that "without his rights of manhood he had better remained a slave. . . . It is adding insult to the long injury of centuries to give them the shadow of liberty without the substance, to invite them to freedom and not give the guarantees."[41] Although there was apparent agreement among most Republicans that emancipation had profoundly altered emancipated African American men's legal status and transformed them into men, congressmen disagreed about exactly which rights these freed men were entitled to possess. Did they, with freedom and manhood, acquire *all* the rights afforded white men? And if not, which ones did (and should) they have?

One way that congressmen dealt with this question was to distinguish between the different kinds of rights they believed men possessed. Particularly in the early days of congressional debate, congressmen sought to maintain the long-held distinction between "civil" and "political" rights and so drafted different legislative proposals to define and protect the different kinds of rights separately. For example, the Civil Rights Act explicitly addressed the basic rights of people within a political community: the rights to the secure possession of freedom, safety, and property. Most nineteenth-century Americans, drawing on American and English legal tradition, understood these civil rights to be the inherent and fundamental possessions of all free individuals. Antebellum Americans had defined political rights, on the other hand, quite differently. These rights, they maintained, were granted to specific individuals within the political community because those individuals were deemed worthy of possessing them; the evolution of their state constitutions reflected this belief.[42] In Congress, legislation dealing with representation (House Resolution 51 and section 2 of House Resolution 127) and with suffrage rights explicitly, as in the District of Columbia (House Bill 1 and Senate Bill 1), sought to define political rights more broadly; the bills' supporters argued that political rights were not earned privileges but were as fundamental as civil rights. Regardless of how this distinction was made, in all rights-related debates throughout the Thirty-Ninth Congress, congressmen used gender to claim or reject black men's possession of both civil and political rights, focusing on their social roles as fathers, household heads, workers, earners, and voters. In so doing, congressmen sought to redefine African American men's relationship to the gendered social institutions of the family, property, and, most particularly, the state.

Family: That Citadel of His Love

Throughout the antebellum period, enslaved people were deprived of familial security as enslavers denied, ignored, or actively thwarted family connections, and southern law failed to recognize familial ties between bondsmen.[43] The slave system's disruption of family life and gender roles was central to abolition arguments in the antebellum years, guaranteeing that protecting African American family life would be a cornerstone of the postwar Republican policy agenda.[44] Throughout debates on the Civil Rights Act, both moderate and radical Republicans pointed to the disruption of the traditional patriarchal family as one of slavery's crimes, arguing that henceforth the secure possession of a family was a fundamental civil right belonging to all people in the United States. Republicans' language when making this argument indicates that they envisioned the possessor of that right as a male head of household. For example, the Michigan Republican Jacob Howard argued that the slave "had no rights nor nothing which he could call his own. He had not the right to become a husband or father in the eyes of the law, he had no child, he was not at liberty to indulge the natural affections of the human heart for children, for wife, or even for friend."[45] The system of slavery not only served to separate African American family members from each other, but worse, Howard argued, it denied African American men the right to benefit from patriarchal family structure.

With emancipation, however, many Republicans contended that black men's status was transformed from "slave" to "freeman," a term used since the earliest days of the nation to define a man eligible for rights within the community. This transformation, they argued, determined that black men were from this point forward entitled to head a household and to securely possess a family. Howard asked, "Is a freeman to be deprived of the right of . . . having a family, a wife, children, a home? What definition will you attach to the word 'freeman' that does not include these ideas?"[46] Howard's rhetorical question implied that the right to possess a family was so closely associated with free manhood that it was unthinkable to separate the two. Implicitly, then, black men's acquisition of freeman status had also meant they acquired legal head-of-household status. Recognizing black men as the heads of their families, Republicans argued, had a further public benefit of helping to stabilize gender relationships in the South among freedmen, relationships that under slavery had not necessarily conformed to nineteenth-century white social norms. Public and legal support for a black man's right to head a household would restore gendered order in the South as it helped to define freedmen's status.

Along with a man's right to head a household, however, came his responsibility and duty to protect that household. For example, the moderate Republican and *New York Times* editor Henry Raymond argued that the Civil Rights Act gave the black man a "defined *status*; he has a country and a home, a right to defend himself and his wife and children."[47] This right reinforced the gendered power of men. All heads of household, Samuel Pomeroy of Kansas contended, had the right to protect their family:

> Every man should have a homestead, that is the right to acquire and hold one, and the right to be safe and protected in that citadel of his love. . . . He should have the right to bear arms for the defense of himself and family and his homestead. And if the cabin door of the freedman is broken open and the intruder enters for purposes as vile as were known to slavery, then should a well-loaded musket be in the hand of the occupant to send the polluted to another world.[48]

Pomeroy was particularly concerned about a man's ability to protect his family from sexual predation, and he associated that right with manhood. Unlike many Democrats, Pomeroy situated that manhood (via the musket) in the hands of African American men in the South, reinforcing both the rights of men as the exclusive heads of families and the rights of African American men to claim manhood status.

Although the right to safely possess a family was not truly a radical demand, white conservatives believed that granting African American men the power accorded to heads of households was the greatest threat to southern gender relationships. The image of a musket in a black man's hands being used to protect his family may have reassured some Republicans, but it was a profoundly threatening image to Democrats and conservatives. In particular, they were concerned that granting black men the power to head households and wield violence meant granting them power over women. Conservative congressmen recognized that independent men with families possessed the legal right to control the labor power of the women and children of their household. But they asserted that granting freedmen this same power would not necessarily be contained by racial boundaries; if black men were given patriarchal familial power over black women, there was nothing to prevent them from claiming this same power over white women. Conservatives were clearly concerned that the patriarchal arrangements of family and marriage that had long benefited white men in the United States, relationships between men and women characterized by one senator as "quasi-servitude," would be shared by black men.[49] This power would be expressed in two ways: as interracial marriage and as rape.

Claiming that patriarchal power over a household would translate into sexual power over white women was evidence of conservative paranoia. Beyond simple racism, however, there was a kind of logic to the Democrats' assertions. Essentially, these conservatives were acknowledging that at the heart of patriarchy lay sexual power, and thus granting black men the right to head a household was the equivalent of granting them the power to control women's sexuality within that household. In many ways, these politicians were recognizing what Republicans had been insisting upon in these debates—that ideas about gender had the potential to obstruct embedded assumptions about race and to override prewar racial boundaries. Just as Republicans claimed that recognizing African American men's manhood rights overrode racial distinctions among men as workers, owners, and citizens, these Democrats and conservatives argued that legally recognizing and protecting those rights would override racial distinctions among men as the possessors of sexual power over women. This would, they claimed, thereby permit black men to access white women sexually with or without those women's consent. Legally protecting black men's manhood rights, Democrats were essentially arguing, would make gender more powerful than race.

More moderate congressmen were concerned that granting black men head-of-household status would translate into legal protection for interracial marriage, which, they implied, would endanger white women. In particular they worried that the rights of states to make race-based laws regulating marriage would conflict with a federally enforced Civil Rights Act. Reverdy Johnson, the moderate Senate Democrat and member of the Joint Committee on Reconstruction, pointed to this potential conflict between state and federal law should the act pass, saying that "there is not a State in which these negroes are to be . . . which does not make it criminal for a black man to marry a white woman, or for a white man to marry a black woman; and they do it not for the purpose of denying any right to the black man or the white man, but for the purpose of preserving harmony and peace of society. Do you not repeal all that legislation by this bill?"[50] Although his central concern seemed to be with federalism, Johnson was also worried that if states recognized the civil rights of men, then legal segregation would not be able to constrain their family rights.

Johnson was unusual among conservatives in acknowledging that the legal restrictions against interracial marriage also applied to white men; most Democrats seemed more afraid that black men would interpret the right to head a household as a chance to take white wives.[51] The way the conservative Republican senator Edgar Cowan of Pennsylvania articulated the legal problem was more typical: "A black man in Maryland, after the passage of this act, marries a white woman, and he is arraigned under the law of Maryland forbidding it. . . . What would the Maryland judge do? . . . Here is an act of Congress which declares that, as to all civil rights and immunities, the negro is to be put upon precisely the same footing as the white man. . . . What is the remedy of this bill?" The states, Cowan argued, should be "competent" enough to define the boundaries of racial interactions and to determine for themselves whether or not black men were entitled to access white women, a problem that Cowan classed as similar to polygamy and incest.[52] Most Republicans denied that civil rights legislation would result in interracial marriage. Instead, they argued that cultural restrictions and social choices would serve to replace legal authority in enforcing racial boundaries. But President Andrew Johnson, in his message to Congress, cited the possibility of interracial marriage as one cause of his veto of the Civil Rights Act. The Illinois Senator Lyman Trumbull, among other Republicans, argued that Johnson's tactics were designed merely to excite racial fears and prejudice.[53]

Whereas moderate conservatives mostly confined themselves to articulating fears about interracial marriage, more extreme Democrats contended that empowering black men with the rights of manhood would result in the rape of white women. In the immediate postwar period the fear of black men's sexual relationships with white women took on an urgency that had not existed in the antebellum years. With the institutions of slavery to uphold southern white men's power to control sexual access to both white and black women, the need for southern whites to carefully regulate black men's sexual relationships was minimized. It was the possibility of sharing that power with black men that pushed conservatives and southerners to use social and sexual interactions between black men and white women as a political weapon.[54] In the Thirty-Ninth Congress the most vehement wielder of that weapon was Garrett Davis of Kentucky, one of the most outspoken opponents of black men's equality. Davis's primary claim was that granting African American men equal civil rights would enable them to commit violent sexual preda-tion because legal equality would prohibit states from making race-based variations in rapists' punishments. "By the law of my State," Davis reported, "a negro who commits a rape upon a white woman is subject to death, as he ought to be; and he ought to die, and I hope he always will die for any such offense."[55] On the other hand, white rapists in Kentucky, Davis told his colleagues, were merely sentenced to a few years in prison. The Civil Rights Act would make this distinction illegal, which Davis argued was "preposterous . . . absurd and unsound to the last degree."[56] Davis seemed to believe that a black rapist was guilty of two crimes: the violation of a white woman and the violation of white privilege. It was, perhaps, the latter with which he was most concerned.

By favoring the death penalty for black rapists of white women, Davis demonstrated his belief that the exertion of sexual power by a black man over a white woman was akin to murder and treason. Moreover, he implied that there was a vital need for the distinction in punishments between the two crimes—that without harsher punishment for black rapists of white women, there would be little states could do to deter the crime. Whereas Davis was slightly oblique on this point, the Wisconsin Democrat Charles Eldridge explicitly declared that states needed harsher punishments for black rapists. He argued that "it may be said that there is no reason for this distinction; but I claim that there is. And there is no man that can look upon the crime, horrid as it is, diabolical as it is when committed by the white man, and not say that such a crime committed by a negro upon a white woman deserves, in the sense and judgment of the American people, a different punishment from that inflicted upon the white man."[57] Eldridge did not actually explain to his colleagues why this different pun-ishment was required, perhaps presuming that they understood his impli-cation that the real crime was racial transgression.[58] Neither Eldridge nor Davis seemingly felt the need to consider the punishment for white rapists of black women or for black men who raped black women. Black women as victims in need of protection did not enter their public rhetoric and perhaps not even their consciousness. They ignored the far more prevalent and socially sanctioned sexual exploitation of black women that had been the foundation of southern slavery in favor of obsessing over a fictional black male rapist threat.[59]

Reading these conservatives' statements, one can speculate about what they were actually attempting to protect—the ostensible sanctity of white womanhood, the purity of the white race, or the right of white men to control *all* women's sexuality. If black men were granted the right to control a household and therefore to have power over and access to women's sexuality, then southern white men's exclusive monopoly on this right of manhood would be disrupted. Although conservative congressmen may have feared for white women's safety and viewed interracial sexual interactions as distasteful and dangerous, it seems likely that they were also concerned that white men would lose power (both sexual and political) if African American men were granted the gender-based right to possess and protect a family.

Property and Contract: The Fruits of His Own Labor

Because conservatives such as Davis and Eldridge centered white male power in the control over the family and emphasized head-of-household status as the core of gender identity, they focused much of their energy on rejecting black men's right to possess this measure of manhood. Republicans, on the other hand, seemed less concerned with this particular issue, not because they favored interracial sexual interactions but because they focused their main arguments on the other two components of manhood: property/contract and connection to the state. The right to contract one's labor power, along with the right to securely possess property resulting from that labor, formed the core of their arguments about civil rights owed to the emancipated, and they conceptualized this connection between citizenship and property rights as a right of manhood.[60]

Although the right to possess property and contract one's labor was a theme Republicans used in many debates, it was particularly central to their arguments for the Civil Rights Act. In the earliest debates on the act, Lyman Trumbull, Chair of the Judiciary Committee, argued that the bill's purpose was to ensure that the emancipated were "entitled to the rights of citizens," which he identified as "the right to acquire property, the right to go and come at pleasure, the right to enforce rights in the courts, to make contracts, and to inherit and dispose of property."[61] When pressed by California Democrat James McDougall for further clarification as to "how he interpret[ed] the term 'civil rights,'" Trumbull pointed to the bill's text: "The first section of the bill defines what I understand to be civil rights: the right to make and enforce contracts, to sue and be sued, and to give evidence, to inherit, purchase, sell, lease, hold and convey real and personal property, and to full and equal benefit to all laws and proceedings for the security of persons and property. These I understand to be civil rights, fundamental rights belonging to every man as a free man, and which under the Constitution as it now exists we have a right to protect every man in."[62] Only the enslaved, married women, children, and the institutionalized could be denied these rights in nineteenth-century America. Black men, by virtue of emancipation, were no longer dependents but free adult men; therefore, it was the duty and mission of the United States government, Trumbull argued, to protect African American men's right to manhood and its accompanying benefits.

Trumbull was not alone among Republicans in arguing for government protection of a man's right to property and contract. Other Republicans also identified contract and property as central to the definition of civil rights. This seemed to Pennsylvania Republican Russell M. Thayer so obvious that he could not believe any man in Congress would oppose the act: "I . . . challenge any man in this House to give me, if he can, a sensible reason . . . which he can reconcile with his own sense of justice . . . why the rights which are enumerated in the first section of this bill should not be extended to the freedmen of the South? The sole purpose of the bill is to secure to that class of persons the fundamental rights of citizenship; . . . those rights which secure life, liberty, and property, and which make all men equal before the law."[63] If the right of property made all men equal before the law, conversely, all equal men must therefore have the right of property.

Even some moderate Republicans who were reluctant to extend manhood rights beyond property and family were fairly vehement that the right to possess property safely and legally was a right that African American men had acquired in the transition from slavery to freedom. The Maryland Republican John L. Thomas declared that even though he could not support social or political equality, his position on the right of property was clear:

> I shall vote for no measure or connect myself with any party that would either deprive the black man of what he already has or that would oppose the conferring upon him all the rights necessary and essential in securing to him life, liberty, the pursuit of happiness, and the enjoyment of the fruits of his own labor. . . . The negro is free. I will do all in my power to make his freedom a blessing to him and to us. As a freeman he is entitled to acquire and dispose of real and other property, to labor and receive the avails and proceeds of his labor. . . . I will go further, and say that as he shall have the right to contract, so shall he have the right to enforce his contract. . . .[64]

Like Thayer and Thomas, Iowa representative James Wilson also viewed property as a fundamental right of men within organized communities.

Referencing *Blackstone's Commentaries*, Wilson declared that all "constituent member[s] of the great national family" had the right to personal security, to liberty, and to "personal property; which [Blackstone] defines to be, 'the free use enjoyment, and disposal of all his acquisitions, without any control or diminution save only by the law of the land.'"[65] Like the right of contract, ownership of property indicated one's status as a man, and so without these rights, Republicans argued, black men would not be secure in their status or safe in their identities as citizens or men.

The language that these congressmen used indicates that they understood property rights to be restricted to men. Thomas's use of the word "freeman" is notable, as is Wilson's point that independence was a critical component of controlling property. Most important, however, is the fact that these arguments did not apply to women. Not all married women had the free use and enjoyment of their property in 1866: in many states they and their property were still subject to their husband's control.[66] This point was not lost on the members of Congress. At least one conservative, Edgar Cowan, used married women to oppose the Civil Rights Act: "The bill has been taken to mean to confer those rights as they are conferred upon white citizens in the several States. That is not so. These rights are not conferred absolutely. . . . Now, a married woman in no state that I know of has a right to make contracts generally. . . . Is it intended . . . that this bill confers upon married women the unlimited right to contract?"[67] Cowan worried that the act would put federal and state law in conflict, but more seriously, it "confers upon married women, upon minors, upon idiots, upon lunatics, and upon everybody native born in all the States, the right to make and enforce contracts, because there is no qualification in the bill. . . . The power given to these people by this bill is unlimited as to persons . . . and to contracts."[68]

Although they feared that the Civil Rights Act would grant contract rights to the unworthy, dependent, and unmanly, Democrats and conservatives like Cowan were more concerned about the impact African American men's civil rights would have on racial hierarchies. Reverdy Johnson, again demonstrating the Democrats' interest in the connection between family, sexual power, and manhood, tied the right of contract to marriage. He argued that the Civil Rights Act, by protecting the right to contract, definitively protected the right of black men to marry white women because marriage was a contractual relationship. When "white and black are considered together, put in a mass," Johnson contended, "the one is entitled to enter into every contract that the other is entitled to enter into. Of course, therefore, the black man is entitled to enter into the contract of marriage with a white woman."[69] Though he was most likely taken less seriously by his colleagues than the respected lawyer

Johnson, Garrett Davis was also concerned with the impact on whites if black men were granted the right to contract. In particular, he expressed concern for the labor market. In debate to override President Johnson's veto of the Civil Rights Act, Garrett Davis declared that if passed, the act would "introduce . . . competition between the white and black laborers for employment, for wages; and this competition on the part of the white men will be limited to the poorer classes who do not wish to employ labor themselves. . . . The passage of such a bill as this is calculated to produce interference between, and disturbance of, the relations of the black laborer and his white employer, to get up feuds and quarrels and contentions between them by interested and sinister persons, to alienate the white employer from the black laborer."[70] This alienation, he claimed, would "induce the employer to resort to the white instead of the black laborer to cultivate his fields and perform his other work."[71] How Davis envisioned a labor system without either slavery or contract rights was unclear, but it was clear that he opposed granting black men any right traditionally held by white men exclusively.

Other conservative members of Congress argued that giving African American men the right to contract would result in their acquisition of other rights such as access to public education, gun ownership, and public transportation. The Indiana representative Michael Kerr argued that civil rights would enable any person to open any kind of business venture. "Under the laws of Indiana, no person except white male inhabitants can be allowed to engage in the business of retailing spirituous liquors. . . . Now, it cannot be said that selling liquor . . . is not a civil right. . . . It is as much a contract or civil right as would be a license to sell meat in their market houses or to run a dray in their streets or to carry on any other business."[72] Perhaps the danger of permitting an African American man to sell liquor was self-evident to Kerr. He seemed to feel no need to explain why this was problematic. Instead, he moved on to argue that equal school attendance would also be mandated by the Civil Rights Act, requiring a mingling of black and white children in the schoolroom—another so-called problem he did not feel warranted explanation. Kerr's argument implies that social disruption would result from equal civil rights, violating a perceived sense of social separation between the races. More important, Kerr was noting that enabling African American men to own property and to contract would disrupt white men's right to control black men's labor and property, thereby reducing white men's social and economic power.

Some Democrats argued much more explicitly that granting African American men the rights of manhood would harm whites and reduce their power. The New York Democrat John Chanler claimed that changing the southern system of labor and social organization would materially damage white workers. "The exclusion of the white laborer of the Northeast and West [from the South]," he argued, "will eventually give the finest and fairest land in the South to the black man in perpetuity to the exclusion of the white working men of this country." This exclusion, he asserted, "is unjust to the white laborer and a mockery."[73] But this was not his greatest concern. Chanler argued that with the elimination of slavery and equalization of civil rights, race would be the only category left by which power differences could be maintained. "Ingraft the black man into the term 'people,'" he declared, "and you surrender the South to the black race, and the question comes up not between slave and free, but between white and black."[74] Although Chanler exaggerated the potential power realignments that could result from a public recognition of black men's right to property, he accurately perceived that with emancipation white men would lose some measure of control over both black labor power and southern property.

This seems precisely what Democratic congressmen feared. Embedded within their arguments was a fear that if the economic and social playing field were leveled, whites in general, and white men in particular, would suffer either the loss of sexual power over white women or economic power in the marketplace. Democrats like Chanler and Kerr recognized that acknowledging black men's right to contract shifted black men's status from dependents to sovereign men and thus threatened white men's exclusive exercise of economic power in the South. Even more worrisome for these conservatives, it also threatened the white man's government.

Participatory Citizenship: The Equality of His Manhood

Although Democrats were concerned that granting black men rights as heads of households and owners of property would lead to social equality, violent predations on white women, and an overthrow of white men's monopoly on economic power, they were most worried about suffrage. Some conservatives grudgingly acknowledged the justice in granting limited manhood rights to black men, and many seemed to believe that it was reasonable to permit black men secure families, property, and labor contracts. But the prospect of sharing political power elicited their most vehement objections.[75] To reassure their conservative colleagues, during debates on the Civil Rights Act both radical and moderate Republicans insisted that civil rights were distinct from participatory citizenship. Anxious not to strain their public support, more conservative Republican congressmen argued that only civil rights should be extended to black men, who would maintain their primary legal relationship with the state via the courts. Simple contract rights, these Republicans declared, did not convey either voting rights or political power.

Despite these protestations, most Democrats remained skeptical that *some* of the rights of manhood could be granted to African American men without granting *all* of those rights. They contended that the close ties between the rights of manhood made it impossible legally to separate family, property, and citizenship. For example, the Delaware senator Willard Saulsbury asked in debate in January of 1866, "What is one means and a very important means of securing the rights of person and property? It is a voice in the Government which makes the laws regulating and governing the right of property."[76] A few days later, he continued this train of thought, challenging the Republican attempts to separate civil rights and suffrage:

It will not do for the honorable chairman of the Judiciary Committee [Trumbull] to say that by specifying . . . the right to sue and be sued, and to give evidence, to lease and hold property, he limits these rights. He does no such thing. . . . When these rights are given to the negro as freely as to the white man, I say, as a lawyer, that you confer the right of suffrage, because under our republican form and system of government, and according to the genius of our republican institutions, one of the strongest guarantees of personal rights, of the rights of person and property, is the right of the ballot.[77]

Conservatives such as Saulsbury were well aware that the same Republicans who were proclaiming so earnestly that the Civil Rights Act was not an attempt to enfranchise black men were, in debates on apportioning representation and expanding the franchise in Washington, also declaring the right of suffrage a necessary right for black men.

In representation and enfranchisement debates, many Republicans who supported black male enfranchisement argued that black men needed full participatory citizenship for purely practical reasons—to defend their rights of manhood by protecting themselves, their families, and their property. Black codes passed in the South since the end of the war indicated the extent to which the rights of African Americans were endangered without the vote. Much like their Democratic critics, these Republicans contended that the rights of manhood could not be separated from each other. Further, they claimed the most effective and natural way to remove the burden of protecting freedmen's rights from the federal government was to give African American men the power to protect themselves. As Samuel Pomeroy of Kansas articulated most simply, the black man "should have the ballot, for he has no security short of it."[78]

Having the political power to protect one's household and property, pro-suffrage Republicans argued, was a critical right of manhood. The Illinois representative John Farnsworth asserted that "the right of self-defense is the first law of nature. The right to vote, the ballot, is the freeman's defense; and if his right to freedom is an inalienable and natural right, then, too, is the right to protect that freedom an inalienable and natural right."[79] Comparing the ballot in political communities to violence in a state of nature, the Kansas Republican Sidney Clarke contended that African American men "must have the means of protection, whether it be the simple force of the savage, or the complex forms of modern civilization. This means of protection belongs to all men, not as a bestowed privilege, but as a right inherent to existence as members of society. . . . The right of suffrage . . . is not to be measured by other men's prejudices."[80] James Wilson also asserted that race was no longer a sufficient reason to deprive a man of his right to access the political community. He asked, "Why should the color of a man's skin deprive him of the political right of defense?"[81] It was up to Congress, Wilson argued, to remedy the injustices of the past "by placing in each man's hands the power to defend his own freedom and rights."[82] The Indiana Republican George Julian also denied the legitimacy of race to divide men from their rights. "Color has nothing whatever to do with the question of suffrage," he argued. "The negro should not be disfranchised because he is black, nor the white man allowed to vote because he is white. Both should have the ballot because they are men and citizens, and require it for their protection."[83]

Prosuffrage Republicans such as Julian interpreted the ballot as the best means by which black men could overcome both racial prejudice and its institutionalized legal forms. The Pennsylvania Republican Glenni Scofield argued that a hypothetical African American man in Washington, D.C., needed the ballot "because . . . he is hated in this city, and justice denied him by prejudiced officials. . . . His vote is necessary for his own protection."[84] Ohio's Martin Welker was also concerned with the impact of prejudice on black men's rights in the South. He argued that black men should have the right to vote because in the South there existed "a spirit of bitterness, a determination to oppress and harass them in every way possible, [that] now pervades the legislation of most of these States. In many of them there is no protection afforded the colored men."[85] The New Hampshire senator Daniel Clark agreed, arguing that guaranteeing civil rights was simply not enough:

You may open the courts to him by law, you may make him a competent witness, you may give him land for a home, you may sweep away all distinction by law between him and others, and leave him at liberty to go and to come, to sue and be sued, to contract and labor when and where and however he pleases . . . and still, in my judgment, you will have failed to do what most of all you need to do—put the black man in a position to protect himself. . . . To do this fully you must give him the ballot.[86]

If the freedmen were not given the power to protect themselves by participating in their own governance, Republicans claimed, then that power would remain in the hands of their former owners—an outcome they surely sought to avoid.

As prosuffrage congressmen styled the ballot as men's best means of self-protection, they used distinctly martial language to describe its power and purpose. Frequently, they argued that the ballot was a weapon appropriately wielded by men in political community. Daniel Clark claimed that by granting a black man some of the rights of manhood but denying him the ballot, "you will have fitted him to use his weapon, but not have supplied him with the weapon." But when black men had the ballot, he declared, they would gain "a feeling of independence and self-respect. There is nothing like the ballot for this. Take it from your northern men and they would feel powerless and degraded. . . . Arm three or four millions of people with this weapon and they will protect themselves and teach their oppressors caution and respect."[87] The Ohio representative and future president James Garfield also depicted the ballot as a weapon of manhood, "the shield, the sword, the spear, and all panoply that best befits a man for his own defense in the great social organism to which he belongs."[88] Given the growing racist violence in the South, that men would need weapons for their own protection in such an environment seemed almost self-evident to Republicans.

Representing the ballot as a political weapon of manhood pointed Republicans to a more literal way in which African American men had recently wielded weapons. Throughout debates on representation and suffrage, prosuffrage Republicans echoed African American activists' claims that black men's service in the Union Army during the Civil War entitled them to the ballot.[89] Because the United States government had called black men to military duty, the argument went, it had acknowledged and accepted their service. This official approval offered a precedent for a similar official acknowledgement of black men's political rights. "Tell me, then," the New Hampshire senator Daniel Clark asked, "why two hundred thousand black men . . . who rushed in to save the burning house of your Government, should not be permitted to participate in that Government which they helped to preserve?"[90] If service to the state was one means by which a man proved his manhood, had not these men done their duty? Charles Sumner stated this point most succinctly: "If he was willing to die for the Republic he is surely good enough to vote."[91]In fact, advocates of enfranchisement claimed that southern black men would be a safer repository of the ballot than former confederates. Clark asked his colleagues which group they would prefer to empower: "Tell me, sir, if called upon to put arms into the hands of men in the disloyal States, into whose hands would you put them? Would you do as they have done, or attempted to do in Mississippi—arm the rebel militia and disarm the loyal black soldier? . . . Surely not, sir. You would retain the arms in the hands of the black men. Let, then, your ballots go where you would intrust your bayonets."[92]

More than offering mere service to the state through their participation in the late war, some Republicans argued, black men had overcome barriers that white soldiers did not face, making their sacrifices the epitome of manly duty. Echoing African American activists, William Windom of Minnesota argued that when black men enlisted, they knew that they faced greater risks than white soldiers, with less chance of reward: "When it was decided to accept the proffered services of the blacks, and to permit them to aid in fighting our battles, we were still unwilling to do them full justice; and they entered the Army with less pay than white soldiers, and without any of that protection which the laws of war accord to belligerents. The black soldier knew full well when he was enrolled in the Army it was with a halter about his neck, and that if taken prisoner no quarter would be shown him."[93] Nevertheless, Windom noted, "two hundred thousand strong arms seized the musket, and two hundred thousand dusky heroes grappled with the foe. Nobly have they performed their part, and largely have they contributed to our victory."[94]

Using the words "strong," "heroes," and "nobly," Windom depicted black men as worthy men who had fulfilled the primary duties of participatory citizenship. Other congressmen followed suit. Like Windom, James Wilson painted a heroic picture of the black male soldier:

> [The] States summoned the black man to fight the battles of the endan-
> gered country, put the musket in his hands, gazed with beaming eye
> upon his glittering steel, and heard the inspiring music of his tramp as
> he moved away to fight, bleed, die, that the nation might live, and saw
> those men come back maimed and wounded. These States know that
> thousands of them are in their graves. . . . And yet, after all the fidelity
> and heroic conduct of these men, prejudice, party spirit, and conserva-
> tism and all that is base and mean on earth combine to deny the right
> of suffrage to the brave soldier of the Republic.[95]

Prosuffrage Republicans like Wilson who argued that black soldiers were brave, self-sacrificing, and virtuous mobilized gender-specific definitions of participatory citizenship to justify their enfranchisement.[96] Some congressmen were quite specific in linking military service, manhood, and the ballot. Burt Van Horn of New York lauded black men who "rose up as one man to the rescue, first of the Government, which had always denied them their liberty, and second, to assert, in the fiery shock of battle, their manhood and their claims to freedom and its immunities."[97] As William D. Kelley of Pennsylvania declared, "The colored man . . . attest[ed] his manhood upon the field of battle."[98]

Whereas military service allowed black men to demonstrate their manhood, some prosuffrage Republicans contended that they were entitled to the ballot by the fact of their gender identity alone. The New Hampshire senator Clark declared, "Not chiefly . . . do I advocate this right of the black man to vote because he fought the battles of the Republic and helped to preserve the union, but because he is a citizen and a man, one of the people, one of the governed, upon whose consent . . . the just powers of the Government rest."[99] Now emancipated, black men were independent and so had no need to earn manhood status—the mere fact of emancipation permitted them to join the male political community. The Radical Massachusetts representative George Boutwell agreed, stating, "I am for dealing justly with [black soldiers] because they have performed service. But I am more anxious to deal justly by them because they are men."[100] Voting rights, Clark argued, were determined by manhood alone: "Man derives the right [of suffrage] from his manhood and the equality of his manhood with his fellow men."[101]

Just as manhood was required for political rights, political rights reinforced manhood. Participatory citizenship, as the ultimate marker of manhood, would cement the transformation of black men from dependents to independent free men. Daniel Clark declared that "when you have given him equal rights, equal privileges, and equal security with other citizens . . . you have opened the way for him to be a man."[102] Charles Sumner proclaimed that "the freedman is no longer a dependent. The ballot comes to him . . . filling him with the strength and glory of manhood."[103] If the ballot were denied to black men, prosuffrage Republicans warned, not only would the state be harmed by its failure to mete out just rewards to men who offered it service, but black men's nascent public manhood would be imperiled. Sumner warned, "The elective franchise [is] essential to the security of the freedman, without which he will be the prey of slavery in some new form, and without which he cannot rise to the stature of manhood. . . . . Suffice it to say . . . that

Emancipation will fail in its beneficence if you do not assure to the former slave all the rights of the citizen. Until you do this your work will be only half done, and the freedman will be only half a man."[104]

In order to overcome race-based objections to black men's enfranchisement, prosuffrage Republicans sought to emphasize the common bonds of manhood among men regardless of race. Many of them argued this connection between men explicitly, in the process articulating an expanding and changing definition of manhood that was not dependent on whiteness. For example, Daniel Clark declared that "the black man has just as much right to his vote as the white man has to his; and it is no more a gift or a boon in the one case than in the other; and the white man has no more authority to confer or withhold it than the black man."[105] Among men, Clark asserted, there were no distinctions of power that meant that one man could dictate the rights of another. Like Clark, John Farnsworth drew the bonds of manhood explicitly between white men and black men:

> Sir, the test of suffrage is manhood, as I have before remarked. . . . Our fathers . . . declared that all men were created equal . . . that one man is equal to any other man. . . . They said that the just powers of the Governments were derived from the consent of the governed. If that be true . . . will some gentleman, in God's name, tell me why this body of men who are under the Government have not the same right as I have to participate in it? What business have I to elbow another man off, and say to him that he has no right here?[106]

Taking this argument a step further, George Julian asserted that there was a common collegiality between white men and black men based on gender, and he challenged his opponents to apply the standards they sought to impose on African American men to themselves: "Are you willing to rest your right to the ballot on the purely contingent fact of your color? Your manhood tells you instantly that *that* is not the foundation. You are a man, endowed with all the rights of a man, and therefore you demand a voice in the Government; but when you say this you assert the equal rights of the negro."[107] Republicans with similar beliefs contended that the commonalities between men were more important in determining the boundaries of the political community than the contingencies that divided them. It was clear to them that race was not a persuasive test of political fitness or participatory citizenship. It was equally clear, however, that gender was.

When a furious Lovell Rousseau cornered Josiah Grinnell outside the Capitol on June 14, 1866, he probably was not thinking about black men and their right to the franchise. Nor is it likely that, as he brought his cane down onto Grinnell's head, he was actively considering the ways that Republicans and Democrats used gender to defend or refute black men's political rights. However, Rousseau's dispute with Grinnell, as much as it depended on ideas about personal honor, was prodded toward its violent, if abortive, conclusion by the way that each man's party engaged in the congressional debates about gender, race, and rights. Like other Republicans who asserted that the rights of manhood must apply to African American men because of their service to the state, their newly acquired right to contract their labor, and their inherent manhood, Josiah Grinnell had faith in a vision of a race-blind postwar voting polity of male equals. Like the conservatives and Democrats, on the other hand, Rousseau believed that the rights of manhood belonged exclusively to white men because those rights were derived from sexual access to white women. He defended a vision of a reconstructed South that preserved white men's exclusive possession of political power. This defense was so vital to Rousseau that he conflated the personal with the political and wound up in a violent altercation with a political opponent.

The way that members of Congress intertwined the rights of manhood with the rights of political participation in the early days of Reconstruction had a far greater impact than merely prodding two relatively insignificant junior congressmen to personal enmity and violence. The Thirty-Ninth Congress's use of the rights of manhood as a model for postwar political relationships put gender at the heart of the national conversation about suffrage and rights. Although they profoundly disagreed about the meanings, qualities, and locales of the rights of men, by using these rights as a template for reconstructing the political community Republicans and Democrats alike defined political rights as dependent upon one's gender. Thus, in their partisan debates, these powerful men explicitly and deliberately linked manhood to suffrage both to defend and to reject its expansion.

By situating gender at the heart of discussion about political rights, members of both parties defined gender identity as the linchpin linking individuals and the polity. This meant that even the most radical congressmen were not necessarily reconsidering the foundations of political citizenship. Rather, insisting on the manhood of black men enabled Republicans to alter the composition of the body politic but not necessarily redefine all of the rules governing its membership. Conflating the rights of manhood with the rights of citizens, these congressmen created a race-neutral male polity and left no room for women.

CHAPTER 5

That Word "Male"

In late December 1865, while many of New York City's citizens were celebrating their first Christmas in four years free from the taint of civil war, at the Stanton family home on West Thirty-Fourth Street Elizabeth Cady Stanton and Susan B. Anthony were preparing for battle. Anthony had arrived at the Stantons' on December 11 after having come to New York to "commence W[omen's] R[ights] work in earnest" and to resume the agitation for gender equality that she and Stanton had set aside during the war. Even Christmas did not interfere with the two activists' plans. In typically pithy diary entries, Anthony described the work that she and Stanton had begun that clear and cold holiday: "Sunday, December 24, 1865. Writing and folding and addressing petitions. Monday, December 25, 1865. Christmas. Mrs. S. and I wrote all the A.M."[1]

Stanton and Anthony sacrificed the 1865 Christmas holiday to their activism because they were deeply concerned that the newly seated Thirty-Ninth Congress would use gender-specific language to define voting citizens in the Constitution. Closely watching congressional actions and noting that three early amendment proposals identified voters as "male," Stanton wrote to her abolitionist cousin Gerrit Smith on New Year's Day 1866 that "the sons of the Pilgrims" were "trying to get the irrepressible 'male citizen' into our immortal Constitution." "What a shame it would be," she declared, "to mar that glorious bequest of the Fathers, by introducing into it any word that would recognize a privileged order." Echoing both the paternal and martial political language of the congressmen themselves, Stanton urged her cousin to "unsheath your sword & [come] to the rescue" to save both "the mothers of the republic" and the nation's sacred Constitution from "this desecration by the recreant sons of the Fathers." For if these recreant sons were successful and "that word 'male' be inserted" into the Constitution's text, Stanton declared, "it will take us a century at least to get it out again."[2]

To prevent the introduction of "male" into the Constitution, Stanton and Anthony turned to a mode of political engagement that they had used successfully in the past—petitioning. As leaders of the Women's Loyal National League's massive petition drive for the Thirteenth Amendment, they became familiar with the process of petitioning Congress and aware of the impact a large number of citizens' petitions could have on the political process.[3] Drawing on this experience, the two activists and their allies followed the Loyal League model for their new women's rights campaign. First, during their work in December the two wrote and had printed over a thousand copies of a petition requesting that Congress "prohibit the several States from disfranchising any of their citizens on the ground of sex."[4] They then disseminated the printed petition widely among their friends and allies, as well as having it duplicated in radical newspapers such as the *Liberator*, the *National Anti-Slavery Standard*, and the *Independent*. The papers' readers were instructed to clip the petition text from the newspaper, attach a signature, and independently forward their own signed copies of the petition to Congress.[5] Although these techniques for petitioning Congress were not new, the substance of Stanton and Anthony's petition was. For the first time in the nation's history, a group of citizens asked the national legislative body to "extend the right of Suffrage to Woman."[6]

Although the underlying goal of this campaign was to advance women's enfranchisement, Anthony told the abolitionist Wendell Phillips in January of 1866 that the petitions' more immediate function was to "awaken the public to the fact that woman demands political recognition in the new order of things."[7] In particular, activists hoped these petitions would alert congressmen that women, like the African American men whose status so dominated national political discourse, were also disfranchised outsiders seeking access to the American political community.[8] Despite the suffragists' hopes, however, awakening Congress to women's demands for the ballot did not translate into support for a gender-neutral franchise. Rather, Stanton and Anthony's woman suffrage petitions alerted Congress that the whole political community no longer understood the long-held associations between gender and voting rights to be "natural." These petitions directly challenged gendered congressional suffrage rhetoric and explicitly contested the connection between manhood and voting just as Republicans were using gender both to argue for black men's enfranchisement and to define their own political actions. Most critically, however, the petitions helped push congressmen framing the Fourteenth Amendment to make their assumptions about gender and voting rights explicit in order to prevent the amendment from inadvertently enfranchising women.

Both the petitions' fate in Congress and congressional discussions about women's right to the ballot between January and June of 1866 demonstrate the impact of the early woman suffrage movement on the Fourteenth Amendment. From the moment the petitions arrived at the Capitol, they changed the way Congress approached suffrage rights. As soon as the targeted congressmen removed the glued-together and tightly rolled pages from their pigeonhole mailboxes and unrolled them enough to read their origins and purpose, they became aware that some people, at least, were challenging the connection between manhood and suffrage. That awareness likely spread to most of the rest of Congress when the petitions were presented to the House and Senate. But when Congress referred eight petitions to the Joint Committee on Reconstruction, it guaranteed that the politicians tasked with drafting the Fourteenth Amendment were fully alerted to women's demands. But for this group of fifteen congressmen, knowledge did not inspire support. Rather, after they received the petitions, the members of the Joint Committee abandoned all amendment drafts with gender-neutral suffrage language and instead identified voters as male in all subsequent proposals, including the second section of House Resolution 127—the Fourteenth Amendment. The woman suffrage petitions that Stanton and Anthony had pinned both their hopes and their emerging movement on during the Christmas holiday of 1865 were partially responsible for creating the very outcome they sought to prevent—the introduction of that word "male" into the Constitution.

Manhood Suffrage Irrespective of Color

Preventing this outcome was a daunting task for supporters of woman suffrage. Outside of Congress, Republicans, at best, showed little interest in women's rights in the early days of Reconstruction. At worst, the language they used to discuss suffrage explicitly excluded women from the political community they were beginning to re-create. In the Republican press, reporters and editors writing about suffrage in the mid-1860s consistently used gender-specific language to define suffrage rights. For example, throughout the summer and fall of 1865, Horace Greeley's *New York Tribune* included in almost every issue an article or editorial advancing the enfranchisement of African Americans in the South. None mentioned woman suffrage, and most used gendered terms for voters. One editorial published on May 26 even acknowledged that vague suffrage language was a problem. When another paper declared that "President Johnson does not think the colored people ought to vote," the *Tribune's* editor subtly corrected his rival's vague use of the term "people," saying instead that he supported "earnest advocacy of Negro Suffrage—or rather of Manhood Suffrage irrespective of color."[9] Even if the rival paper was linguistically careless, the *Tribune's* editor clearly understood the question of voting rights as a gendered issue, even to the point of recognizing that "negro suffrage" was a term so general it could include African American women.

Greeley's paper was not the only partisan publication in late 1865 to envision the ideal voter as male. Other Republican-leaning periodicals also used gender-specific language when discussing suffrage. A June 1865 article in *Harper's Weekly* discussing President Johnson's Reconstruction policy asserted that although the states' constitutions determined voting rights for their members, the essential spirit of the federal Constitution determined that the "adult male population [was] the constitutional 'people' of the State."[10] The editors of *Harper's* implied that even the *people* of a state, the political actors in "We, the people," were male.[11] In an August 1865 editorial advocating an expanded franchise, the weekly magazine even more specifically defended the relationship between gender and political power. It declared that when Congress convened, it should "[entrust] the political power, according to the principle of our Government, to the whole adult male population."[12] These select examples, just a few among many, reveal that many Republicans outside Congress collectively assumed that manhood was a necessary component of a voter's identity.

Throughout the summer and fall of 1865, some Republicans and abolitionists were privately conveying the same message to Stanton and Anthony. While Anthony visited her brother Daniel in Kansas, some prominent western politicians and activists warned her that women's rights were not on the Republican Party agenda. On August 4 and 5, Anthony reported in her diary that she had met with the Kansas senator Samuel C. Pomeroy and the Republican representative Sidney Clarke to discuss the fact that "no class can be trusted to legislate for another though that other be wife, daughter, mother, etc." Whereas Pomeroy generally supported woman suffrage, Clarke echoed the abolitionists' and partisan press's rejection of women's enfranchisement and, Anthony wrote, "advised me *not* to bring in W. Rights."[13] Friends and abolitionist allies were also warning Stanton against raising the topic of women's rights in Congress. In early January of 1866 as Stanton gathered petitions to send to Congress, Wendell Phillips quite plainly told her that the petition campaign could have unintended consequences that she had not foreseen. In response to Stanton's request that he join in a spring lecture tour for woman suffrage, Phillips refused and suggested that any national activism for women's voting rights could actually hurt both of their causes. "Indeed," he wrote to Stanton, "do you need more than a few good sized petitions just to awaken Congress and block wheels that are only too willing to be blocked?"[14]

Despite such discouragement, the suffragists were cautiously hopeful that congressional action on African American voting rights would create a "universal" franchise that would also benefit women.[15] With good reason—most of the early congressional suffrage-related proposals to expand the franchise used gender-neutral language to discuss voters. But three specific Republican resolutions offered in early December indicated that the suffragists' hope for a gender-neutral franchise was a fragile one. On December 5, the former Union general and Ohio Republican Robert Schenck submitted a joint resolution that would base congressional representation on the number of voters in each state. The same day, the Pennsylvania Republican John Broomall also sought a constitutional amendment enumerating representatives by voters (House Resolution 6).[16] Though these two proposals were disturbing enough because they failed to count women as members of the polity, to Stanton and Anthony the most egregious resolution was one submitted by the Rhode Island Republican Thomas Jenckes on December 11 (House Resolution 11) proposing that only literate "adult males" could vote.[17]

Jenckes's proposal indicated that early in the Thirty-Ninth Congress Republicans were neither identifying universal suffrage as gender-neutral nor including women in the polity as they thought about voting and representation. Most critically, however, this resolution raised the prospect that as Congress amended the Constitution, it could actively create a new barrier to women's enfranchisement by using the word "male" to identify voters. Stanton, for one, was particularly disturbed by this possibility. She denounced "Schenck & Jenckes & Broomall" to Wendell Phillips's wife, Ann, in early January as "the guilty trio who have insulted the mothers of the republic by bringing such joint resolutions before the nation for consideration."[18] To Gerrit Smith, Stanton complained that even the politicians' names reflected their flawed politics: "I'm glad that the men who are doing so base an act are named Schenck and Jenckes. Say their names slowly & see how indicative the sound is of pettiness & cruelty."[19] But whether their names or their politics were to blame, in the earliest days of the congressional session, some

Republicans, at least, were already attuned to the possibility that if they were not linguistically careful any action they took could have significant consequences for the gender composition of the polity. And this is precisely what Stanton and Anthony, and their petition campaign, hoped to address.

The Broad Ground of Republicanism

To convince the Republican-dominated Thirty-Ninth Congress to enfranchise women or at least not to use the word "male" in the Constitution, the suffragists' petition campaign had to make women's claim to the ballot seem reasonable to their congressional audience. Further, their arguments had to be sufficiently persuasive that a majority of Republicans would reconsider their negative position on women's voting rights.[20] The suffragists sought to achieve these goals by appropriating the ideas and language Republicans were using to discuss suffrage, using rhetoric about citizenship, justice, the family, and protection to argue for women's right to the ballot. Anthony's correspondence reveals that this language was not merely a coincidence but a deliberate political and ideological strategy. In a letter to Caroline Healey Dall on December 26 Anthony described this rhetorical plan, proclaiming that for the suffragists, "the broad ground of republicanism is the one true place for all advance[d] minds to occupy."[21] By adopting "republicanism," in both the partisan rhetorical sense and the broader theoretical sense, the suffragists crafted an appeal to the Republican-dominated Congress that they hoped would produce positive results.

Stanton initiated this strategy in December of 1865 in the *National Anti-Slavery Standard,* a forum Radical Republicans and abolitionists were likely to see. In a letter to the paper's editor on December 26, 1865, she argued that the ballot was a vital tool for self-protection—but unlike abolitionists and Republicans, she claimed that it was a tool women should possess. She asked her readers, "As self-preservation is the first law of nature, would it not be wiser to keep our [women's] lamps trimmed and burning, and when the Constitutional door is open, avail ourselves of the strong arm and blue uniform of the black soldier to walk in by his side, and thus make the gap so wide that no privileged class could ever again close it against the humblest citizen of the Republic?"[22] Stanton's argument shows the influence of Republican constructions emphasizing the masculinity of black men; she implies that strong black soldiers should help women achieve the goal of enfranchisement.

In addition to capitalizing on black men's manhood, Stanton also adopted Republican arguments about citizenship and suffrage. In her letter to the

Standard, she explicitly referenced the Republican assertion that suffrage was a fundamental right of citizenship, arguing that "in changing the status of the four millions of Africans, the women as well as the men should be secured in all the rights, privileges, and immunities of citizens. . . . The disfranchised all make the same demand, and the same logic and justice that secures Suffrage to one class gives it to all." If, as Republicans were arguing, it was unjust to deny citizenship rights to southern black men, then it was equally unjust to deny those same rights to women. "If our rulers have the justice to give the black man Suffrage," she claimed, "woman should avail herself of that new-born virtue to secure her rights."[23]

Although newspaper articles generated important publicity for the suffragists' cause, the best way to ensure that politicians saw their arguments was to petition Congress directly. To ensure that Republican politicians understood their claims, the suffragists appealed to the partisans on their own terms: the text of the woman suffrage petition adopted almost every rhetorical justification Republicans were wielding for black men to assert women's right to the ballot. Every justification, that is, except manhood. First, the petition claimed that women were entitled to suffrage because they were citizens. It stated that the "undersigned, Women of the United States . . . represent . . . one half the entire population of the country—intelligent, virtuous, native-born American citizens; and yet stand outside the pale of political recognition." If the government denied women this fundamental right of citizenship, then it would perpetrate a patent injustice: "The Constitution classes us as 'free people,' and counts us *whole* persons in the basis of representation; and yet are we governed without our consent, compelled to pay taxes without appeal, and punished for violations of law without choice of judge or juror." In case the congressional recipients of the petition missed the connection between equal suffrage rights and justice, the last line made such a relationship specific, closing with the statement "For justice and equality your petitioners will ever pray."[24]

Congressional Republicans often claimed that denying African American men the ballot violated Article IV, Section 4 of the Constitution, which declared that "the United States shall guarantee to every state in this union a republican form of government."[25] The woman suffrage petition also asserted that to fulfill this same constitutional obligation, Congress needed to expand the franchise to women. "As you [members of Congress] are now amending the Constitution," it said, "and in harmony with advancing civilization, placing new safeguards round the individual rights of four millions of emancipated slaves, we ask that you extend the right of Suffrage to Woman—the only remaining class of disfranchised citizens—and thus fulfill your Constitutional obligation 'to Guarantee to every State in the Union a Republican form of Government.'" If Congress refused to meet this obligation, it would endanger the nation because "all partial application of Republican principles must ever breed a . . . discontented people."[26]

Paralleling the argument put forth by Radical Republican congressmen who claimed the safety of the nation depended on granting African American men citizenship rights, the 1866 petition suggested that woman suffrage was just as vital to the ideological and physical safety of the nation. "We would pray your Honorable Body, in order to simplify the machinery of government, and ensure domestic tranquility, that you legislate hereafter for persons, citizens, tax-payers, and not for class or caste." This reference to domestic tranquility, engaging all possible interpretations of the term "domestic," indicated that if women did not receive justice from the government, tranquility within the home, as well as outside it, would be disrupted. The petition also claimed that individual women's safety was at risk as well: "The experience of all ages, the Declarations of the Fathers, the Statute Laws of our own day, and the fearful revolution through which we have just passed, all prove the uncertain tenure of life, liberty, and property so long as the ballot—the only weapon of self-protection—is not in the hand of every citizen."[27]

The petition followed Republican suffrage rhetoric only so far: it simply could not argue that women's manhood entitled them to the ballot. But it could awaken the public to women's demand for suffrage rights and alert those amending the Constitution that the relationship between manhood and voting was being challenged. Although Anthony hoped that the petitions would bring woman's voting rights into the public consciousness, she presumed that awareness would result in acceptance. Both she and Stanton seemed fairly confident that if congressmen, Republicans, and their abolitionist allies could simply see the logical links between the analogous, anomalous positions of women and African American men, then by reasonable principle they would move to enfranchise both. If only their claims could be expressed in the right way, the suffragists reasoned, then perhaps the majority party would support women's enfranchisement. Instead, by pointing to the fact that women claimed the right to vote, the woman suffrage petition of 1865–66 indicated to Congress that a new degree of ideological caution and linguistic specificity would be required when addressing any change in the franchise.

Blocking Congressional Wheels

Charles Sumner, the *History of Woman Suffrage* reported, once recalled that he "wrote over nineteen pages of foolscap to get rid of the word 'male' [in the second section of the Fourteenth Amendment] and yet keep 'negro suffrage' as a party measure intact; but it could not be done."[28] In fact, for the first three months of the amendment's lifetime in Congress the word "male" was not a permanent or an original feature of the Fourteenth Amendment's early drafts. It did not appear as a sustained, recurrent component of the amendment's language until Congress had received, introduced, and passed to committee the petitions for woman suffrage. But Sumner's assertion was undoubtedly true. Republicans' reliance on gender to justify black men's enfranchisement meant that the only suffrage expansion consistent with party policy in the earliest days of reconstruction was universal manhood suffrage.

In early 1866, however, only the most radical Republicans, such as Sumner, were actually considering extending congressional control over suffrage nationally to directly enfranchise black men. The majority of Republicans were more concerned with the question of congressional representation. Constitutionally, Congress had complete control over how representation was apportioned, so linking suffrage rights to congressional representation seemed an ideal way to protect African Americans' civil rights while encouraging southern states to enfranchise black men. Further, linking suffrage to representation enabled Republicans to avoid disrupting the long-established balance of power between the states and the federal government. But making this connection did require Congress to reconsider the nature of citizenship, to define civil and political rights, and to determine the limits of membership in the political community. The group charged with this task, and with determining the best plan for tying suffrage to congressional representation, was the Joint Committee of Fifteen on Reconstruction (JC15). As such, it was the primary recipient of the woman suffrage petitions.

The composition of the Joint Committee reflected the wide range of political opinions present in the Congress. The House cochair Thaddeus Stevens was the acknowledged senior statesman and representative radical on the committee. Dictatorial, hard-edged, and humorless, he was a passionate and often unyielding advocate for racial equality. Having shepherded the antislavery cause to fruition, he hoped to use his considerable congressional clout to shape a radical reconstruction policy.[29] The Senate cochair and presiding officer of the committee, William Pitt Fessenden, on the other hand, was a far more moderate Republican, more political strategist than idealist. He had served as Lincoln's secretary of the treasury and was one of the most powerful Republicans in the Senate. Although Fessenden was no radical, he did offer some qualified support for black suffrage.[30] Perhaps influenced by a vehement personal hatred of his fellow New Englander Charles Sumner,

Fessenden scorned the radical vision of Reconstruction favored by Stevens and Sumner, promoting instead what he viewed as more pragmatic policies that favored the federal balance of power over the goal of racial equality.[31] The Senate's choice of Fessenden to chair the committee indicated its more cautious approach to Reconstruction than the House's.

Five senators and eight representatives joined Stevens and Fessenden on the Joint Committee. The wide-ranging political alignments of the committee members reflected broader coalitions within Congress. Following their chamber's more conservative leanings, none of the committee's senators were as fervent as Stevens about freedmen's equality. The most radical were James Grimes of Iowa and Jacob Howard of Michigan. Howard was an early supporter of enfranchising African American men, but neither he nor Grimes always voted for the most radically egalitarian positions in roll call votes.[32] The two other Senate Republicans were significantly more conservative: George Williams of Oregon had been a Democrat until 1864, and his voting record reflected this background.[33] The New York lawyer Ira Harris also voted conservatively, perhaps reflecting his stronger commitment to legal issues than to partisan maneuvering.[34] The only Democrat the Senate appointed to the committee was the attorney Reverdy Johnson, one of the most universally respected legal minds in the nation.[35] Johnson generally opposed any expansion of the franchise but often argued his opposition in terms of legal precedent rather than the more blatant racial prejudice wielded by other Democrats.

Like the Senate, the House also appointed mostly centrist members to the committee. Roscoe Conkling of New York, a rising politico who would move into Ira Harris's Senate seat in the next Congress; John Bingham of Ohio, who would write the civil rights portion of the Fourteenth Amendment; and the Missouri abolitionist, a contributing financier to Dred Scott's legal defense, Henry T. Blow, all voted in a mostly moderately fashion throughout the session.[36] Elihu B. Washburne, an antislavery Whig and close Lincoln colleague, who would be critical in maneuvering Grant to the presidency, also held fairly moderate political views.[37] The House Democrats, Henry Grider of Kentucky and Andrew J. Rogers of New Jersey, though not as temperate as the moderate Republicans nor as learned as their Senate colleague Reverdy Johnson, also lent their weight to the most conservative views.[38] Rogers, in particular, was a volatile speaker with a penchant for a creative use of racist invective. All together, the conservatives and moderates outnumbered the House radicals on the committee—the former Massachusetts governor George Boutwell and the chair of the important Ways and Means Committee, Vermont representative Justin S. Morrill.[39]

In their confidential meetings, the committee members sorted through the various proposals brought to the floors of the House and Senate for apportioning representation.[40] This was no easy task. Because there were such varied opinions about the best way to accomplish Reconstruction more broadly and how to replace the three-fifths clause and regulate apportionment particularly, many congressmen presented proposals for reapportioning representation.[41] Between the Joint Committee's first meeting on January 6 and its last meeting on April 30, before the final version of the Fourteenth Amendment (House Resolution 127) was submitted, its members considered seventeen different proposals for restructuring congressional representation. These can be broken down into two main categories: proposals that based representation on voters and those that based it on population but assigned penalties to states that withheld the franchise from African Americans.

In the Joint Committee's first few meetings, the group favored plans that based representation on states' voting populations. The first proposal came from Thaddeus Stevens on Tuesday, January 9, 1866. It determined representation on a state's "legal voters" and so consequently had to carefully define exactly who was qualified to be a "legal voter." Its full text declared that "Representatives shall be apportioned among the several States, which may be included within this Union, according to the number of their respective legal voters; and for this purpose none shall be considered as legal voters who are not either natural born or naturalized citizens of the United States, of the age of twenty-one years."[42] Identifying adult citizens as legitimate voters, Stevens recycled antebellum understandings of the franchise as determined by national membership and age, but he pointedly left off references to voters' race or gender.[43] This omission may have reflected his more liberal attitude toward women's enfranchisement, or it may have been an oversight.[44] In any case, the committee did not wait long to correct the problem. After some discussion, the New York Republican Roscoe Conkling offered an amendment to "[insert] the word 'male' between the word 'naturalized' and the word 'citizens,'" which was immediately adopted.[45] Though the clerk did not record the details of debate on this issue, the committee's subsequent rejection of both Justin Morrill's amendment to add a literacy qualification and George Williams's suggestion to eliminate the definition of voters shows that the committee's choice to include the word "male" in the proposal was deliberate.

The Stevens/Conkling proposal did not last long, however. It was soon replaced by an amendment that based representation on population but omitted any group from enumeration that was denied the franchise because of race or color. Resolutions of this type, unlike Stevens's amended proposal, were mostly gender-neutral, perhaps because they did not require a clause to define voters. Instead, population-based amendments implicitly accepted the states' existing populations of voters but determined that any race-based discrimination would be politically costly. At the committee's third meeting on January 12, Justin Morrill proposed a substitute for the Stevens/Conkling voter-based representation plan. It stated that "Representatives and direct taxes shall be apportioned among the several States, which may be included within this Union, according to their respective numbers of persons, deducting therefrom all of any race or color, whose members or any of them are denied any of the civil or political rights or privileges."[46] Neither Morrill's plan nor the four different amendments to and variations on this resolution that followed used gender-specific language.[47]

Given these two completely different methods for calculating representation and encouraging enfranchisement, it became clear by the end of the January 12 meeting that the committee's members needed to find a way to evaluate their various options. With too many proposals on the table to vote on, the committee appointed a five-member subcommittee consisting of Stevens, Conkling, Fessenden, Howard, and Bingham to examine both the committee members' representation plans and referred proposals from the House and Senate. On January 16, the subcommittee reported back their agreement upon a population-based model of representation. After some discussion and amendment, the committee adopted this text: "Representatives and direct taxes shall be apportioned among the several States which may be included within this Union, according to their respective numbers, counting the whole number of persons in each State, excluding Indians not taxed; provided that, whenever the elective franchise shall be denied or abridged in any State on account of race or color, all persons of such race or color, shall be excluded from the basis of representation."[48] On January 22, 1866, Stevens presented this plan to the House as Resolution 51.[49] It did not use gendered language.

A Strife of Unbridled Suffrage

While the Joint Committee was developing Resolution 51, Congress as a whole was also considering the same ideas, debating which was a better solution to the representation dilemma, calculating representation based on a state's voters or based on its full population. Population-based models seemed to offer the best of both worlds: they allowed states to count all their inhabitants toward congressional representation, including women and children, but did not allow them to count populations who were denied the ballot. But they also raised an ideological conundrum: why was it acceptable in principle to include some nonvoting groups of people in representation totals (i.e., white women and children) but not others who were similarly disfranchised (i.e., African American men, women, and children)? Voter-based models offered a way around this logical inconsistency as they counted only officially recognized political persons—men. But they were also problematic because of gender: states with skewed male-to-female gender ratios could either gain or lose representation if a voter model was adopted. Congressmen whose states' political influence depended on the number of representatives they fielded in the House would be fairly reluctant to relinquish a population-based system if the number of male voters in their states was comparatively low.

The Republican James Blaine of Maine was the first congressman to point out that gender was a significant obstacle for reapportioning representation. On January 8, 1866, he argued that voter-based representation could shift the regional balance of power from the currently dominant eastern states with large proportions of women and children to the male-majority western states. Because, he said, "the ratio of voters to population differs very widely in different sections, . . . [from] a minimum of *nineteen percent* to a maximum of *fifty-eight per cent* [of the population] . . . the changes which this fact would work in the relative representation of certain states would be monstrous."[50] To prove his point, Blaine noted that although California and Vermont had roughly the same number of representatives under the current population-based system, if voters were "assum[ed] . . . as the basis of apportionment," California's 207,0000 voters would give the state eight representatives, while Vermont 87,000 voters would merit only three.[51] Although Blaine's central concern was the loss of congressional power in his region and state, he also argued that a voter-based representation model violated women's and children's right to be represented in the government: "As an abstract proposition no one will deny that population is the true basis of representation; for women, children, and other non-voting classes may have as vital an interest in the legislation of the country as those who actually deposit the ballot."[52] Although he acknowledged that women were not permitted to participate in the political system as actors, Blaine defended their stake in political decisions and used this as another reason to reject voter-based representation.

His concern resonated with many eastern congressmen but was not really borne out by the evidence. As soon as Thaddeus Stevens finished presenting Resolution 51, his fellow committee member Roscoe Conkling addressed the gender question. First, Conkling offered his fellow easterners some reassuring math. Having carefully analyzed the population in all states, he demonstrated that there would be little or no difference in the number of representatives apportioned to eastern states regardless of the way representation was calculated. He dismissed Blaine's concern that "New England would lose very largely should men be made the basis of representation in place of including women and children," claiming that it had "no foundation."[53] Given the census numbers from 1860, he noted that California was the only state whose population was so imbalanced that a voter-based enumeration system would impact its representation. But Conkling agreed with Blaine and objected to the voter-based model because it denied representation to those who did not vote: "Restricting the enumeration to male citizens of the United States twenty one years old and upward . . . would shut out four-fifths of the citizens of the country—women and children, who are citizens, who are taxed, and who are, and always have been represented."[54] In this way he identified women as vital members of the political community.

Conkling's support for women's representation did not mean that he favored their enfranchisement. Rather, to the man who first introduced "male" language to the Joint Committee on Reconstruction, the main downfall of the voter-based model was that it offered an incentive to states to expand their franchise to the unqualified, such as women. "If voters alone should be made the foundation of representation . . . one State might let women and minors vote. Another might—some of them do—give the ballot to those otherwise qualified who have been residents for only ten days. Another might extend suffrage to aliens. This," he said, "would lead to a strife of unbridled suffrage."[55] Although Conkling defended women's right to be enumerated as members of the political community for representative purposes, actually including them within the political community as decision makers would, he thought, lead to a disastrous breakdown in social relations. Where would such a suffrage expansion stop? If the Constitution structurally encouraged states to expand their franchise without limitation, what would prevent them from giving the right to vote to women, children, immigrants, Indians, or Chinese aliens in California?[56] But there was a simple solution for preventing a reckless expansion of the ballot: gendered language. On January 23, the Wisconsin Republican Ithamar C. Sloan suggested an amendment to Resolution 51 to "get rid [of Conkling's] objection . . . that some of the States may give the right of suffrage to women. The word "male" inserted will obviate that objection. . . . The amendment I propose is that "qualified male electors, citizens of the United States of the age of twenty-one years and upward, shall be the basis of representation."[57]

Over the next two days two other congressmen pointed to gendered language as a way to prevent women's enfranchisement. Moderate Ohio Republican William Lawrence rejected Resolution 51 because it lacked any explicit acknowledgment of the link between men and political power. By enumerating whole populations, it gave "representation to women, children, and unnaturalized foreigners, all declared by the laws of the States unsafe or unnecessary depositories of political power."[58] Conflating representation and political participation and ignoring the fact that women, children, and foreigners had been counted toward representation since the nation's founding, Lawrence argued that if women were not voters, they should not be represented. "It has never been deemed necessary for the protection of females that they should be regarded as an element of political power," he said, "and hence, they should not be an element of representation. If the necessity shall come, or, if our sense of justice should so change as to enfranchise adult females, it will be time enough then to make them a basis of representation."[59] Despite his incorrect interpretation of the current representation system, Lawrence's sentiment that women were not legitimate members of the political community was a widely shared one. Moreover, his arguments indicate how intertwined many believed representation and the franchise already were.

For some congressmen, House Resolution 51's gender neutrality remained a fundamental problem. The resolution proposed to allow states to count their female inhabitants who were not full members of the political community and yet punish states for failing to enfranchise the African American inhabitants who were also not full members of that community. Not everyone was comfortable with this inconsistency. As the Joint Committee member John Bingham declared, "I am by no means sure that the East is entitled to count its women and children in its basis of representation unless it gives them a voice in the Government, any more than the people of South Carolina ought to count their negroes without giving them a voice in the Government." Yet despite his discomfort, Bingham, like his Republican colleagues, did not think that enfranchising women was a desirable outcome. Lest anyone mistake him as an advocate for woman suffrage, Bingham quickly followed his critique of Resolution 51 with a disclaimer: "But I am not here now to advocate that provision."[60] Most Republicans, like Bingham, had no interest in advocating women's enfranchisement and so seemed fully prepared to overlook the resolution's double standard if for no other reason than that it closely followed the existing formula for apportioning representation based on population while also simultaneously indirectly encouraging states to expand their franchises to African American men, a goal dear to many Republicans' hearts.

In Behalf of the Fairest Portion of Creation

Democrats, on the other hand, were not willing to let this inconsistency pass unnoticed. They seemed delighted to point out Republicans' ideological irregularity on this issue and adopted the cause of gender equality to do so. They did this in two ways: by occasionally advocating for women's enfranchisement and by referencing the petitions of Stanton, Anthony, and their allies. For example, on January 23 the New York Democrat James Brooks critiqued House Resolution 51 because it excluded women from participatory citizenship yet still counted them toward representation.[61] The fact that women were petitioning Congress for the right to vote, Brooks claimed, made the resolution even more problematic. As evidence, he asked the clerk of the House to insert into the record a recently received letter from Susan B. Anthony, along with the text of its accompanying petition.[62] This was the first recorded woman suffrage petition in congressional history.[63] In her letter, Anthony told Brooks that as a member of the minority party, he had the duty to "drive the Republicans to do good works . . . to hold the party to a logical consistency that shall give every responsible citizen in every State equal right to the ballot."[64] Brooks seemed to be taking Anthony's advice by prodding the weakest point of House Resolution 51—its confusing position on voting rights: "In order to make [the] resolution consistent," he declared, "I raise my voice here in behalf of fifteen million of our countrywomen, the fairest, brightest portion of creation, and I ask why they are not permitted to be represented under this resolution?"[65]

Roscoe Conkling rose to answer Brooks's question and to defend the resolution. When Brooks asked why women were not represented under the provisions outlined by the resolution, Conkling interjected, "They are."

BROOKS: Persons are.
CONKLING: I thought they were persons.
BROOKS: And so they are, but they are excluded from all voting. . . . This is a new era; this is an age of progress. . . . Why not, in a resolution like this, include the fair sex too, and give them the right of representation?[66]

Here Brooks confounded women's status as legal persons and as voters, as well as equating representation with voting. But in so doing he noted that the resolution's intent toward women was exclusionary at best. The resolution deemed women persons and counted them toward congressional representation totals but implicitly permitted their disfranchisement. It deemed unacceptable only race or color as a basis for denial of voting rights. In light of this exclusion, Brooks proclaimed Anthony's suffrage claim legitimate and so worthy of support that he promised at a future date to offer an amendment to House Resolution 51 proportionally reducing the congressional representation of any state that did not enfranchise women.[67] Strong words indeed. However, Brooks never did offer this amendment, which likely indicated that he was more interested in using woman suffrage to irritate Republicans than in actually giving women the ballot. Nevertheless, in the midst of the representation discussion woman suffrage had come to the forefront.

Fortunately for the suffragists, the petition drive did not end with Brooks. Because he read the woman suffrage petition only in debate, it was not registered for consideration at that time. Nor was it ever. Other members of the House, however, did officially submit the petitions they received throughout the weeks that Congress debated House Resolution 51. Between January 22 and January 31, three different congressmen and two different senators presented petitions to the clerk of the House or Senate; they were then entered into the congressional journals and passed on to the appropriate committees. In the weeks between these January discussions and March 14, when the Senate rejected House Resolution 51 and returned the problem of representation to the Joint Committee on Reconstruction, fourteen more congressmen officially presented woman suffrage petitions. By the time the Joint Committee introduced House Resolution 127 (the Fourteenth Amendment), a total of sixteen different congressmen had submitted twenty-seven petitions for woman suffrage. Half of those were presented on days that Congress was debating House Resolution 51.[68] Table 2 shows where the petition originated, which congressman presented it, what his party affiliation was, and the committee to which it was referred.

During the Thirty-Ninth Congress, the Senate referred almost all petitions relating to the apportionment of representation and reconstruction to the Joint Committee on Reconstruction. Twenty-five of the Senate's twenty-six general petitions on representation sent before April 30, 1866, were referred to that committee. The Senate also sent most petitions it received about black men's enfranchisement to the same committee. Between January and April of 1866 sixteen petitions were introduced in the Senate advocating black men's suffrage rights alone, as well as nineteen additional petitions that discussed enfranchisement in connection with other Reconstruction issues. Of those thirty-five petitions, twenty-nine were referred to the Joint Committee on Reconstruction.[69] Thus by early 1866, the Senate had established a consistent pattern of referring any suffrage- or representation-related petition to the Reconstruction committee.

On January 24, Benjamin Gratz Brown of Missouri officially presented the first copy of Stanton and Anthony's woman suffrage petition to Congress.[70] The Senate, following established precedent, forwarded it to the Joint Committee. It did not vary this pattern for the remaining five petitions

Table 2 Woman suffrage petitions

Petition #	Chamber	Date of petition	Member of Congress	Party and state	Action taken	Committee	Petitioners
1	S	1/24/66	Brown	UU§ (MO)	Referred	JC15	Women of the United States
2	H	1/25/66	Clarke, S.	R (KS)	Referred	Judiciary	Lizzie A. Sanderson and other women, of the State of New York
3	H	1/29/66	Stevens	R (PA)	Referred	Judiciary	Elizabeth Cady Stanton and other women
4	S	1/31/66	Lane	R (KS)	Referred	JC15	Women of Lawrence, Kansas
5	H	1/31/66	Clarke, S.	R (KS)	Referred	Judiciary	Men and women of the State of Kansas
6	H	2/1/66	Ferry	R (MI)	Referred	Judiciary	Michigan Ladies
7	H	2/6/66	Farnsworth	R (IL)	Referred	Judiciary	Women of the United States
8	H	2/10/66	Laflin	R (NY)	Referred	Judiciary	One hundred ladies of Philadelphia, Jefferson County, New York
9	H	2/13/66	Jenckes	R (NY)	Referred	Judiciary	Women of the State of Rhode Island
10	H	2/14/66	Hart	R (NY)	Referred	Judiciary	Women of the State of New York
11*	S	2/14/66	Sumner	R (MA)	Referred	JC15	3 petitions, citizens of New England
12	S	2/14/66	Sumner	R (MA)	Referred	JC15	Women of the United States
13	H	2/20/66	Humphrey, J.	D (NY)	Referred	Judiciary	Ladies of the State of New York
14	S	2/21/66	Henderson	R (MO)	Tabled		
15†	H	2/21/66	Humphrey, J.	D (NY)	Referred	JC15	Women of Erie County, New York
16	H	2/26/66	Hart	R (NY)	Referred	JC15	Women of the State of New York
17	H	2/26/66	Marvin	U (NY)	Referred	Judiciary	Women of the State of New York
18†	H	2/27/66	Van Horn	R (MO)	Referred	Judiciary	Ladies of the State of New York

(Continued)

Table 2 (Continued)

Petition #	Chamber	Date of petition	Member of Congress	Party and state	Action taken	Committee	Petitioners
19	H	3/5/66	*Defrees*	R (IN)	*Referred*	*Judiciary*	*Women of Steuben County, Indiana*
20†	H	3/9/66	*Washburne*	R (MA)	*Referred*	*JC15*	*Women of the State of Illinois*
21	H	3/12/66	*Laflin*	R (NY)	*Referred*	*Judiciary*	*Women of the State of New York*
22†	H	3/16/66	*Marvin*	U (NY)	*Referred*	*JC15*	*Ladies of Johnstown, New York*
23	H	3/26/66	*Laflin*	R (NY)	*Referred*	*Judiciary*	*Citizens of the State of New York*

Source: House: *Journal*; Senate: *Journal*.

Note: Petitions in italics were presented as universal suffrage petitions, rather than as woman suffrage petitions. See discussion following.

* This petition requested no discrimination in voting based on race, color, or sex.

† Ambiguous petition without confirmation as a woman suffrage petition.

§ Unconditional Unionist.

presented before April 30. By referring woman suffrage petitions to the Joint Committee on Reconstruction, the Senate both indicated its belief that there was a fundamental connection between suffrage rights for women and black men and representation and ensured that those congressmen responsible for determining the limits of that connection understood that suffrage was a question with unclear gendered boundaries. The petitions must have prompted the committee to take gender into account as it made further decisions about representation.[71]

Because the chamber rules permitted senators time to comment on the petitions they were presenting and allocated time for questions, the petitions sparked some of the Thirty-Ninth Congress's most direct discussions about women's rights.[72] In these, the senators revealed both their biases about enfranchising women and their faith in the link between gender and voting rights. Primarily, those who presented petitions took care to reject women's enfranchisement even as they brought the suffrage movement's first efforts to the attention of their colleagues. For example, Charles Sumner presented two woman suffrage petitions to the Senate on February 14, 1866, but claimed that he did so under protest: "I present this petition at this time, as it has been sent to me for this purpose; but I take the liberty of saying that I do not think this is a proper time for the consideration of that question."[73]

When the Republican Senator John Henderson of Missouri presented a petition on February 21, 1866, his initial comments may have led listeners to believe he advocated the women's cause: "I present this petition without any apology. Indeed, I present it with pleasure. It is respectful in its terms, and is signed by ladies occupying so high a place in the moral, social, and intellectual world, that it challenges at our hands at least a respectful consideration." However, as he continued, he undermined his initial support: "The petitioners claim, that as we are proposing to enfranchise four million emancipated slaves, equal and impartial justice alike demands the suffrage for fifteen million women. At first view the proposition can scarcely be met with denial, yet reasons 'thick as blackberries' and strong as truth itself may be urged in favor of the ballot in the one case, which cannot be urged in the other."[74] Although Henderson did not fully elaborate on what those abundant reasons were, he did assert that his primary objection to woman suffrage was that "it is wholly unnecessary as a means for their protection."[75] Perhaps perplexed by this mixed message, one of his colleagues asked the senator if he supported the petition's cause. Henderson took refuge in procedure, replying that debating the merits of a petition was not in order. Concluding the exchange, the president pro tempore asked him what he would wish to do with the petition: Henderson requested that it be tabled.[76]

Just as Republican senators presented Stanton and Anthony's petitions half-heartedly, House Republicans' treatment of the petitions likewise demonstrated their party's lack of interest in women's enfranchisement. Some representatives even disguised the women's petitions as ones supporting black men's enfranchisement. Eleven of the nineteen House petitions from women were submitted and identified in the House *Journal* and *Congressional Globe* merely as petitions for "universal suffrage," a term most congressmen were using to mean "universal male suffrage." (Those petitions are shown in italics in table 2.)[77] The actual petitions that were submitted, housed in the committee records at the National Archives, show that these eleven petitions were copies of the petition that Stanton and Anthony had printed—most likely they were a few of the thousand copies they had disseminated.[78] Whether the members of Congress presenting these petitions sought to deliberately obfuscate their nature in order to add the weight of those signatures for universal manhood suffrage or whether this was a simple legislative oversight is unclear. Nevertheless, it is plain that as a rule congressional Republicans did not have any great passion for presenting woman suffrage petitions, just as they had no great passion for enfranchising women.

However reluctantly presented, those petitions that were properly submitted and referred pushed Republicans to change their suffrage rhetoric. Prior to the presentation of the petitions, Republicans could safely refer to "black suffrage" and know that they meant "black male suffrage." After the presentation of Stanton and Anthony's petitions, however, that generalization was no longer safe. The senator James Lane of Kansas demonstrated this potential danger on January 31. In submitting a woman suffrage petition, Lane first drew upon the rhetorical and collegial masculinity of the Senate, expressing his pleasure in presenting a petition from "one hundred and twenty-four beautiful, accomplished, and intelligent ladies of the city of Lawrence, Kansas" and asking that "a gallant Senate may hear it read."[79] After reading the petition into the record, Lane then suggested it be referred to "the committee that is considering the subject of extending the right of suffrage to the blacks, the male blacks of the United States . . . the proper one to which to refer the petition of the white women of the United States on that subject."[80] Here Lane stumbled. By initially declaring that the committee was considering black suffrage, he adopted typical suffrage language to discuss the ballot—language that did not mention gender. But catching himself, he realized that he had to rephrase exactly which blacks were being considered for suffrage (i.e., only the males). Lane's blunder was revealing. Had there been no women formally asking for the ballot, he and the rest of his congressional colleagues could have blithely continued imagining that universal suffrage applied only to men. They could then have drafted a constitutional amendment like House Resolution 51 that did not explicitly define legitimate voters as male. But woman suffrage petitions had made both this linguistic nonchalance and a gender-neutral representation provision impossible.

Given these petitions, the problem of women's representation, and Democratic opposition rhetoric as Congress debated House Resolution 51, hardly any congressman could fail to realize that the resolution had a gender problem. But in early 1866, gender was the least of the resolution's troubles. Although the House had passed it on January 31 over the objections of radicals who thought it too vague about suffrage rights and of Democrats who thought it imposed overly harsh conditions on southern states, it did not fare so well in the Senate. First, the Senate tabled the resolution until it had finished debating the Civil Rights Act. Then, when it did begin to debate House Resolution 51 on February 5, the problems the proposal had faced in the House were amplified. Most important, Senate radicals such as Sumner opposed the resolution because it tacitly permitted states to disfranchise African Americans and most likely disregard their basic civil rights as well, with only a loss of congressional representatives as punishment. To object to this permissive approach, some radicals argued that the resolution fundamentally violated the link between taxation and representation because it permitted states to collect tax revenues from disfranchised African Americans who were not included in the basis of representation.[81]

This concern with taxation and representation brought gender directly into the Senate discussions of representation. In these debates moderate congressmen used women's status to reject the radicals' critique of House Resolution 51. They argued that the resolution did not violate any fundamental democratic principle because there already existed a separation between taxation and representation as women were disfranchised taxpayers who were nevertheless represented. William Pitt Fessenden offered the best example of this argument in early February, using women to rebut Charles Sumner's lengthy and passionate objections to the resolution:

The [theory that the] honorable Senator from Massachusetts argued . . . that taxation and representation should go together, would just as well apply to women as to men; but I noticed that the honorable Senator dodged that part of the proposition very carefully. . . . When it came to the question whether females should vote or not, I did not hear that he expressed any opinion upon that subject whatever; and yet his argument goes to that extent. If a necessary connection between taxation and representation applies to the individuals in a State. . . . I should like to have him tell me why every female that is taxed ought not to vote.[82]

Common practice since the ratification of the Constitution, Fessenden argued, both taxed and represented women even though they did not vote. Certainly anyone elected to represent others, he claimed, did not envision himself as representing only voters. "I do not know how the honorable Senator from Massachusetts feels, but I could hardly stand here easily if I did not suppose I was representing the ladies of my State. [Laughter.] I know, or I fancy I know, that I have received considerable support from some of them, not exactly in the way of voting, but in influencing voters. [Laughter.]"[83] Fessenden used gender here primarily to embarrass a colleague who supported all manner of radical changes short of woman suffrage, posing himself in stark contrast to Sumner as a manly and gallant protector of women. But he also adopted an approach to women's political engagement that would be wielded with greater frequency in the next fifty years, contending that women did not require enfranchisement because they already had vast political power in their ability to influence men.

Radical and Democratic senators allied on March 9, 1866, to defeat House Resolution 51 by a vote of twenty-five to twenty-two, falling well short of the two-thirds required for passage.[84] This returned the problem of representation to the Joint Committee on Reconstruction and inspired new representation proposals from the floor. Unlike the reapportionment proposals submitted in the earlier months of the congressional session, these new proposals prominently featured gendered language.[85] Even population-based models with suffrage restrictions that had until this point been articulated in gender-neutral terms now contained language identifying voters as male. For example, on March 12 James Grimes, a moderate Republican and member of the Joint Committee on Reconstruction, offered a gendered population-based representation resolution:

> Representation shall be apportioned among the several States which may be included within this Union according to their respective numbers, counting the whole number of persons in each States, excluding Indians not taxed; but whenever in any State the elective franchise shall be denied to any portion of its male citizens above the age of twenty-one years, except for crimes or disloyalty, the basis of representation of such State shall be reduced in the proportion which the number of male citizens so excluded shall bear to the whole number of male citizens over twenty-one years of age.[86]

Grimes's proposal upheld the notion that representation was gender-neutral, but his use of the word "male" in the resolution simultaneously affirmed that voting rights were not; "persons" were counted toward representation, but only male citizens could not be denied the right to vote. Grimes's plan connected a gendered definition of voters with the population-based model of representation. When it returned to representation in April, the Joint Committee on Reconstruction also began to make this connection.

Mature Manhood

On April 21, Thaddeus Stevens proposed to the Reconstruction committee that a Fourteenth Amendment incorporate civil rights, representation, repudiation of Confederate debt, and suffrage rights for the emancipated. This multipart amendment did not use gendered language in any of its provisions, referring to voters as "persons," rather than as men or males.[87] But on April 28, George Williams offered a substitute means of apportioning representation, identifying voters as male:

> Representatives shall be apportioned among the several states which may be included within this Union according to their respective numbers, counting the whole number of persons in each State excluding Indians not taxed. But, whenever in any State the elective franchise shall be denied to any portion of its male citizens, not less than twenty-one years of age, or in any way abridged, except for participation in rebellion or other crime, the basis of representation in such State shall be reduced in the portion which the number of such male citizens shall bear to the whole number of male citizens not less than twenty-one years of age.[88]

Following Grimes's earlier lead and echoing Conkling's January 12 proposal for House Resolution 51, Williams's representation provision blended the gendered specification of the voter-based models with the population-based means of determining representation.[89] It thus offered the committee a way to base representation on a state's population and yet convey its preference for a political community of male participants. The committee adopted the amendment—only Stevens, Washburn, and Jacob Howard opposed it. Two days later Williams's proposal was sent to the House as section 2 of House Resolution 127.

This representation provision was not all that radicals had hoped for. Like the earlier House Resolution 51, it steered a middle course between

population-based and voter-based representation, and compromising significantly on the question of suffrage, it failed to enfranchise the emancipated.
Thus, like most compromise measures, House Resolution 127 garnered little
passionate support. Those Republicans supporting it in the two-day House
debate most frequently expressed their disappointed resignation that the resolution was so moderate. Thaddeus Stevens, the first to speak on the resolution
in the House, set the tone when he acknowledged that the committee had
hoped for a more radical measure but settled on this as a compromise, one
that he privately had called "shilly-shally" and "bungling."[90] "This proposition is not all that the committee desired," Stevens publically declared. "It
falls far short of my wishes, but it fulfills my hopes. I believe that it is all that
can be obtained in the present state of public opinion."[91] Like Stevens, other
members of the House seemed resigned to the compromise representation
provision. When they discussed it specifically, they recognized that public
opinion would not support direct congressional enfranchisement, and they
conceded that the proposed measure was the best they were likely to achieve.
The Massachusetts Republican Thomas Eliot's statement is representative of
most House members' feelings: "The second section, Mr. Speaker, is, in my
judgment, as nearly correct as it can be without being fully, in full measure, right." With statements like these for the most part, House members
showed little interest in debating representation; it was an issue they had
already thoroughly covered. After two days of relatively uneventful debate,
the House passed Resolution 127 by a vote of 128 to 37, with nineteen
abstentions.[92]

On May 23, 1866, the Senate began its more extensive discussions of
House Resolution 127. In these debates, the senators explicitly connected
woman suffrage and the proposals' gendered language, indicating that the
word "male," as the primary critical difference between Resolution 51 and
Resolution 127, had been deliberately adopted to prevent women's enfranchisement. The first incident illustrating the connection between woman
suffrage and Resolution 127's gendered language was an exchange between
the Reconstruction Committee members Jacob Howard and Reverdy Johnson when the resolution was first presented to the Senate. Their conversation
shows the assumptions that members of the Joint Committee were making
about the relationship of women to the new American polity.

On the first day of the Senate's debate, Howard presented the resolution
for the Senate committee chair Fessenden, who was indisposed. After briefly
discussing the first section on civil rights, Howard confessed that the second
section was not all that he would have wanted: "It is very true and I am sorry
to be obliged to acknowledge it, that this section of the amendment does not

recognize the authority of the United States over the question of suffrage in the several States at all. . . . If I could have had my own way . . . I certainly should secure suffrage to the colored race to some extent at least."[93] But, Howard, like Stevens, acknowledged that the state legislatures were "not yet prepared to sanction so fundamental a change as would be the concession of the right of suffrage to the colored race." Because of this lag between congressional and public opinion, he suggested that the representation provision outlined in the proposed amendment's second section was the best that the committee could do.[94] Thus Howard did not dismiss the provision as a mere compromise measure. He argued instead that House Resolution 127 offered an optimal way of organizing apportionment that was consistent with the founders' understanding of representative democracy. To support this assertion, he cited James Madison's discussion of suffrage in his then recently published writings: "It seems indispensable that the mass of citizens should not be without a voice in making the laws which they are to obey, and in choosing the magistrates who are to administer them." If, Howard claimed, one applied this principle broadly and consistently, "how can any man of true republican feeling, attached to the essential principles of our system of government, refuse the right of suffrage to the whole negro population as a class?"[95]

Howard's sweeping interpretation of Madison's principle prompted Reverdy Johnson to interrupt to ask if the principle applied to all citizens, to the *whole* class of the "negro population." He tersely asked Howard, "Females as well as males?" Howard dismissed this question out of hand: "Mr. Madison does not say anything about females." The fact that Madison did not say anything specific about African Americans either did not seem to bother Howard. Johnson's reply was pointed and simple: "Persons." Howard seemed exasperated by having to explain on record what must have seemed obvious: the difference between men, whatever their race, and women.

> I believe Mr. Madison was old enough and wise enough to take it for granted that there was such a thing as the law of nature which has a certain influence even in political affairs, and that by that law women and children were not regarded as the equals of men. Mr. Madison would not have quibbled about the question of women's voting or of an infant's voting. He lays down a broad democratic principle, that those who are to be bound by the laws ought to have a voice in making them; and everywhere mature manhood is the representative type of the human race.

With this, Howard ended his defense of the resolution's representation provision, perhaps deeming it wise to move on before he found himself ensnared by the controversial woman suffrage issue. No great supporter of women's rights, Johnson did not press Howard further.[96]

What to Howard seemed patently obvious was also clear to most members of the Senate chamber: women and infants were equivalently qualified as voters. No matter how broad an interpretation was given to the principle of representative democracy, no matter how Congress sought to delimit the boundaries of the franchise, they believed that a higher "law of nature" precluded women from political participation.

To Throw Out the Ladies

On June 8, the Senate passed House Resolution 127, 33 to 11.[97] The radicals supported the amendment despite their principled objections; some conservative Republicans, despite their partisan affiliation, did not. There were 10 votes to spare for its required two-thirds majority. A few days later, the House overwhelmingly agreed to the few Senate amendments by a vote of 128–36. On June 15, the resolution was enrolled and sent to the states for ratification as the Fourteenth Amendment to the Constitution.[98] The second section's language had been finalized in the Senate Committee of the Whole by George Williams on June 7. It declared:

> Representatives shall be apportioned among the several States according to their respective numbers, counting the whole number of persons in each State, excluding Indians not taxed. But when the right to vote at any election of the choice of electors for President and Vice-President of the United States, representatives in Congress, the executive and judicial officers of a State, or the members of the legislature thereof, is denied to any of the male inhabitants of such State, being twenty-one years of age and citizens of the United States, or in any way abridged, except for participation in rebellion, or other crime, the basis of representation therein shall be reduced in the proportion which the number of such male citizens shall bear to the whole number of male citizens twenty-one years of age in such State.[99]

Given how similar this provision was to the one in House Resolution 51, why had members of Congress rejected the earlier resolution but accepted its gendered replacement? Certainly there were many complex partisan and political reasons. Between dissatisfaction with the president, pressure from constituents, fear of further party schism, the need for a comprehensive Reconstruction policy, and the looming end of the congressional session, there were significant pressures for senators to accept House Resolution 127's arrangement of representation, though they had previously rejected the earlier version.[100]

But what role did gender play? Did congressmen reject House Resolution 51 solely because it lacked gendered language? It would be a stretch to say so. Did they prefer the representation provision in House Resolution 127 because it was gendered? It seems likely that this was at least a contributing factor, as the language of the resolution better reflected the way members of the Thirty-Ninth Congress were defining the limits of their political community.[101] Moreover, the issue of women's voting rights in particular, and gender more broadly, was never far from Congress's collective consciousness as it debated suffrage and representation. Adopting the political rhetoric that had linked manhood and the ballot for decades, members of the Thirty-Ninth Congress conceptualized political action, theirs and others, as explicitly gendered. They defined the newly reforming American political community as a male family consisting solely of fathers, sons, and brothers. They deemed political actions they approved of as manly acts, those they opposed as unmanly. They argued that African American men's wartime military service, their newly acquired roles as household heads in the South, and their fundamental personal identity as independent men—all duties or rights of men—entitled them to the ballot. And they articulated deep disapproval of the woman suffrage petitions they received. The Fourteenth Amendment's language reflected all of this, demonstrating that the members of Congress believed that manhood and voting were, and should be, synonymous. In this way, members of Congress definitively declared that gender, and not race, would be the central criterion for membership in the postbellum body politic.

Yet the ultimate question remains: Was the use of "male" to refer to voters in the second section of the proposed Fourteenth Amendment a deliberate attempt to exclude women who were starting to explicitly ask Congress for the franchise, or was it simply a reflection of the politicians' generalized belief in a natural law that deemed men more qualified for political thought and action? The arguments of one conservative senator from Pennsylvania hint at an answer. While complaining about Congress's redefinition of political rights, the Republican Edgar Cowan revealed his belief that gendered suffrage language was intended to prevent women's enfranchisement. Unlike most of the Republican senators who conceded that some sort of constitutional change linking enfranchisement and representation was necessary, Cowan disagreed. All the Constitution required, he argued, was that the states have a republican form of government. But because congressmen could not seem to agree on how to define "republican," Cowan, like his fellow Democrats, argued that the states should determine the matter themselves: "Now we are told that a republican form of government is this, that, and the other. One man says it is 'universal suffrage'; another man says it is 'universal manhood suffrage,' so as to throw out the ladies; another says it is 'universal white suffrage,' and so on. Who can agree as to what a republican form of government is?"[102] Although Cowan's discomfort with the varying ways that Congress sought to define a republican form of government is interesting, his statement hints at some of his colleagues' motivations as they made critical linguistic choices. He implies that gendered language was used to reference suffrage in order to prevent women's inclusion in the postwar community of voters. At the very least, he strongly suggests that congressmen fully understood that using "that word 'male,'" as Stanton put it, would have the consequence of throwing out the ladies and making gendered distinctions between Americans a permanent part of the United States Constitution.

CHAPTER 6

White Women's Rights

For women's rights activists, the Fourteenth Amendment was a call to arms. With its passage, Susan B. Anthony declared in an open letter to Congress in 1866, Congress had sold women's "birthright" of equality to "save from a timely death an effete political organization."[1] In other words, party politics was to blame for the gendered Fourteenth Amendment. The amendment's drafting process illustrated how problematic women's influence was on partisan politics; its language indicated how central gender was to that politics. So how should advocates of women's equality respond? Because Republicans had rejected women's petitions and, Anthony argued, prevented an effective "protest against the propositions . . . to introduce the word 'male' into the Federal Constitution," a new political strategy was in order.[2]

On May 10, 1866, Anthony and her fellow activists began by reactivating the women's rights organizations and networks that had lain mostly dormant during the Civil War, convening the first National Women's Rights Convention since 1860. At this meeting, Anthony proposed a new political strategy: women's rights advocates should consolidate their efforts with those of supporters of black men's enfranchisement. This collaboration, she argued, would "concentrate all our forces for the practical application of our one grand, distinctive, national idea—Universal Suffrage." The convention agreed and formed the American Equal Rights Association (AERA). The AERA's primary goal, Elizabeth Cady Stanton declared, would be to "bury the black man and the woman in the citizen."[3]

Between 1866 and 1868, the AERA sought to convince American politicians that gender and race were irrelevant to American participatory citizenship. In two state-level campaigns in particular, in New York and Kansas, AERA leaders advocated for the removal of all legal racial and gender distinctions between voters. However, in the course of these campaigns the AERA came up against the cornerstones of American democracy: the connection of identity to citizenship and partisan politics. Descendants of the authors of the white man's government, neither Republicans nor Democrats understood political citizenship to be race- and gender-neutral. Rather, both were relying on identity to define both partisan distinctions and political strategies. Thus from its founding moment, the AERA faced an even greater challenge than merging two separate social movements in a hostile political climate. To bury specific gender and racial identities within the category of citizen, it had to persuade lawmakers and partisans that despite decades of common belief and despite current political practice and theory, the social meanings attributed to whiteness and manhood were not commensurate with the fundamental requirements for voters in a democracy. Further, the new organization had to convince majority-party Republicans in both states that using gender to obfuscate the racial meanings that had disfranchised black men in the past, redefining voting as a male privilege rather than as a white male privilege, was both ideologically wrong and a flawed political strategy.

In New York, the AERA leadership began this process by making gender- and race-neutral claims to the ballot based on traditional democratic principles, as they had done in the congressional petition campaign of 1865–66. Republican delegates to the convention rejected these arguments and the AERA's request for women's enfranchisement by claiming that not only would female voters disrupt the polity, but they would transform fundamental gender relations. Stanton and Anthony responded by adapting their political rhetoric and tactics and attacking manhood directly. This represented their first significant steps away from the Republican/abolitionist alliance that had characterized their work since 1863.

In Kansas, where referenda were on the ballot to enfranchise both African American men and women in the fall of 1867, that alliance became even more strained. Republican infighting among state politicians led to a schism between supporters of black men's and women's enfranchisement. Some state Republicans also turned to gender to attack women's rights advocates, claiming that the men and women who supported woman suffrage were gender deviants. Again, Stanton and Anthony responded by shifting tactics and rhetoric. This time, they opted for partisan politics, aligning themselves in the late days of the campaign with an openly racist Democratic-leaning demagogue. Throughout the following year, the two openly pursued Democratic connections by adopting Democratic racist language to advocate for white women's enfranchisement exclusively. This led to strained relationships between Stanton and Anthony and other AERA leaders.

Why did Stanton and Anthony turn to racism to advocate for white women's political equality? Their actions as reformers seeking access to the American political system were constrained both by their contemporary partisan political culture and by the rhetorical norms of that culture. Because they wanted to become legitimate participants in this system, suffrage activists had to work within it, regardless of how it restricted their actions, ideas, and language. In other words, suffragists who wanted the ballot could have as many radical ideas as they liked, and they could articulate those ideas in whatever terms they wished, but to succeed they had to persuade those with power to share it. And yet they still had to critique the political system that excluded them. It was a tricky balance. By 1868, Stanton and Anthony thought that perhaps the best way to achieve their goals would be to make arguments that would appeal to partisan political insiders. Rejected by Republicans, by 1867 they turned to Democratic insiders as a viable target for their energies and attention.

Members of the State

Between its formation in May of 1866 and the start of the New York constitutional convention, the AERA spent thirteen months campaigning for universal suffrage, "ma[king] a thorough canvass of the entire State, with lecturers, tracts and petitions" and convening forty-eight meetings in over thirty locations across the state.[4] In these meetings, AERA speakers had two overlapping goals: to advocate for universal suffrage for the upcoming special election and to persuade the upcoming convention to bestow "the right of suffrage upon equal terms to both men and women."[5] There was some indication that the first goal was within reach. New York's two previous special constitutional convention elections, in 1801 and 1821, had allowed all men to choose convention delegates regardless of their net worth, even though general elections had a property-based franchise. Because constitutional conventions reconstituted the whole political community and so required all of the community members' consent, all men were permitted to participate. By the winter of 1866, most Republicans in the New York Senate and Assembly supported applying this same principle to African

American men who did not meet the current $250 property restriction for general elections. The AERA noted these trends and thus pursued the special election as an opportunity for women, as well as African American men, to acquire a political voice.[6]

To claim that New York's women had a right to select constitutional convention delegates, the AERA activists made arguments that echoed those of the congressional petition campaign, situating gender as incidental to American democratic citizenship. They claimed that because men and women were equally alike as citizens, they were entitled to the same rights. As Anthony argued, "If men will talk . . . of impartial suffrage, universal suffrage, we mean to have them understand that women are to be included in its impartiality and universality."[7] Fundamental law classified women as a part of "we, the people," AERA activists argued; therefore, women were equally subject to and equally entitled to participate in the making of the laws of the state. For example, attendees at a Syracuse meeting on December 12, 1866, declared that because "women as well as men, are made to bear the burdens of, and to yield obedience to the government" they were equally entitled to the franchise.[8] Auburn delegates resolved on January 7, 1867, that since

> a State Constitution should . . . be assented to by a majority of the people, including as well those whom it disfranchises as those whom it invests with the suffrage; and . . . there is nothing in the present Constitution of the State of New York to prevent women from voting for, or being elected as delegates to the Convention about to assemble to revise the Constitution of the State; therefore, *Resolved*, That we recommend to the people to elect their delegates to said Convention, *irrespective of sex or complexion;* and we shall call on the Legislature to enact that women, as well as men, shall be admitted to vote for such delegates.[9]

At a meeting in Troy, New York, on February 18, Anthony called the state to task for failing to implement its own democratic principles. Men and women were equally taxed, she argued, and so should be equally entitled to the franchise. "The property of women is assessed to pay for canals, for the support of militia, for bridges, railroads, and public works, and yet she has not a voice in aiding these enterprises or saying how they should be carried [out]."[10] Anthony argued, as others had done before her, that America's "second revolution" offered the nation a chance to fulfill the founders' vision of equality and properly align America's policies with its principles.

These general assertions, consistent with the suffragists' immediate postwar strategy, sought to convince those New Yorkers attending AERA meetings that the ideas they already believed in and treasured could and should be applied to American women. And in some places, the arguments seemed to be working.[11] For example, the *Yates County Chronicle* reported of Stanton's December twenty-third appearance in Penn Yan that her lecture "was attended by a very small audience, but was an excellent entertainment for each as did attend. . . . The cause [Stanton] supports is rapidly gaining adherents these days, and those who oppose it will soon be in the minority, unless they had better arguments against it than those heretofore in vogue."[12] In an article published a few days after Stanton's appearance, the paper declared female suffrage to be a good idea, despite the fears of the "fogies [who] tremble at the mention of this further step." "We believe," the *Chronicle* reported, that "the influence of women will be as salutary, as constitutional and as legitimate at the polls as at the fireside."[13]

Although public support was essential to their movement, Stanton and her colleagues also needed to persuade New York's political leadership that women should vote in the special election selecting convention delegates. Despite their general skepticism, New York's legislators granted Elizabeth Cady Stanton a hearing before the state assembly on behalf of the AERA on January 23, 1867. Stanton began by claiming that because the state constitution was being revised, the political community of the state was being remade; therefore the voices of *all* its citizens were needed for that remaking. Further, she argued, women's and poorer African Americans' exclusion from the franchise violated article 1, section 1 of the existing New York Constitution which stated, "No member of this State shall be disfranchised or deprived of any of the rights or privileges secured to any citizen thereof, unless by the law of the land and the judgment of his peers." Stanton asserted, "Now, women, and negroes not worth two hundred and fifty dollars, however weak and insignificant, are surely 'members of the state.'" In fact, these two "minority" groups together, Stanton contended, constituted a majority: "On our republican theory that the majority governed, women and negroes should have a voice in the government of the State; and being taxed, should be represented."[14] Here Stanton echoed the ideas articulated in the upstate meetings and speeches and emphasizing the essential equality of all individuals. But she quickly moved beyond this basic claim.

Throughout the rest of the speech, Stanton argued that *either* men and women were the same citizens under the law, and therefore were entitled to the same right to the franchise, *or* they were so profoundly different that men could not adequately represent women and their interests, and women should therefore represent themselves. Either way, she claimed, women must have a voice in the government. For example, in her consideration of article 1, section 1, Stanton asserted, "The law of the land is equality. The question of disfranchisement has never been submitted to the judgment of [the peers of women and African Americans with little property]. A peer is an equal. The 'white male citizen' who so pompously parades himself in all our Codes and Constitutions, does not recognize women and negroes as his equals; therefore, his judgment in their case amounts to nothing."[15] If these groups were so unlike white men, then they needed political autonomy. Perhaps more disturbing to her listeners, Stanton declared that "women and negroes constituting a majority of the people of the State, do not recognize a 'white male' minority as their rightful rulers."[16] That white male minority "have legislated as unjustly for women and negroes as have the nobles of England for their disfranchised classes."[17] "If the 'white male' will do all the voting," she grumbled, "let him pay all the taxes."[18]

Stanton recognized that in the current political climate, New York's Republicans, at least, were seriously considering permitting African American men to represent themselves, particularly because of the change in southern freedmen's status from dependent to independent taxpayers. "In demanding suffrage for the black man of the South, the dominant party recognizes the fact that as a freedman he is no longer a part of the family, therefore his master is no longer his representative, and as he will now be liable to taxation, he must also have representation." New York also actively recognized the link between taxation and representation, Stanton claimed, because black men who had less than $250 could not vote and so were not taxed. But women, she noted, had never been exempt from taxation. "Is it on the ground of color or sex, that the black man finds greater favor in the eyes of the law than the daughters of the State?"[19] Unfortunately for Stanton and the AERA, the answer was sex.

The privilege and power Reconstruction-era politicians were attributing to sex frustrated Stanton. In her speech to the legislature, this frustration showed, particularly in her sarcastic use of the term "white male."[20] But Stanton also explicitly objected to New York's white man's government. The state's constitution placed such emphasis on whiteness and manhood, she argued, that it enabled many "unfit" voters simply because they were white and male: "What an unspeakable privilege to have that precious jewel—the human soul—in the setting of *white manhood*, that thus it can pass through the prison, the asylum, the alms-house . . . and come forth undimmed to appear at the ballot-box at the earliest opportunity there to bury its crimes, its poverty, its moral and physical deformities all beneath the rights, privileges, and immunities of a citizen of the state."[21] Stanton also contended that the growing number of urban poor were also suspect voters, yet were permitted to vote simply because of their gender and race. "Just imagine the motley crew from the ten thousand dens of poverty and vice in our large cities, limping, raving, cringing, staggering up to the polls, while the loyal mothers of a million soldiers whose bones lay bleaching on every southern plain, stand outside sad and silent witness of the wholesale desecration of republican institutions."[22] Vehemently distancing herself (and other white women) from these unfit voters, she added, "I, for one, gentlemen, am not willing to be thus represented. I claim to understand the interest of the nation better than yonder pauper in your alms-house, than the unbalanced graduate from your asylum and prison." She continued, "No wonder that with such voters, sex and color should be exalted above loyalty, virtue, wealth, and education."[23]

Unfortunately for Stanton and the AERA, the New York Legislature did not share her concern that gender and race were inappropriate measures of voting citizens. Instead, it reaffirmed the centrality of gender to politics by deciding in March to prohibit women from participating in the election to select convention delegates.[24] With this defeat, Stanton, Anthony and the other AERA activists turned their whole attention to the upcoming constitutional convention. They continued touring the state through the spring and into early summer, speaking on universal suffrage and gathering petition signatures. This campaign was fairly successful; the suffragists later claimed that the AERA had gathered about twenty thousand signatures for equal suffrage for black men and women to send to the convention.[25]

Radical Transformations

Almost as soon as New York's constitutional convention began on June 4, 1867, the delegates began to debate the connections between gender, race, and voting rights in the state. Women's enfranchisement was in the forefront of these discussions: only seven days after the convention began, Ezra Graves, a delegate from the Twentieth Senate District, offered a resolution for the convention to appoint a committee to decide whether a special election should be held among the state's women to determine whether they themselves wanted the ballot.[26] A more encouraging sign for the AERA was the early appearance of some of the suffrage petitions they had gathered during the spring tour. Longtime woman suffrage advocate George William Curtis presented the first petition on June 19, and more followed throughout the early weeks of the convention.[27] But for the AERA the best news was that the convention appointed Horace Greeley, the influential newspaper publisher and delegate at large from Westchester, to chair the committee on suffrage. Greeley, a former radical and a Republican, had in the past endorsed women's rights as well as equal rights for African Americans.[28] Although there were some indications that he was becoming more conservative, since he supported the amnesty of all former Confederates and had posted bail for Jefferson Davis, his long record on equal rights seemed to situate him ideally to support the AERA's goals.[29] When Greeley granted the AERA an early hearing before his suffrage committee, it looked as if there might actually be a chance for it to persuade the committee, and hence the convention, to eliminate any franchise exclusions based on gender or race.

On the evening of June 27 in the assembly chambers in Albany, Anthony and Stanton, as the representatives of the AREA, addressed "a very large audience" of convention delegates and interested onlookers. Their initial presentation reflected the AERA's ongoing strategy of emphasizing the similarities between men and women and their equal entitlement to the ballot.[30] But in the question-and-answer session, Stanton's critique of the link between manhood and the franchise came to full fruition. The first few questions, from Greeley and another Republican member of the suffrage committee, Stanton B. Hand, addressed the obligations of citizenship. Greeley and Hand asked whether women would accept all the duties that accompanied the privilege of voting, burdens heretofore undertaken only by men. Anthony replied that women would certainly accept jury duty. Hand followed this up by asking whether or not women would be willing to submit to a military draft if given the right to vote.[31] Anthony's response challenged the idea that military service was restricted to men alone: "Yes, I am opposed to war; but if it must be, let them both serve. Yes, sir, we are ready to submit to a draft."[32] Furthermore, Anthony argued, not only were women willing to serve, but they already *had* served in the Civil War, disguised as men. She cited numerous examples of women who had donned male dress and fought as soldiers during the war but were dismissed when their sex was revealed. These cases, Anthony argued, were evidence that women could and would assume the duties to the state that accompanied the franchise.[33]

Here Anthony challenged the delegates' assumption that manhood and military service were synonymous. If military service conveyed manhood, were the women who had served in the military now men? Although with this argument Anthony sought to separate the connections between manhood and military service, her example of women who donned a male identity in order to fight pointed the committee members to the gender transgression engaged in by these women, perhaps encouraging them to think of similar transgressions that could occur if women were enfranchised. Rather than demonstrating a logical inconsistency, as she had clearly hoped, Anthony instead may have confirmed the worst fears of the politicians who were closely associating political activity with manhood: that women's enfranchisement would result in gender disruption.

Stanton's reply to the same question characteristically took a more aggressive approach. Instead of basing her arguments on women who did serve in the military, she instead turned to men who did not. After Anthony answered Hand's question, Greeley pushed the suffragists further on the idea of women's military service, asking Stanton, "If you vote are you ready to fight?" She replied, "Yes . . . we are ready to fight sir, just as you did in the late war, by sending our substitutes."[34] With this declaration Stanton pointed out a logical inconsistency to those who believed that military service conveyed manhood and manhood conveyed political power, observing that in New York the most politically powerful men, had not, for the most part, served in the military. Yet these men still voted. Stanton hoped that by making this argument she had delivered "a crushing blow," as she called it in a letter to a friend describing the incident, to the delegates' assumption that only men could vote.[35]

But Stanton and Anthony's efforts to disconnect manhood, suffrage, and military service fell on deaf ears. In fact, by the date of the AERA's hearing, Greeley's suffrage committee had already finished a report recommending that the convention not enfranchise women.[36] It declared that "adult rational manhood" was the best means of determining voters' qualifications, so the ballot should be wielded by "every man of the age of twenty one years" who met residency requirements. Although this was troubling enough for the cause of woman suffrage, the report went further, explicitly rejecting the enfranchisement of women because it would "involv[e] transformations so radical in social and domestic life" that most people in New York would not accept them.[37] The report claimed that enfranchising women would cause a profound disruption in gender identity. It was a change "so openly at war with a distribution of duties and functions between the sexes as venerable and pervading as government itself."[38]

After the suffrage committee submitted its report, the question of New York's franchise was turned over to the whole convention. Debates on the committee's proposal indicate that the delegates fully supported its recommendation to maintain an all-male body politic. In particular, the convention's Republican delegates situated the link between gender and the franchise at the heart of their arguments for granting black men the right to vote in New York, arguing that black men's military service during the Civil War indicated their manhood and therefore their voting fitness. These arguments began with the committee's report. To explain its recommendation to eliminate any distinction among male voters based on race, when he presented the suffrage report on June 28 Greeley argued that "whites and blacks were indiscriminately drafted and held for service to fill our State's quotas in the war whereby the Republic was saved from disruption" and so should be equally enfranchised.[39] He was not alone in making this claim. Supporters of black male suffrage in the New York convention frequently argued that the Civil War had transformed black men from slaves and virtual children to men—connecting manhood, military service, and the franchise.[40]

For example, on Saturday, July 13, 1867, Theodore Dwight, a Republican from the Nineteenth Senatorial District, made this argument by sharing a personal conversion story describing his first encounter with African American soldiers. He admitted that he had opposed the 1860 state referendum to enfranchise black men but that when he saw black soldiers, "men clad in the United States Uniform, standing erect with a manly port . . . I saw that . . . they thought the time had come when their race should show that they were men, and thus should be enfranchised. And from that hour, sir, I have felt that the negro was a man."[41] Dwight recognized that the soldiers he had seen were "go[ing] forth to protect me and my wife and children, and my friends and society, and above all his country. . . . And men who have done that for me I believe, sir, to be men. I have no doubt about it."[42]

Whether or not Dwight's story was true or merely a clever use of narrative for partisan purposes, his notion that black soldiers were manly and therefore required the most important privilege that adhered to manhood—voting—was an idea shared by many of his fellow delegates. Like Dwight, the convention's Republicans repeatedly argued in suffrage debates that voting eligibility should be determined only by adult male status, regardless of one's race.[43] For example, on July 9, Jerome Fuller, a Republican from the Twenty-Eighth Senatorial District, argued that "the qualification for the elective franchise, undoubtedly, as a general proposition is manhood."[44] On the same day of debate, Seth Wakeman, a Republican from the same district, stated, "I am disposed to base the right to vote upon manhood, without reference to color. . . . I must vote for the amendment . . . doing away with all property qualifications, for the white as well as for the colored man, and put each on his manhood."[45] Even some Democrats recognized the connection between manhood and voting. Joseph Masten, Democrat-at-large, in debate called the vote a "manly privilege."[46]

This perception, of voting as a male privilege, was the essence of what Anthony and Stanton and the AERA sought to challenge. The two activists continued their attack on the link between manhood and voting in New York even after their appearance before the suffrage committee. On July 4, both women spoke at a massive rally for the AERA in Westchester, near

Horace Greeley's home.[47] In her speech Stanton continued to challenge the link between voting rights, manhood, and military service. This link did not exist, she argued, because she "presumed not a member in the Constitutional Convention had gone to the war, or could show the scar of a bullet received in battle. The ballot and the bullet certainly did not go together."[48] By pointing out that convention members were men and voters but probably not veterans, Stanton critiqued the convention's political leaders for not practicing what their party was preaching. It also demonstrated her developing ability to use social differences to argue for women's enfranchisement. Clearly, only the wealthy could pay poorer men to fight in their place.[49] If the tie between military service, manhood, and voting rights was simply a formality that could be overcome by men with money, Stanton cleverly noted, that the wealthiest women with money could overcome such a formality just as easily.

But the convention's delegates were not associating social class with suffrage; they were linking manhood to the ballot, and the AERA leaders' attempts to challenge this link were not working. Therefore, in mid-July Stanton and Anthony tried a different line of attack. On July 16, the suffrage leaders persuaded George William Curtis, whom Anthony considered the best woman suffrage advocate at the convention, to present a particularly critical petition.[50] Unlike the many earlier AERA petitions submitted to the convention, this one gained significant public attention because of one particular signature. The petition came from "Mrs. Horace Greeley and other citizens of Westchester County, asking for equal suffrage for men and women."[51]

As the convention was currently debating Horace Greeley's suffrage committee report, recommending that New York not implement equal suffrage for men and women, Mrs. Horace Greeley's petition caused quite an uproar. Greeley had not been informed that this petition was coming to the floor, and when its presentation occasioned "much amusement" in the rest of the convention, the ambushed Greeley became quite upset. When the convention adjourned for the day, the suffragists later recalled, he "had disappeared through some side door, and could not be found."[52] Greeley's embarrassment was noted in all the major New York papers, providing the perfect opportunity for partisan ridicule.[53] The *New York World* headlined the incident in very large, bold print on the front page: "Mrs. Horace Greeley Petitioning for Female Suffrage" and reported that the petition's "announcement created a general laughter in the convention at the expense of Greeley."[54] The editors of the *New York Herald* wrote that the petition was "clearly a domestic protest against the tyranny of that gay deceiver Horace." Later in the editorial, in the racist language typical of their party in this period, the Democratic editors stated that "there is room enough for the women on the broad platform of universal suffrage, and we have a poor idea of the manhood that would crowd these gentler ones away to make room for the niggers."[55]

Attacking Greeley personally was a deliberate political strategy. Stanton and Anthony had persuaded Mary Cheney Greeley to sign one of the AERA's universal suffrage petitions early in their petitions drive. But by holding on to the petition until after Horace Greeley's suffrage committee report had indicated his disfavor of the issue, they (through Curtis) ensured the petition would garner significant attention for their cause. Further, by presenting the petition from "Mrs. Horace Greeley" rather than from "Mrs. Mary Greeley," as many women signed petitions at the time, the three sought to make clear exactly which Mrs. Greeley supported women's enfranchisement.[56] Consequently, this petition emphasized the differences in opinion on woman suffrage within the Greeley household and exposed marital discord there for the entire state to see. It revealed that Horace Greeley did not control, or perhaps was not even aware of, his wife's opinions. Most vital, however, it implied that Greeley was not an effective head of his household—that he simply could not control his wife.[57]

Ridicule of Greeley's manhood was not limited to the press—it also emerged in the convention itself. On July 18, during the debate on the suffrage committee's proposal, George Curtis proposed removing the word "male" from the constitution's suffrage provision.[58] This led the convention to explicitly debate woman suffrage on July 22–23, and again briefly on July 25.[59] On two different occasions during these debates, delegates obliquely referenced Greeley's public embarrassment. The first came on July 22, five days after Mrs. Greeley's petition was offered to the convention, when Marcus Bickford argued that if women voted, they would also then have the right to hold office. The election of women, Bickford argued, would result in a dramatic spectacle, "when the Speaker recognizes 'the Lady from Westchester.'" The records of debate indicated that at this, the convention laughed.[60] Horace Greeley, as the most prominent representative from Westchester County, was likely Bickford's target. Greeley, Bickford implied, was less than a man, either because his role could be readily supplanted by a woman or because Greeley himself was implied to be the lady in this scenario.

The second reference was more oblique. On July 25, one of the last days that woman suffrage itself was explicitly debated in the convention, the Democrat Erastus Brooks from the First Senatorial District argued that women did not wish to be enfranchised. "There are in this convention one hundred and sixty household gods, so to speak, representing our homes and firesides," he stated. "All of these are represented by us in our respective heads of families. How many of these homes, how many of our wives and daughters and sisters desire to be intrusted with this right of franchise?"[61] Only nine days before, at least one of the "household gods" of the convention, Horace Greeley, was shown to have a wife who did desire to be entrusted with the right.

The presentation of Mrs. Greeley's petition as an attempt to challenge the connection between manhood and voting was unsuccessful and problematic. As an intentional strategy designed to point out logical inconsistencies in the link between manhood, political power, and the franchise, it instead played out as a personal attack. This made it seem more of an angry reaction born of spite, hurt, and feelings of betrayal than a reasoned political strategy. Further, it did not transform the opinions of delegates at New York's constitutional convention. Instead, it may have played into their worst fears: that woman suffrage would result in domestic discord, undermining the natural authority of men as the heads of households, disrupting existing gender arrangements.

In the floor debates on woman suffrage, the delegates revealed their fear that women's enfranchisement would transform gender relations and reaffirmed their faith in the link between gender and the franchise. For example, the Republican Horace Smith of the Fifteenth Senate District argued that suffrage was not a natural right for women because gender was not an "unjust or invidious distinction." He stated that the Declaration of Independence "demands the same rights and privileges for the colored man that belong to the white man, other things being equal. But, sir, it does not ignore natural distinctions, nor does it involve necessarily an identity of sphere or sameness of functions."[62] Perceiving gender, but not race, as a natural distinction, Smith argued that "we demand the right of suffrage for colored men because they are *men*, and exclude women because they are *women*. The distinction," he said, "depends upon sex and not upon color."[63] In case there was any confusion, Smith repeated his assertion and reiterated his party's position: "We claim the right of suffrage for colored men because they are men, the same measure of political rights for black as for white, under the principles of our government and the Declaration of Independence; but we object to women, both white and black, participating in government because they are women."[64]

Other delegates agreed with Smith and foresaw gender chaos if women voted. For example, John Francis, a Republican from the twelfth district, bemoaned the loss of sacred masculine space if women were permitted to vote: "Why, sir, if we admit this exercise of the franchise we are substantially told that the ladies shall wrangle at the bar, shout in the auction room, speculate at the Bourse, and be present at the bickering of the gold room. . . . There will be no door to office so concealed or jealously guarded upon which there will not be the gentle but peremptory knock of woman."[65] Francis feared that the vote could enable women to break down the boundaries separating the gendered public and private spheres so valued by nineteenth-century Americans.

The Republican Francis Silvester agreed, but he feared women's preemptory knock on the military's door. Clearly influenced by Stanton and Anthony's argument that enfranchised women would serve in the military, Silvester entertained his fellow delegates with a hypothetical scenario:

> Suppose we consider [women] enrolled in the militia, what uniform are they to support? Are they to don the regulation pattern of the national guard of the State of New York, or are they to appear in expansive crinoline, in flowing train, in head dress and waterfall? [Laughter]. . . . Here is a regiment composed of male and female; here is a rank . . . the inspector stations himself next to private William Brown, and ranges his eyes along the line of warriors to test its straightness, but the poor masculine soldiers are completely hidden by the crinoline of the feminine warriors, and the inspector, completely baffled, is obliged to relinquish his task.[66]

Although Silvester intended to amuse his colleagues, the problem of women joining the male sphere was far more worrisome to the delegates than choosing appropriate uniforms for feminine warriors. These warriors, by their very presence, would undermine military discipline and order. But Silvester also raised a specter of soldiers in drag, a fundamental transgression of the boundaries between masculine and feminine behavior and dress. Women voters would result in women soldiers, both trespassing in the male sphere and generating political and social chaos.

Silvester and Francis expressed a fear of gender disruption caused by women's enfranchisement because for them voting was fundamentally defined as a male privilege, and manliness was fundamentally tied to voting. Giving women the vote would defeminize women, as Marcus Bickford inadvertently indicated by calling the suffragist and AERA leader Lucy Stone "Mr." when she spoke before the convention on July 10.[67] But it would also feminize men. Acting on this fear, the convention overwhelmingly defeated Curtis's proposal for enfranchising women, first by a vote of 133 to 9, then by a vote of 125 to 19.[68] Immediately before the final vote was taken, Horace Greeley rose and took the floor to explain his opposition to enfranchising women. In particular, he protested against the gender disruption that he felt would result: "I wish the women of this State to be heard as women, and not to be mixed up with and commingled with men in caucuses, on nominating committees, and at the polls, but allowed to have their views heard as women of the State. . . . I am very sure they will be heard as women."[69]

Ultimately, Stanton and the AERA could not persuade New York's 1867 convention delegates that burying the woman in the citizen would not also bury all gendered distinctions; the delegates simply did not believe that citizenship was neutral ground into which gender identities could be buried. Despite this failure, the AERA's attacks on manhood, military service, and Horace Greeley at the convention represented important attempts to seek an alternative argumentative framework outside the abolitionist/radical Republican alliance. By challenging the link between manhood and the franchise, Stanton and Anthony challenged the Republicans' partisan rhetorical hegemony and foreshadowed their forthcoming split with the party of Lincoln. But within the partisan world of Reconstruction politics, there were limited alternatives to Republican alliances and rhetorical culture. To successfully navigate this world, the suffragists had to work within the constraints it imposed. Thus, in Kansas when they began looking away from the Republicans, the only remaining option was the other political party competing with the Republicans for institutional control—the Democrats.

Such a Fearful Deglutition

As New York was rejecting the AERA's request for a revolution in voting rights in the summer of 1867, the organization was already looking to its next campaign.[70] In Kansas the Republican Party had placed a referendum for black suffrage onto the November ballot. More importantly for woman suffragists, the influential state senator Samuel N. Wood had persuaded his colleagues to add a referendum to enfranchise women to the same ballot. In the spring and summer, Wood extended invitations to several prominent eastern suffrage advocates to come to Kansas and stump for his referendum.[71] The AERA sent Olympia Brown, Lucy Stone, and Henry Blackwell to speak for equal rights across the state.[72] However, they found little support among many Kansas Republicans, some of whom, like the New York and congressional Republicans, feared that the association of woman suffrage and black male suffrage would defeat both. Consequently, most Kansas Republicans sought to distance the black suffrage campaign from woman suffrage. By early summer, Stone and Blackwell had returned to the East, discouraged by the lack of support they found in the state.[73] Upon further urging from Wood, Stanton and Anthony came to Kansas in September hoping to revive the lagging woman suffrage campaign.[74]

They arrived in Kansas late in the game, but there was enough activity among Kansas Republicans to keep their hopes for success alive. Two prominent Republicans, Senator Samuel Pomeroy and the state's ex-governor

Charles Robinson, actively worked for universal suffrage: Robinson accompanied Stanton for the first few weeks of her state lecture tour, and Pomeroy prompted forty-four other politicians and editors to sign a document indicating their support for both suffrage referenda. In late September the eastern radical papers finally chimed in: Theodore Tilton's *Independent* endorsed woman suffrage in Kansas. On October 1, the notable eastern radicals Benjamin Wade, Theodore Tilton, Wendell Phillips, Gerrit Smith, and Henry Ward Beecher published in Horace Greeley's *New York Tribune* a plea to Kansas voters to vote favorably on both referenda.[75]

But this lukewarm support was far too little and way too late. Although officially the party declared itself neutral on women's enfranchisement, permitting each party speaker to "express his individual opinion on all 'side issues'" led many local Republicans to campaign actively against woman suffrage at Republican-sponsored events.[76] Some of these politicians, a supporter argued to the party's state central committee "used ungentlemanly, indecent, and infamously defamatory language when alluding to a large and respectable portion of the women of Kansas, or to women now engaged in canvassing the State in favor of impartial suffrage."[77] One group in Emporia even cited Greeley's New York convention suffrage report as support for their opposition.[78] Even worse was the active negative campaigning engaged in by some party papers. Calling woman suffrage a "nauseating dose," the editor of the Atchison *Daily Champion* suggested that "the stomach of our State . . . is, as yet, too tender and febrific to allow such a fearful deglutition."[79] Other newspaper editors followed suit. Charles Eskridge of Emporia, who sought to leverage tensions between supporters of black men's and women's suffrage to take over the practically leaderless Kansas Republican Party, initiated a relentless press campaign that challenged the gender identity of supporters of women's voting rights—calling one man a "poodle pup" and women "male women."[80] Eskridge declared that the voting referenda would "bring about a conflict of races and sexes" and echoed the oft-expressed sentiment that enfranchising women would be the end of American society.[81] Those who shared his views put this sentiment into action, forming an Anti-Female Suffrage State Committee to campaign actively against women's rights.[82] Divided and weak, the state party's leadership refused to censure speakers who were attacking women activists, which some AERA supporters interpreted as a clear indication of a broad Republican hostility to their cause.[83] Feeling abandoned by local Republicans and frustrated by national radicals' inaction and late action, some suffragists in Kansas started to look for a different constituency.

As early as 1866, woman suffrage supporters had sought support from the Democratic Party.[84] Early in the Kansas campaign, ex-governor Robinson discovered that some Democrats were "disposed to talk favorably of the male proposition," meaning Wood's referendum to remove the word "male" from the state constitution.[85] In an April 10 letter, Lucy Stone reported to Stanton that although the Republicans were setting aside woman suffrage, "the Democrats all over the State are preparing to take us up."[86] Despite these hints of support, in September the Democrats officially rejected both suffrage referenda. Although some local Democrats continued to support woman suffrage, it was the appearance in late October of a well-known and popular figure associated with the Democrats—George Francis Train—that fueled the hopes and garnered the attention of the woman suffragists.[87] Train, a railroad financier wealthy enough to be funding his own private campaign for president, was an energetic and outlandish speaker who rarely restrained himself to one subject in his public speeches. Known for his impromptu short poems, called epigrams, that ridiculed prominent political figures, Train had been invited to stump Kansas in favor of woman suffrage by a state suffrage organization, as well as by Samuel Wood.[88] Although critical of both parties, Train had close ties to the Irish-American community, which guaranteed that wherever he went in Kansas, some Democrats at least would turn out to hear him speak.[89] His national reputation for eccentricity likewise ensured that wherever he went, hundreds of others would turn out simply for the spectacle.[90]

Train's appearance in Kansas to support woman suffrage was a surprise to Stanton and Anthony, but the two AERA leaders soon embraced him for the publicity, attention, and financial backing that he offered their cause.[91] They also accepted his racism. For the last two weeks of the campaign, Anthony toured the state with Train, speaking on the same platform, as Train openly wielded racist arguments to support white women's enfranchisement.[92] This was not the first time the AERA leaders had turned to race to support their quest for partisan alliances. In the spring campaign, when Stone and the other AERA lecturers had sought Democratic partisan support, they argued for woman suffrage in racist terms that would appeal to Kansas's Democrats. For example, Henry Blackwell circulated a pamphlet in April suggesting to the southern states that they could "counterbalance" the votes of the emancipated men the North was seeking to enfranchise with the ballots of "your four million Southern white women." Adding white women's votes to that of white men, Blackwell seemed to be suggesting, would be one way to maintain white supremacy in the face of northern pressure for racial equality.[93]

In October, Train echoed these ideas, pitching woman suffrage to Democrats as a weapon for white supremacy. For example, in Johnson County he composed the following epigram:

> White women work to free the blacks from slavery / Black men to enslave the whites with political knavery, / Woman votes the black to save, / The black he votes, to make the woman slave, / Hence when blacks and "Rads" unite to enslave the whites, / 'Tis time the Democrats championed woman's rights.[94]

Train's intent was clear: unless Democrats enfranchised white women, black male voters would turn white women into slaves. He repeated this theme throughout his tour of Kansas, particularly emphasizing a race-based social hierarchy. In Leavenworth on October 15, he polled his audience: "All those in favor of lifting women up to the level of negroes *politically*, by giving them votes say aye. (Cries of aye, and laughter.). . . . Now then . . . all those in favor of placing the women below the negro politically . . . say aye. (No response.)."[95] In Ottawa, Train argued that an antiwoman suffrage Republican who intended "to vote for *negro suffrage* and against *woman suffrage*" was endangering white women: "Not satisfied with having your mother, your wife, your sisters, your daughters the equals *politically* of the negro—by giving him a vote and refusing it to woman; you wish to place your family politically still lower in the scale of citizenship and humanity."[96] By emphasizing a social hierarchy, Train, like other Republicans and Democrats in Kansas, depicted the enfranchisement of black men and of white women as oppositional. This depiction and its accompanying tensions persisted throughout the rest of the Kansas campaign, as Republicans fragmented, as African American activists grew increasingly frustrated, and as Stanton and Anthony increasingly turned to the Democrats.[97]

Defining white women's rights and black men's rights as oppositional benefited neither cause in Kansas. On November 5, Kansas voters rejected both referenda by a significant margin. Black male suffrage was defeated by a vote of 19,421 to 10,483, woman suffrage by 19,857 to 9,070. State and national Republican Party support failed to guarantee the passage of black suffrage; Train's racist appeals failed to secure the Democrats for woman suffrage.[98] But in spite of this defeat, Stanton and Anthony did not end their association with Train. Instead, the two activists accepted his offer both to fund their return trip east and to finance a new suffrage newspaper they would edit and manage upon their return to New York. As Stanton later recalled, "We saw that our only chance was in getting the Democratic vote," and Train, it seemed, was their ticket to the Democrats.[99]

Stanton and Anthony's continued connection with Train was troubling to many of their radical friends and erstwhile allies. William Lloyd Garrison was shocked that the two activists could "have taken such leave of good sense" to abandon the Republican Party fold for "that crack-brained harlequin and semi-lunatic, George Francis Train!" Train, Garrison said, "is as destitute of principle as he is of sense, and is fast gravitating toward a lunatic asylum. He may be of use in drawing an audience; but so would a kangaroo, a gorilla, or a hippopotamus."[100] Despite a chorus of criticism like this, Train's offer of a newspaper was too tempting to pass up. The historian Faye Dudden has argued that a woman suffrage newspaper offered Stanton and Anthony an independent and autonomous forum in which to express their views, but even more important, if successful and profitable it would provide them with a long-term, stable source of funding for suffrage activism.[101] Train's paper, the *Revolution,* also offered them a way to pursue new political alliances. In the next few years, their articles and editorials continued to appeal to Democrats, adopting Democratic arguments, rhetoric, and racism.

An Antidote to Political Arsenic

Although the Democrats in Kansas had made anemic overtures to woman suffrage supporters, they were not the first to do so. Throughout suffrage-related debates in the Thirty-Ninth and Fortieth Congresses, numerous Democrats advocated white women's enfranchisement both to oppose black suffrage and as a tool for maintaining the white man's government. Many of these congressmen used white women's voting status negatively to argue against the connection between citizenship and suffrage. In congressional debates on suffrage and representation in 1866, Democrats refuted the Republican Party assertions that the ballot was a right of citizenship by pointing to women's disfranchised status. For example, the Representative John Chanler of New York argued, "The right to vote is not an inalienable right. . . . It is not a natural right at all. . . . Women, minors, and aliens are excluded from its exercise. Yet no disgrace attaches to them in being deprived of the privilege to vote, nor is any injustice committed on them. If the right to vote be, as asserted by some, an inalienable right, it naturally belongs to every human creature who lands on our shores, and should be granted to them without limitation of time or distinction of sex. This is denied by the friends of negro suffrage."[102] But excluding women from the franchise, Chanler claimed, "does not fix disgrace on the fair sex . . . it is rather an honor to them that they suffer this 'constraint which sweetens liberty.'"[103]

Most Democrats were not so bold as to argue that the lack of the ballot "sweetened liberty" for African American men. But, drawing on their long-held partisan tradition of using race to define themselves as a party and adopting their party's traditional racist rhetoric, Democrats deemed African Americans to be racially inferior, morally depraved, and ignorant, unfit voters.[104] Manhood, they claimed, was insufficient to balance the natural and inherent disabilities of race. For example, on June 16, 1866, the Indiana representative William Niblack declared, "The negro race is inferior to the white race, and . . . anything like social or political equality between the two races is neither practicable nor desirable."[105] Senator James Doolittle of Wisconsin echoed this argument, situating a race-based disability at the heart of his objection to enfranchising black men: "We are Caucasians and represent that race. From history, from our education, from our experience, every man of full age of the Caucasian race in this country, as a general rule is competent. . . . When a man tells me that the Africans in this country just set free on the plantations . . . are competent to exercise the right of suffrage and help shape the laws of this great Republic, he states what is perfectly abhorrent to my sense of justice, reason, or propriety."[106]

Doolittle's association of whiteness with competence, and of African-Americans with incompetence, was echoed throughout Democratic suffrage arguments. By arguing that African Americans were inherently ignorant, Democrats could justify rejecting their enfranchisement because of the important responsibilities that accompanied political rights in a democracy. Indeed, the New Jersey representative Andrew Rodgers argued early in the Thirty-Ninth Congress that African Americans' supposed ignorance was such an inherent impediment to suffrage that no country had ever allowed the black man to have the right to vote: "It has become a settled notion of the people . . . that the negro race were not sufficiently intelligent to exercise the right of suffrage, and they have not been allowed that right since the formation of the government. . . . The wisdom of more than five thousand years had refused to allow the political equality of the negro race as exercised by the white; and no civilized people of any country have allowed universal suffrage to the negro throughout their governments."[107] Paralleling the circuitous argument made by Democrats that because women lacked the right to vote, voting was not a right of citizenship, Rodgers asserted that because black men had never had the right to vote, it therefore must not be a right to which they were entitled.

Depicting African American men as uneducated at best and inherently intellectually deficient at worst, Democrats drew on American fears about the safety of their democracy. Like the Republicans, congressional Democrats suggested that the ideological and physical safety of the nation was at stake in any change to the franchise. Unlike Republicans, however, Democrats claimed that danger resulted not from a denial of the ballot but from the extension of it. The Indiana representative Michael Kerr argued that not only was the nation's safety threatened by African American men's enfranchisement, but whiteness itself would be endangered by black voters: "We may thus, by the [enfranchisement of the freedmen], become substantially *Africanized, Mexicanized, or Coolyized* and all our glorious institutions and national and personal individuality give place to anarchy and weakness."[108] National safety was of particular concern for Democrats in light of recent war and the fragile state of reunification. The newly reformed body politic, they argued, could not handle the dangerous political poison of black voters. As Senator Garrett Davis of Kentucky asserted,

> A healthy man may take into his stomach one or two, or three drops of arsenic without serious detriment to his health; but if he were to swallow one, two, or three hundred drops it would destroy his life. Negro suffrage is political arsenic. . . . The tranquility, prosperity, and freedom of a country depend much upon the homogeneousness of its people. . . . But in our country a race of people that is essentially inferior to the Caucasian race in its physical, mental, and moral structure, and that no cultivation can bring to an approximation of that high standard; that has by nature so low an organization as to be wholly incapable of self-civilization . . . should never have any political power conferred on it.[109]

The American political republic, Democrats claimed, could not survive if its people did not share common interests or common abilities. But the most dangerous difference between people, Democrats such as Davis argued, was measured and determined by race.

Not only would the presence of African American men in the body politic threaten national safety, but, Democrats argued, black male voters would threaten the personal safety of individual Americans. In particular, they inverted Republican arguments that the physical safety of southern freedmen depended on their enfranchisement and asserted instead that the safety of white women and not that of black men was being determined in the enfranchisement debates. Drawing on (and simultaneously helping to reinforce) the myth of the black rapist, Democrats argued that enfranchisement would inappropriately empower African American men and give them license to perpetrate violence against southern white women.[110] The first "fearful outrage" upon white womanhood that Democrats predicted was interracial marriage. Without legal distinctions between the political rights of men, they asserted, race mixture would inevitably result. Representative Rodgers, in February of 1866, stated that if the federal government mandated equal political and civil rights,

> a white citizen of any State may marry a white woman, but if a black citizen goes into the same State he is entitled to the same privileges and immunities that white citizens have, and therefore . . . a negro might be allowed to marry a white woman. I will not go for . . . giv[ing] a power so dangerous, so likely to degrade the white men and women of this country, which will . . . allow the people of any State to mingle and mix themselves by marriage with negroes so as to run the pure white blood of the Anglo-Saxon people of the country into the black blood of the negro or the copper blood of the Indian.[111]

However frightened the Democrats were of interracial marriage, some professed to be even more worried that enfranchisement would empower black men to rape white women. For example, Senator Garrett Davis of Kentucky claimed that granting African American men equal citizenship rights would lead to greater numbers of assaults on white females: "A few weeks since, in Louisville, a negro man violated a girl of only eight years of age; and within a few days, in my county, a similar outrage was committed on a white girl ten years old, after which the black monster cut her throat and disemboweled her."[112] If, as Davis alleged, such "monsters" were committing crimes while the death penalty for black rapists was on the law books, what possibilities could be imagined if those laws were removed by enfranchised black men? By arguing that white womanhood was endangered by black equality, either through voluntary miscegenation or rape, and by capitalizing on the stereotypes of vulnerable white womanhood and sexually predatory black men that were becoming increasingly potent in the post–Civil War period, Democrats applied already existing rhetoric that combined sexual meaning and a particular vision of gender and racial identity to discussions of public political rights.[113]

Yet although many Democrats used gendered stereotypes of both black men and white women to claim the sanctity of the white man's government, a few sacrificed their adherence to traditional white gender roles and expanded their conceptualization of voting "men" to include white women. As Andrew Rodgers declared, Democrats believed that the government of the United States was "intended especially for the benefit of white men and white women, and not for those who belong to the negro, Indian, or mulatto race."[114] Those women, the Pennsylvania Democrat Benjamin Boyer argued, should have the right to vote: "If the negro has a natural right to vote because he is a human inhabitant of a community professing to be republican, then women should vote, for the same reason; and the New England States themselves are only *pretend* republics, because their women, who are in a considerable majority, are denied the right of suffrage. Some of the reformers do say that after the negro will come the women. But I protest against this inverse order of merit; and if both are to vote I claim precedence for the ladies."[115] The conservative Pennsylvania senator Edgar Cowan concurred, arguing that if African American men were to vote, then white women should be enfranchised as well.[116]

> I say you have not demonstrated that it is safe to give the ballot to men . . . who it is not pretended anywhere have that intelligence which is necessary to enable them to comprehend the questions which agitate the people of this nation . . . [but Republicans] are determined to do it, and . . . I want to put along with that . . . doubtful element, that ignorant element, that debased element, that element just emerged from slavery, I want you to put along with it into the ballot-box, to neutralize its poison if poison there be, to correct its dangers if danger there be, the female element of the country.[117]

If, as Democrats had argued, the safety of the country was at stake if freedmen were enfranchised, Cowan posited white women voters as an antidote to the possible influence "dangerous blackness" would have at the polls. The whiteness of the female voters he sought was certainly deemed strong enough to counteract the influence of the gender that had heretofore rendered them unfit voters.

Even Republicans' arguments about military service did not deter Democrats from arguing that white women were more qualified voters than black men. Following Republicans' logic that black men's military experiences entitled them to the ballot, some Democrats made the same claim for women. For example, New Jersey representative Rodgers argued that "if you have to have these men vote because they have fought in the Army, then I want all the women who went down into the Army to administer to the suffering soldiers to be equally entitled to vote."[118] With arguments like these, Democrats challenged the gendered association Republicans were making between African American men and voting rights, emphasizing instead the importance of whiteness as a determinant of political privilege. By consistently making white women the subjects of Republican claims, whether those claims were about citizenship, safety, or military service, Democrats created a racist political rhetorical culture that valued whiteness above all else in potential voters—even above gender. The themes developed in this culture offered a model for some woman suffrage activists to draw on as they sought to turn Democrats from rhetorical and theoretical advocates into actual allies.

Cast under the Heel of the Lowest Orders of Manhood

That most Democrats considered the idea of woman suffrage only as an unwanted yet necessary antidote to the political arsenic of the black male voter did not disturb Stanton and Anthony's enthusiasm for new partisan allies in late 1867. Angry and frustrated with Republicans' rejection in Congress, in New York, and in Kansas, the two suffragists stubbornly defended their new alliance, and Train had provided them with a public means in which to do so. In January of 1868, the three began publication of the *Revolution*.[119] In its pages the two women, although never completely abandoning egalitarian and Republican-leaning arguments for woman suffrage, also began to wield overtly racist arguments that directly mirrored the Democrats' arguments privileging white women's enfranchisement. They sought to appeal to Democrats, Stanton wrote in the paper's second issue, because "the party out of power is always in a position to carry principles to their logical conclusions, while the party in power, thinks only of what it can afford to do; hence, you can reason with minorities, while majorities are moved only by votes."[120] To reason with the minority Democrats, Stanton and Anthony strategically used racism to advance white women's claims to the ballot.

Most frequently, the racist statements in the *Revolution* claimed that the enfranchisement of African American men would rearrange the social hierarchy in America, placing white women beneath black men on a metaphorical ladder of political and social power. To reject this potential reordering, the articles' authors, like the Democrats, deemed black men ignorant and unworthy of the power that enfranchisement would convey. For example, in a January 1868 editorial, Stanton declared, "To what a depth of degradation must the women of this nation have fallen to be willing to stand aside, silent and indifferent spectators in the reconstruction of the nation, while all the lower stratas [*sic*] of manhood are to legislate in their interests, political, religious, educational, social and sanitary, molding to their untutored will the institutions of a mighty continent. . . . What an insult to the women who have labored thirty years for the emancipation of the slave, now when he is their political equal, to propose to lift him above their heads."[121] In May 1868 she restated this argument more explicitly and in a more overtly racist way. To defend her decision to defect from the Republican Party and seek Democratic assistance, Stanton stated that she had done so because she saw "that the women of virtue, wealth, and character in this country were to be made the subjects of every vicious, ignorant, degraded type of manhood, [so] we unfurled a new banner to the breeze, 'immediate and unconditional enfranchisement for women of the republic.'"[122] By implying that black men were "vicious, ignorant, and degraded," Stanton disputed both their fitness for the ballot and the justice in privileging their rights over the rights of upper-class, educated white women. Furthermore, she claimed that black men's enfranchisement would give unqualified freedmen power over the rights and futures of wealthy white women. In February 1869, Stanton again rejected the precedence in enfranchisement that was being given to black men by Republicans, protesting that "suffering under the wrongs of Saxon men, you have added insult to injury by exalting another race above her head: slaves, ignorant, degraded, depraved, but yesterday crouching at your feet, outside the pale of political consideration, are to-day, by your edicts, made her rulers, judges, jurors, and lawgivers!"[123]

Anthony also decried a race-based social hierarchy while directly appealing to the Democrats for support. In June she wrote an open letter to the Democratic Party requesting that it add woman suffrage to its 1868 national platform. In the letter she expressed indignation, which she fully expected Democrats to share, that black men had taken precedence within the Republican Party: "While the dominant party have with one hand lifted up TWO MILLION BLACK MEN and crowned them with the honor and dignity of citizenship, with the other they have dethroned FIFTEEN MILLION WHITE WOMEN—their own mothers and sisters, their own wives and daughters—and cast them under the heel of the lowest orders of manhood."[124] By positioning African American men as the lowest order of manhood and implying that Republicans threatened white women's status, Anthony sought Democratic support for returning the national gendered and racial social hierarchy to its prewar form. In all of these statements, Anthony and Stanton challenged the Republican Party's emphasis on manhood, arguing that the Republican strategy would undermine the importance of race in national politics. These assertions were designed to resonate with the deepest fears of Democrats who relied on whiteness to construct their constituency, political culture, and partisan language.

Further echoing Democrats' racist arguments, Stanton and Anthony suggested in the *Revolution* that because the majority of black men were so recently emerged from the ignorance and degradation of slavery, their enfranchisement would endanger the physical and ideological safety of the already embattled nation. White women voters, they argued, would protect the nation from the danger of governance by the "lowest stratum of manhood."[125] For example, in April of 1868, Stanton argued that America's free institutions had been weakened by the recent war and the challenges of Reconstruction and so required white women's stabilizing influence:

> To-day the ship of state is tempest tossed on an uncertain sea. The men at the helm, lacking the spiritual intuitions of women by their side, are steering without chart or compass. . . . Seeing the nation's danger and the men's need, shall women, with the charts spread out before her, knowing all the dangerous coasts and isles, meekly remain in the vessel's hold, while ignorant hands lay hold the ropes and sails, capable of giving no new light or inspiration to those already bewildered there? To us it would be the height of wisdom for such women to rush on deck and say, let not another man touch the ropes until those more skilled have tried what they can do. . . . So we say to-day, educated women first, ignorant men afterward.[126]

Stanton used this metaphor to depict white women as not merely more educated than black men but more skilled in the maneuverings of government. Because of women's skill, their suffrage would protect the nation from the danger of black men's votes. "Universal suffrage is safe," she said, "because you have the wealth, the virtue, the education of woman to outweigh ignorance, poverty, and vice. You have too, that peculiar elevating and civilizing power found in the difference of sex. But to extend suffrage to ignorant manhood, is to invert the natural order of things; it is to dethrone the Queen of the moral universe, and subjugate royalty to brute force."[127]

In claiming that women's votes would protect the nation, Stanton's language hinted at a more insidious argument made by the Democrats—that giving black men the ballot would result in the sexual endangerment of white women. A week after she made the argument about royalty and brute force in the *Revolution*, Stanton repeated this language in another coded attack on black men. This time, Congress came under fire for enfranchising black men in Washington, D.C. She stated that "in removing all political disabilities from the male citizens of the District, [Congress has] established . . . a government based on the aristocracy of sex . . . invading as it does our homes; desecrating our family altars; dividing those whom God has joined together . . . and subjugating, everywhere, moral power to brute force."[128] The verbs she chose to use in these statements are particularly telling. While "desecrate" and "invade" are sufficiently suggestive, "subjugate" explicitly means to conquer, bring under the power of another, to make submissive, and to subdue.[129] In how many contexts could a black man subdue a white woman, making her submit to his will? In case this coded language was lost on some of her readers, in the same issue of the *Revolution* Stanton articulated her meaning is less ambiguous terms: "Just as the democratic cry of a 'white man's government,' created the antagonism between the Irishman and the negro, which culminated in the New York riots of '63, so the republican cry of 'manhood suffrage' creates an antagonism between black men and all women, that will culminate in fearful outrages on womanhood, especially in the Southern States."[130]

Just as Democrats were utilizing the myth of the black male rapist to define black men as unworthy voters, Stanton also drew on this racist buga-boo to create a reason for women's voting that carried sufficient emotional power. She and Anthony had long understood that women's claim to the ballot lacked the urgency that could be claimed by black southern men. But they demanded that woman suffrage receive equal attention, if not priority over the enfranchisement of those men. Without the immediate and palpable threat of violence against white women to push their suffrage claims, those claims lacked political and moral power. To give women's enfranchisement emotional weight, Stanton fused the Republicans' assertion that black men needed the right to vote as protection against the racist violence in the South with the Democrats' claim that enfranchisement would result in sexual dan-ger for white women. This argument, she hoped, would persuade Democrats to support white women's enfranchisement if for no other reason than to protect white social and political power.

Then Stanton took her appeals to Democrats one step further. On October 1, 1868, she endorsed the policies and politics of the Democratic vice presiden-tial candidate, Frank Blair, in the *Revolution*.[131] In the early fall of 1868, Blair gave a campaign speech in Indianapolis that, Faye Dudden argues in *Fighting Chance*, Stanton found appealing. In this speech, Blair touched on all the ideas that she was promoting in her *Revolution* editorials. In particular, he used the Democrats' most racist argument to reject black men's enfranchisement, claim-ing that if they were empowered as voters, miscegenation and the rape of white women would result. A reporter for the *Cincinnati Commercial* noted that in the speech, Blair "drew a picture of the moral, political, and social evils which he believed would result from negro suffrage, especially the degradation of the female sex."[132] But white women's vulnerability to sexual predation was not Blair's only reference to women; he spent a considerable portion of his text reprimanding Republicans and radical abolitionists for abandoning the cause of white woman suffrage. In particular, and perhaps most interesting to Stanton, Blair pointed to Kansas as a key site of Republican betrayal, saying that "at the late election in Kansas, where the question of female suffrage and of negro suffrage were presented . . . the Radicals showed that they preferred to extend the right of suffrage to the brutal negro race, rather than to place the ballot in the hands of their own wives, mothers, daughters, and sisters."[133] Later in the speech, he particularly praised the efforts of women's rights activists who had been working "within a year or two past to obtain the right of suffrage," efforts he attributed to "an instinctive dread of coming danger."[134]

Given the numerous disappointments and setbacks women's rights advocates had had in the past few years, it had to gratify Stanton to see a major party candidate acknowledging the justice of women's claims and recognizing that the Republicans had abandoned women's rights in favor of, as Blair put it, "manhood suffrage, which . . . means suffrage for the negro man and disfranchisement for the white man."[135] The fact that Blair was parroting the worst of Democratic Party racist propaganda about African Americans did not seem to bother Stanton; rather, she seemed willing to accept his assessments. In her endorsement, she noted, "If you would know, women of the republic, how little trust you can put even in the men of your own race, look at your statutes and constitutions, and see the barbarous laws for women. If Saxon men have legislated thus for their own mothers, wives, and daughters, what can we hope for at the hands of Chinese, Indians, and Africans?"[136]

Stanton's endorsement of Blair was the culmination of her efforts to appeal to Democrats. As she had done with congressional Democrats, she chose to interpret Blair's race-baiting as a genuine expression of support for women's rights. It is most likely, however, that he had no more interest in actually enfranchising women than did congressional Democrats in 1866. Instead, he advanced his own candidacy by using white women as both potential victims and voters, appealing to the party rank and file with its particular partisan rhetoric. Dudden has argued that Stanton's acceptance of Blair's claims, and her endorsement, was "political opportunism of the worst sort: ill-informed, ineffective, and unprincipled."[137] It is hard to disagree with this assessment. However, it is also important to see Stanton's endorsement of Blair as a continuation of her ongoing Democratic-leaning campaign hinted at in Congress and in New York, born in Kansas, and fully pursued in the *Revolution*. In this campaign, Stanton, and Anthony to a lesser degree, accepted Democratic rhetoric as political reality, sought allies among the Democratic camp, and appropriated Democratic partisan language to articulate white women's claims to the ballot in what they hoped would be politically meaningful terms.[138]

Every Argument for the Negro

On January 14, 1869, the *Revolution* published a letter from Stanton's cousin Gerrit Smith declining Anthony's request that he sign a new universal suffrage petition for Congress. Smith said he could not "sign a paper against the

enfranchisement of the negro man. . . . The removal of the political disabilities of race is my first desire,—of sex, my second. If put on the same level and
urged in the same connection neither will be soon accomplished." The events
in New York and Kansas of the previous two years had persuaded Smith,
and most other abolitionists and Republicans, that associating woman suffrage with the enfranchisement of African American men would cause both
to fail. Despite Smith's reservations, after three frustrating years of outright
rejection by Republicans in positions of national and local power, Stanton
clearly had had enough. Angrily she declared in an editorial responding to
Smith's letter that "every argument for the negro is an argument for woman
and no logician can escape it.[139] But by January of 1869 she had also amply
demonstrated that in Reconstruction party politics every argument against
"the Negro" could also be used as an argument for the woman.

Although Stanton and Anthony's racist turn was acutely problematic, if
not immoral, it does show the two suffragists navigating the complex waters
of Reconstruction-era identity and partisan politics. As they watched Republicans use gender to delineate the limits of the polity, subsuming the racial
identity of African American men in their manhood, they sought to do the
opposite—to subsume white women's gendered identity in their race and
use whiteness to define the political community. Their ability and willingness to shift fluidly between the political rhetoric of the Republican and
Democratic parties was a calculated political move designed to make white
women's claim to the ballot bear meaning in the intensely partisan world of
nineteenth-century politics. This strategy—though elitist, controversial, nasty,
and ultimately self-defeating—was a strategic choice that seemed reasonable
to these suffrage activists given the constraints on their available political
options. It was a calculated decision made by political actors attempting to
navigate their complex partisan world. And like many political choices, it
relied more on expediency than morality.

That Stanton and Anthony were willing to sacrifice the high ideals of
the AERA so soon after its founding, to surrender the cause of universal
suffrage and advocate exclusively for white women's rights, is one of the
ugliest moments in the early woman suffrage movement.[140] Their racist language caused an uproar among their fellow reformers and ultimately caused
a schism in the woman suffrage movement, a division that set back the cause
of women's enfranchisement for decades. Worse, perhaps, it laid a foundation
of inequality in the movement that would persist throughout the history of
feminism.[141]

CONCLUSION

By Reason of Race

On January 11, 1869, the Republican George Boutwell of Massachusetts, former member of the Joint Committee on Reconstruction and current member of the House Judiciary Committee, presented to Congress a joint resolution that would eventually become the Fifteenth Amendment to the Constitution. Designed to bolster the Fourteenth Amendment's second section and further protect southern African American men's access to the ballot, the proposal (House Resolution 402) declared that "the right of any citizen of the United States to vote shall not be denied or abridged by the United States or by any State by reason of race, color, or previous condition of slavery."[1] It did not mention sex or gender.[2]

Yet the question of women's enfranchisement was consistently present as congressmen debated the amendment's language. Some members raised the issue to defend or oppose it. One good example: the first amendment offered to the Judiciary Committee's proposal explicitly proclaimed women's right to vote, declaring that "the right of any person of the United States shall not be denied or abridged by the United States or any State by reason of his or her race, sex, nativity, or age when over twelve years, color, or previous condition of slavery of any citizen or class of citizen of the United States."[3] By adding "sex" and "nativity," New York's conservative Democratic representative James Brooks most likely sought to make the whole resolution unpalatable to a majority, rather than to truly advocate women's enfranchisement. Less duplicitous, the other congressmen who raised women's voting rights did so most frequently to challenge their political opponents as they debated the resolution, using women's disfranchised state to note that not all adult citizens should possess the right to vote. But regardless of political party, most congressmen who discussed the connection between gender and the ballot demonstrated their belief that women's exclusion from the polity was natural, legally appropriate, and even advantageous to both women and the nation. For example, the Ohio Republican John Sherman used woman suffrage to argue in favor of leaving some restrictions to the states: any suffrage rule, he said, ought to "operate universally and withdraw from the States all power to exclude any portion of the male citizens of the United States, leaving to them if they choose, to regulate the length of residence, whether females shall participate in the elective franchise, at what age males shall vote, &c."[4] In other words, the federal government would protect the fundamental right of all men to access the ballot, but states should feel free to restrict the rights of women.

Like Sherman, Senator George Edmunds, Republican of Vermont, saw no problem with excluding women from the franchise. He claimed that in this he was supported by the nation's courts, which deemed it normal to defend the "right of manhood citizenship" and yet deny those same rights to women. This perspective on women was not restricted by party. Democratic senator Garrett Davis from Kentucky also rejected women's enfranchisement, but he did so by emphasizing domesticity rather than the law. Davis declared that "woman now occupies her proper domain. She is the priestess of the altar of the household. . . . He is a most mistaken man, if not a positive misanthrope, who would bring to that altar the defilements of party politics."[5] Delaware Democratic senator James A. Bayard Jr. agreed. If women were enfranchised and "the sex is dragged down into the political arena," he said, it "will demoralize women's nature, and . . . her real influence over man will gradually but certainly fade, and be lost, and with that loss we shall, as a people, retrograde in civilization."[6] Bayard rejected the "folly" and "fanaticism," of the "communists, socialists, and women's rights party" who advocated women's enfranchisement and instead declared women's domestic role to be paramount. "Inordinate vanity and the love of notoriety may have tempted some women to unsex themselves, both in their dress and in their pursuits," he said, "but woman's heart and the instincts of maternity will keep her true to the greatest duties in life, the culture and formation of the character of her offspring."[7]

Despite Bayard's assumptions to the contrary, throughout the Fortieth Congress there were plenty of "unsexed fanatics" asking for the ballot. During debates on the Fifteenth Amendment, petitions were presented almost daily from groups of women and men "praying that in any amendment of the Constitution extending or regulating the right of suffrage no discrimination shall be allowed as between men and women." On February 15 alone, four petitions signed by more than 3,600 people were submitted to the House.[8] Large petitions like these kept the problem of women's enfranchisement present in the minds of congressmen debating the Fifteenth Amendment. It was so prominent that some proposed alternatives even included gendered language. For example, the Ohio Republican John Bingham, author of the Fourteenth Amendment's first section, offered a version of the Fifteenth Amendment that protected the voting rights of all "male citizens."[9] And Bingham was not alone. Between January 23 and February 26, as Congress evaluated the Fifteenth Amendment's language, at least one other proposed version included the word "male."[10]

Not all alternatives included gendered language, however. And for at least one congressman this omission posed a problem. On February 17, 1869, Roscoe Conkling, now a Republican senator from New York, was defending his preferred version of the Fifteenth Amendment when the connection between women's voting rights and gender-specific constitutional language was again raised. Conkling's version of the amendment declared that "Citizens of the United States of African descent shall have the same right to vote and to hold office in the State and Territories as other electors." In the midst of defending this language, the Indiana Democratic senator Thomas Hendricks interrupted Conkling to ask why the term "elector" was used. He answered that "elector" had been chosen rather than "citizen" to describe the default possessor of rights because "the word 'citizen' it was suggested, might refer to minors or to women, and therefore, the right to vote by comparison with other citizens would not be guarantied." Hendricks then suggested that even without revision the language of the proposed version would enfranchise "all citizens of the United States of African descent—and that includes the women, of course." Conkling rejected this interpretation outright and offered a quick and simple solution to the problem: "If the honorable Senator thinks that is true it would involve the insertion of the word "male," which I believe has been inserted in a number of these amendments other than this. I do not think this is important enough to discuss. I make no comment upon it, except that if there is any danger of that [then] this amendment ought to be perfected in that respect."[11]

Conkling had ample cause to know that one simple word could easily prevent women's enfranchisement. Just three years earlier he himself had been the first person to suggest "perfecting" the Fourteenth Amendment by adding the word "male." Perhaps it was this experience that made him so confident that women's voting rights could be easily avoided in the Fifteenth Amendment's text. Or perhaps it was the repeated failures of the women's rights movement of the past few years that assured him that the issue was not a political problem worth commenting upon. In any case, this brief exchange indicates that by 1869 members of Congress were fully aware that the issue of women's voting rights was, at the very least, an open question. It also indicates that they were fully prepared to ensure that that question would be answered negatively. Clearly, by 1869, members of Congress had learned the power of gender-specific language and were not afraid to use it.

I began this book began with two related questions: Why was the word "male" used in the second section of the Fourteenth Amendment, and why did Elizabeth Cady Stanton and Susan B. Anthony adopt racist suffrage arguments in the late 1860s? Or put another way, how did the words of politicians, congressmen, and activists become legal standards and rhetorical norms that determined the distribution of political and social power? The answers I found indicated that while race and gender had both come to substitute for property during the antebellum period of suffrage expansion, during Reconstruction, for some powerful partisans, race lost a degree of its political salience as a marker of voting status. Instead, to define the newly reforming political community, those in positions of political and social power followed the lead of African American activists and adopted gender as their guiding principle. This principle was explicitly declared in the Fourteenth Amendment. In the face of a politics and partisan culture that so privileged manhood, Stanton and Anthony, to define white women as voters, turned to race as an equally powerful and equally malleable identity that also had deep roots as a determinant of voting status. That they did so to craft an alternate partisan relationship does not mitigate the most troubling long-term consequence of that act—placing racism at the heart of the woman suffrage movement.

Both the centrality of manhood to politics and the suffragists' racism suggest that changing categories of identity rather than broadening understandings of equality drove the Reconstruction era expansion of suffrage rights. Republicans were not fundamentally redefining voting rights on the basis of a new interpretation of democratic ideals. Instead, they were wielding flexible, constructed identity categories to justify their own partisan policies and interests. That they opted to expand the franchise in this way, rather than simply issuing a positive declaration of enfranchisement, would in the future raise a number of problems. Primarily, by grounding black men's right to vote in such a shifting and socially determined category as gender identity, Republicans during Reconstruction made it all the easier to revoke that franchise when Reconstruction came to an end. If black men's right to the franchise was based not in the right of all adult American citizens to participate in the making of the laws that govern them but rather in their contingent identity as men, then redefining their gender identity could call into question their right to vote, as whites in the Jim Crow South demonstrated with such tragic results.[12]

Further, by using the word "male" in the text of the Fourteenth Amendment and tacitly permitting gender distinctions among voters in the Fifteenth Amendment, Republican Reconstruction politics codified a gendered vision of the voting polity in America's fundamental law. This constitutional language embedded in the nation's primary text a vision of an ideal American political community as gendered, as restricted by the meanings attributed to sexual difference in the mid-nineteenth century. While the representation provision of the Fourteenth Amendment was never actively enforced, its definition of voters as "adult male citizens" contributed to and legally enshrined women's ongoing exclusion from American politics until 1920. Although Elizabeth Cady Stanton's prediction in 1865 that it would take a "full century, at least" to remove "that word 'male'" from the Constitution was wrong, it did take almost fifty years for women to gain equal access to the American political system and to remove the association between manhood and voting rights from the American political consciousness.[13]

Of course, the project of defining the limits of America's franchise certainly did not stop there. It took almost a full century for African American men and women to gain full enforcement of the legal, civil, and political protections the Fourteenth and Fifteenth Amendments promised. Indeed, determining who should and who should not vote in America is an ongoing process. From the millions of explicitly disfranchised convicted felons and prisoners, excluded undocumented immigrants, and tacitly disfranchised poor Americans, today there remain substantial groups with limited or no access to the mechanisms of democracy. How we shall choose to address this, and what qualities we identify as necessary for a legitimate voter, remains one of the most vital political questions of the American democracy as we continue to reconstruct *our* suffrage.

ACKNOWLEDGMENTS

I am deeply grateful to the many institutions and people who helped me as I wrote this book. I received essential financial support from Hobart and William Smith Colleges, Cornell University, and the Dirksen Foundation. I was aided by many archivists and librarians at the Library of Congress and the National Archives, as well as those at Cornell University, Hobart and William Smith Colleges, the Massachusetts Historical Society, New York University Library, the New York State Archives, and the Wisconsin State Historical Society.

I would also like to thank the wonderful editorial staff at Cornell University Press. Michael McGandy and Sara Ferguson are fantastically patient and generous editors. I would also like to thank Jamie Fuller for excellent copyediting and Lisa DeBoer for compiling the index.

I owe so much to the teachers who have guided my work over the years: Keith Fitzgerald and Victoria Brown at Grinnell College; Tom Dublin, Kathryn Kish Sklar, and Tiffany Patterson at SUNY Binghamton; Joel Silbey, Ed Baptist, Derek Chang, Isaac Kramnick, Mary Beth Norton, Glenn Altschuler, Stewart Blumin, Joan Brumberg, Sherman Cochran, Maria Christina Garcia, Sandra Greene, Larry Moore, Nick Salvatore, and the late Michael Kammen at Cornell.

I am profoundly grateful for my lovely colleagues in the history department at Hobart and William Smith Colleges: Maureen Flynn, Clif Hood, Derek Linton, John Marks, Susanne McNally, Colby Ristow, Dan Singal, Liz Thornberry, and Lisa Yoshikawa. Our department seminars helped immensely with the books' development, and I thank all my colleagues for their input. Special thanks go to my colleagues Matt Crow, Will Harris, and Matt Kadane for their insightful contributions to the project. Judy Mahoney also deserves special thanks for her incredibly able editorial assistance and unflagging support. I am indebted to the faculty in the Women's Studies Program at HWS: Etin Anwar, Betty Bayer, Lara Blanchard, Kathryn Cowles, Anna Creadick, Donna Davenport, May Farnsworth, Karen Frost-Arnold, Jessica Hayes-Conroy, Alla Ivanchikova, Charity Lofthouse, Liliana Leopardi, Michelle Martin-Baron, and Leah Shafer. They are excellent colleagues. The

Works-In-Progress Group helped especially with the book's last chapter. My students Lou Guard and Kathryn Lawton lent their excellent research assistance to the project.

My deepest thanks to those who read and commented on the manuscript, in whole or in part, as it evolved through the years: Jean Baker, Rebecca Edwards, Carroll Smith-Rosenberg, Martha Solomon Watson, and Judith Wellman. Thanks to the reviewers at the University of Georgia Press and at Cornell University Press who offered excellent suggestions for revision. I am most grateful to Faye Dudden for reading the entire manuscript so thoroughly and for offering such useful suggestions for improvement.

Thanks to the many friends and family who have shouldered some of my burdens and lightened my heart along the way. It most certainly takes a village. Thank you to Grace An, Ryan An, Amy Attima, Sara Barker, Casey Benson, Tre Berney, Carla Bittel, Russ Charif, Irina Chernykov, Alex Chernykov, Garbi Coleman, Robin Coleman, Darren Dale, Chantelle Daniel, Sara Ferguson, Brad Free, Heather Free, Stephen Frug, Scott Grover, Dawn Grover, Aaron Grzywinski, Amelia Habicht, Oliver Habicht, Ginia Harris, Will Harris, Kate Haulman, Shannon Hedtke, Alice Heise, Emily Hopkins, Marshall Hopkins, Beth Howard, Lenore Hoyt, Linda Janke, Carrie Lang, Connie Lew, John Patrick Locklear, Rachel Nottingham Miller, Michelle Mills, Jenna Milner, Monica Murphy, Paul Murphy, Jessica Rice, Dana Roberts, Laura Ward, Leigh Whitaker, David Whitmore, Whitney Wiggins, Linnie Wieselquist, Sarah Wright, Brandon Woll, Sara K. Woll, and H. Roz Woll.

I am beyond grateful to my parents for their unflagging support and love, manuscript reading, and free child care: my father and step-mother Michael Free and Stephanie Haskell Free, my mother Susan Lee, and my parents-in-law Bruce and Ruth Woll. I also am grateful to my late grandmother, Carolyn VanCamp, for reading and editing an early draft of the book.

I owe more than I can say to Arthur Woll. I simply cannot imagine how I would have finished this project without him. I am so thankful to have him in my life. And finally, I wish to thank Lucy Elizabeth Woll for her patience, her peaceful soul, her lively mind, her joyous heart, and her willingness to share her mother with this project.

Notes

Introduction

1. Carol Berkin, "'We, the People of the United States': The Birth of an American Identity, September 1787," *OAH Magazine of History* 20, no. 4 (2006): 53–54; Gordon S. Wood, *The Creation of the American Republic, 1776–1787* (New York: Norton, 1969), 532–536.

2. Akhil Reed Amar argues that despite the narrow electoral population intact when the Constitution was written, its very flexibility in permitting any expansion of the franchise is testament to its democratic nature. Amar, *America's Constitution: A Biography* (New York: Random House, 2005), 18–19.

3. The constitutional ratifying conventions were an important exception to this general rule. Historians have found that they were remarkably more democratic than the regular voting population. Amar, *America's Constitution,* 17. For a full discussion of the democratic nature of the conventions, see Pauline Maier, *Ratification: The People Debate the Constitution, 1787–1788* (New York: Simon & Schuster, 2010).

4. Casey Miller, Kate Swift, and Stephanie Dowrick, *The Handbook of Non-Sexist Writing for Writers, Editors, and Speakers* (London: Women's Press, 1981); Anne Curzan, *Gender Shifts in the History of English* (Cambridge: Cambridge University Press, 2003).

5. The amendment was ratified in 1868 but drafted in the early months of 1866.

6. Journal of the Senate, 39th Cong., 1st sess. 501 (June 8, 1866).

7. Whereas identifying voters as male was new for national politics, the states had used gender-specific language for the franchise since the early 1800s. See chapter 1.

8. Constitutional scholars have consistently noted this fact in their histories of the amendment and commented on the impact that gendered language had on women in subsequent judicial interpretations of the amendment's clauses. See, for example, Raoul Berger, *The Fourteenth Amendment and the Bill of Rights* (Norman: University of Oklahoma Press, 1989); Akhil Reed Amar, "Women and the Constitution," *Harvard Journal of Law & Public Policy* 18 (1994): 465–474; Akhil Reed Amar, "The Bill of Rights and the Fourteenth Amendment," *Yale Law Journal* 101, no. 6 (1992): 1193–1284; Judith A. Baer, *Equality under the Constitution: Reclaiming the Fourteenth Amendment* (Ithaca, NY: Cornell University Press, 1983); Reva B. Siegel, "She the People: The Nineteenth Amendment, Sex Equality, Federalism, and the Family," *Harvard Law Review* 115, no. 4 (2002): 947–1046; Nina Morais, "Sex Discrimination and the Fourteenth Amendment: Lost History," *Yale Law Journal* 97, no. 6 (1988): 1153–1172.

9. Nina Morais comes the closest to exploring the origins of this change in her 1988 *Yale Law Review* article. Although Morais considers a few causes for the inclusion of gendered language, her central concern is using the amendment's terms for

litigating contemporary sex discrimination cases. Morais, "Sex Discrimination and the Fourteenth Amendment."

10. By political community, I mean the group of people commonly understood to be eligible participants in American political life.

11. Roger B. Taney, *The Dred Scott Decision: Opinion of Chief Justice Taney, with an Introduction by J. H. Van Evrie. Also, an Appendix, Containing an Essay on the Natural History of the Prognathous Race of Mankind, Originally Written for the New York Day-Book by Dr. S.A. Cartwright* (New York: Van Evrie, Horton & Co., 1859), http://hdl.loc.gov/loc.law/llst.022. See also Don E. Fehrenbacher, *The Dred Scott Case: Its Significance in American Law and Politics* (New York: Oxford University Press, 1978).

12. 14 Stat. 27 (1866).

13. Nineteenth-century Americans did not believe voting to be a fundamental right of all people but understood it as a restricted, political privilege, able to be applied or taken away at the will of the government.

14. Howard Ohline, "Republicanism and Slavery: Origins of the Three-Fifths Clause in the United States Constitution," *William and Mary Quarterly,* volume 28, no. 4 (1971): 563–584; U.S. Const., art. I, § 2.

15. U.S. Const., amend. XIII.

16. I have opted to focus on these two particular women's rights activists because they reacted so strongly to the Fourteenth Amendment. This pulls me away from other suffrage activists in this period who were equally engaged with the cause but who, like Lucy Stone, did not respond with racism to the Fourteenth and Fifteenth Amendments. These women and men were in the majority among the activist community. However, Stanton's and Anthony's fame and later importance to both the suffrage movement and feminism justify a focus on their postwar activities. On other early women's rights activists see Andrea Moore Kerr, *Lucy Stone: Speaking Out for Equality* (New Brunswick, NJ: Rutgers University Press, 1992); Joelle Million, *Woman's Voice, Woman's Place: Lucy Stone and the Birth of the Woman's Rights Movement* (New York: Praeger, 2003); Colleen C. O'Brien, "'The White Women All Go for Sex': Frances Harper on Suffrage, Citizenship, and the Reconstruction South," *African American Review* 43, no. 4 (2009): 605–620; Alison M. Parker, *Articulating Rights: Nineteenth-Century American Women on Race, Reform, and the State* (DeKalb: Northern Illinois University Press, 2010); Michael Stancliff, *Frances Ellen Watkins Harper: African American Reform Rhetoric, and the Rise of a Modern Nation State* (New York: Routledge, 2011); Margaret Washington, *Sojourner Truth's America* (Urbana: University of Illinois Press, 2009); Nell Irvin Painter, *Sojourner Truth: A Life, a Symbol* (New York: Norton, 1996); Carol Faulkner, *Women's Radical Reconstruction: The Freedmen's Aid Movement* (Philadelphia: University of Pennsylvania Press, 2004); Carol Faulkner, *Lucretia Mott's Heresy: Abolition and Women's Rights in Nineteenth-Century America* (Philadelphia: University of Pennsylvania Press, 2011).

17. Ellen DuBois argues that this quest resulted in the first independent feminist movement in the United States. DuBois, *Feminism and Suffrage: The Emergence of an Independent Women's Movement in America, 1848–1869* (Ithaca, NY: Cornell University Press, 1978; with new preface, 1999).

18. The earliest historians of suffrage did not engage with the problem of the suffragists' racism, perhaps taking their cues from the suffragists themselves. See

Elizabeth Cady Stanton, Susan B. Anthony, Frances Dana Gage, and Ida Husted Harper, *History of Woman Suffrage: 1861–1876* (Rochester, NY: Susan B. Anthony, 1881); Eleanor Flexner, *Century of Struggle: The Woman's Rights Movement in the United States* (Cambridge, MA: Belknap Press of Harvard University Press, 1975). But since then, historians have started to consider the racism inherent in Stanton's work during the 1860s. Angela Yvonne Davis, *Women, Race, & Class* (New York: Random House, 1981); Bettina Aptheker, *Woman's Legacy: Essays on Race, Sex, and Class in American History* (Amherst: University of Massachusetts Press, 1982); Barbara Hilkert Andolsen, *"Daughters of Jefferson, Daughters of Bootblacks": Racism and American Feminism* (Macon, GA: Mercer University Press, 1986); Nancie Caraway, *Segregated Sisterhood: Racism and the Politics of American Feminism* (Knoxville: University of Tennessee Press, 1991); Rosalyn Terborg-Penn, *African American Women in the Struggle for the Vote, 1850–1920* (Bloomington: Indiana University Press, 1998); Louise Michele Newman, *White Women's Rights: The Racial Origins of Feminism in the United States* (New York: Oxford University Press, 1999); Kathi Kern, *Mrs. Stanton's Bible* (Ithaca, NY: Cornell University Press, 2001); Lori D. Ginzberg, *Elizabeth Cady Stanton: An American Life* (New York: Macmillan, 2010); Sue Davis, *The Political Thought of Elizabeth Cady Stanton: Women's Rights and the American Political Traditions* (New York: NYU Press, 2010); Ann D. Gordon, "Stanton and the Right to Vote: On Account of Race or Sex"; Michele Mitchell, "'Lower Orders,' Racial Hierarchies, and Rights Rhetoric: Evolutionary Echoes in Elizabeth Cady Stanton's Thought during the Late 1860s"; and Christine Stansell, "Missed Connections: Abolitionist Feminism in the Nineteenth Century," in *Elizabeth Cady Stanton, Feminist as Thinker: A Reader in Documents and Essays*, ed. Ellen Carol DuBois and Richard Cándida Smith (New York: NYU Press, 2007), 111–127, 128–151, 32–49; Sue Davis, *The Political Thought of Elizabeth Cady Stanton: Women's Rights and the American Political Traditions* (New York: NYU Press, 2010); Faye E. Dudden, *Fighting Chance: The Struggle over Woman Suffrage and Black Suffrage in Reconstruction America* (New York: Oxford University Press, 2011); Lisa Tetrault, *The Myth of Seneca Falls: Memory and the Women's Suffrage Movement, 1858–1898* (Chapel Hill: University of North Carolina Press, 2014).

19. This does not mean that private opinions or behind-the-scenes political actions were irrelevant, merely beyond the scope of this project. For analysis of the private partisan motives and back room political decision making behind the Fourteenth Amendment see Joseph B. James, *The Framing of the Fourteenth Amendment* (Urbana: University of Illinois Press, 1956); William E. Nelson, *The Fourteenth Amendment: From Political Principle to Judicial Doctrine* (Cambridge, MA: Harvard University Press, 1988); and Earl M. Maltz, *Civil Rights, the Constitution, and Congress, 1863–1869* (Lawrence: University Press of Kansas, 1990).

20. For some of the many ways that gender was used in post-war American life, see Kathleen Ann Clark, *Defining Moments: African American Commemoration and Political Culture in the South, 1863–1913* (Chapel Hill: University of North Carolina Press, 2005); Catherine Clinton and Nina Silber, *Divided Houses: Gender and the Civil War* (New York: Oxford University Press, 1992); Glenda Elizabeth Gilmore, *Gender and Jim Crow: Women and the Politics of White Supremacy in North Carolina, 1896–1920* (Chapel Hill: University of North Carolina Press, 1996); Laura F. Edwards, *Gendered Strife & Confusion: The Political Culture of Reconstruction* (Urbana: University of Illinois Press, 1997); Peter W. Bardaglio, *Reconstructing the Household: Families, Sex, and the*

Law in the Nineteenth-Century South (Chapel Hill: University of North Carolina Press, 1998); Hannah Rosen, *Terror in the Heart of Freedom: Citizenship, Sexual Violence, and the Meaning of Race in the Post-Emancipation South* (Chapel Hill: University of North Carolina Press, 2009); Mary Farmer-Kaiser, *Freedwomen and the Freedmen's Bureau: Race, Gender, and Public Policy in the Age of Emancipation* (New York: Fordham University Press, 2010).

21. In focusing on language and public speech, I join scholars in what has been inelegantly labeled "new, new political history," or the "newer political history." This history seeks to incorporate consideration of language and culture into traditional political history. A discussion of its origins can be found in the introduction to Jeffrey L. Pasley, Andrew W. Robertson, and David Waldstreicher, *Beyond the Founders: New Approaches to the Political History of the Early American Republic* (Chapel Hill: University of North Carolina Press, 2004). See also Liette Gidlow, "Delegitimizing Democracy: 'Civic Slackers,' the Cultural Turn, and the Possibilities of Politics," *Journal of American History* 89, no. 3 (2002): 922–957, esp. 927–929; and Steven Pincus and William Novak, "Political History after the Cultural Turn," *Perspectives on History,* May 2011, http://www.historians.org/perspectives/issues/2011/1105/1105for3.cfm.

1. The White Man's Government

1. Judd, "The Constitution—No. V," *Times* (Hartford, CT), August 18, 1818, vol. 2, issue 86, 3.

2. "Judd" was a pseudonym that honored Connecticut's early advocate of constitutional reform William Judd (d. 1804). Richard Buel and George J. Willauer, *Original Discontents: Commentaries on the Creation of Connecticut's Constitution of 1818* (Hamden, CT: Wesleyan University Press, 2007), 112–113.

3. Connecticut held a convention to draft its first constitution between August 26, 1818, and September 16, 1818. Until this time the state had relied on its colonial charter. Ralph Gregory Elliot, foreword to *Annotated Debates of the 1818 Constitutional Convention* by Wesley W. Horton, *Connecticut Bar Journal, Special Issue* 65 (January 1991), SI-1; Judd, "The Constitution—No. V."

4. Ibid.

5. Ibid. John Walker's 1818 dictionary defined complexion as "Involution of one thing in another; the colour of the external parts of any body; the temperature of the body." It seems most likely that Judd was referring to skin color. Walker, *A Critical Pronouncing Dictionary, and Expositor of the English Language* . . . (New York: Collins and Hannan, 1818), 146.

6. On race and violence in the early Republic see Carroll Smith-Rosenberg, *This Violent Empire: The Birth of an American National Identity* (Chapel Hill: University of North Carolina Press, 2010).

7. On the founders' ideology in the early Republic, see Gordon S. Wood, *Empire of Liberty: A History of the Early Republic, 1789–1815* (New York: Oxford University Press, 2009); on the democratic impulse, Sean Wilentz, *The Rise of American Democracy: Jefferson to Lincoln* (Norton, 2005).

8. J. G. A. Pocock, *The Machiavellian Moment: Florentine Political Thought and the Atlantic Republican Tradition* (Princeton, NJ: Princeton University Press, 2009);

Bernard Bailyn, *The Ideological Origins of the American Revolution* (Cambridge, MA: Belknap Press of Harvard University Press, 1967); and Gordon S. Wood, *The Creation of the American Republic, 1776–1787* (New York: Norton, 1969). On state constitutions' evolution in the early revolutionary era see Willi Paul Adams, *The First American Constitutions: Republican Ideology and the Making of the State Constitutions in the Revolutionary Era* (Lanham, MD: Rowman & Littlefield, 2001); and Marc W. Kruman, *Between Authority and Liberty: State Constitution-Making in Revolutionary America* (Chapel Hill: University of North Carolina Press, 1999). On the tensions between varying strains of political ideology, see Rogers M. Smith, *Civic Ideals: Conflicting Visions of Citizenship in U.S. History* (New Haven: Yale University Press, 1999).

9. Alexander Keyssar, *The Right to Vote: The Contested History of Democracy in the United States* (New York: Basic Books, 2000), app. A.9. Of the three states—Rhode Island, South Carolina, and New York—none applied property restrictions to all native white male citizens. Rhode Island's requirement was restricted to immigrants, New York's to African Americans. South Carolina permitted voters to substitute residency for property. Ibid., app. A.3.

10. James Madison famously warned against the dangers of democracy in Federalist 10, stating that "democracies have ever been spectacles of turbulence and contention; [they] have ever been found incompatible with personal security or the rights of property; and have in general been as short in their lives as they have been violent in their deaths." James Madison, "No. 10: The Same Subject Continued, the Union as a Safeguard against Domestic Faction and Insurrection, From the *New York Packet,* Friday, November 23, 1787," *The Federalist Papers,* http://avalon.law.yale.edu/18th_century/fed10.asp.

11. There was some variation in the personal considerations required. Most states required residency, restricted the ballot from the mentally ill or the completely impoverished. Some required a voter to be able-bodied and others a U.S. citizen. Barbara Young Welke, *Law and the Borders of Belonging in the Long Nineteenth Century United States* (Cambridge: Cambridge University Press, 2010). On the origins of the gendered state see Mary Beth Norton, *Separated by Their Sex: Women in Public and Private in the Colonial Atlantic World* (Ithaca, NY: Cornell University Press, 2011); Mark E. Kann, *The Gendering of American Politics: Founding Mothers, Founding Fathers and Political Patriarchy* (Westport, CT: Praeger, 1999).

12. Georgia, Massachusetts, New Hampshire, New York, South Carolina, and Virginia identified voters as "male." Maryland, North Carolina, Pennsylvania, and Vermont identified them as "freemen." Race restrictions were fewer before 1800. Only Georgia, South Carolina, and Virginia restricted their franchise to "whites." Keyssar, *Right to Vote,* app. A.1.

13. Of the six states without race restrictions, five were in New England (Maine, Massachusetts, New Hampshire, Rhode Island, and Vermont.) Of the four states that did not use "male" to define voters (Georgia, North Carolina, Pennsylvania, and Vermont), only Georgia did not use any gendered language at all. North Carolina, Pennsylvania, and Vermont all identified voters as "men," "freemen," or in the singular, "man." Benjamin P. Poore, *The Federal and State Constitutions, Colonial Charters, and Other Organic Laws of the United States,* 2 vols. (Washington, D.C.: U.S. Government Printing Office, 1878). Keyssar notes that despite the state's neutral constitution,

there is no evidence that African Americans or women ever voted in Georgia before the Civil War. Keyssar, *Right to Vote,* app. A-4, n5.

14. Jan Lewis critiques historians for being slow to see the connection between the franchise's expansion for white men and its contraction for others. Lewis, "Rethinking Women's Suffrage in New Jersey, 1776–1807," *Rutgers Law Review* 63 (2010): 1017, 1033n100.

15. Rosemarie Zagarri, *Revolutionary Backlash: Women and Politics in the Early American Republic* (Philadelphia: University of Pennsylvania Press, 2011), 180.

16. The poorest Americans were an important exception. As states expanded to include adult white men of little property, Delaware, Louisiana, Maine, Massachusetts, New Hampshire, New Jersey, Rhode Island, South Carolina, and Virginia all implemented pauper restrictions, excluding those with no property at all from casting ballots. Keyssar, *Right to Vote,* app. A.6. On pauper restrictions see Robert J. Steinfeld, "Property and Suffrage in the Early American Republic," *Stanford Law Review* 41, no. 2 (1989): 335–376; and James W. Fox Jr., "Citizenship, Poverty, and Federalism: 1787–1882," *University of Pittsburgh Law Review* 60 (1998): 421, and especially 470–479.

17. Keyssar, *Right to Vote,* 26–29, 52. For more on increasing voting populations, see Stanley L. Engerman and Kenneth L. Sokoloff, "The Evolution of Suffrage Institutions in the New World," *Journal of Economic History* 65, no. 4 (2005): 891–921, especially table 2.

18. James Horton and Lois Horton note that "the emphasis on mature manhood and independence as the preeminent qualifications for full citizenship in the republic provided the logical basis for the denial of such rights to dependent population groups such as women, children, and blacks." Horton and Horton, *In Hope of Liberty: Culture, Community and Protest among Northern Free Blacks, 1700–1860* (New York: Oxford University Press, 1996), 166.

19. Jacob Katz Cogan calls this "the look within," arguing that beliefs about a voter's capacity replaced property as the standard for voting rights. Cogan, "The Look Within: Property, Capacity, and Suffrage in Nineteenth-Century America," *Yale Law Journal* 107, no. 2 (1997): 473. Rogers Smith similarly argues that as "egalitarian republican conceptions of citizenship" were adopted in the Jacksonian period, it became "imperative to make ascriptive disqualifications [like gender and race] explicit." Smith, *Civic Ideals,* 213.

20. Keyssar, *Right to Vote,* 26–27. See also Chilton Williamson, *American Suffrage: From Property to Democracy, 1760–1860* (Princeton, NJ: Princeton University Press, 1960); Kirk Harold Porter, *A History of Suffrage in the United States* (Chicago: University of Chicago Press, 1918).

21. In Maryland and New Jersey, the state legislatures first made changes in their legal codes, which were later confirmed in constitutional conventions: Maryland in 1810 and 1851, New Jersey in 1844. Poore, *Federal and State Constitutions,* 1:832, 840, 2:1315.

22. In debates the delegates rarely considered women's voting, and when they did, it was only as a theoretical counterpoint to natural-rights suffrage arguments. They claimed that because women did not vote, voting was therefore not a natural right of all persons.

23. This despite the request for women's enfranchisement in at least one of the constitutional conventions (New York, 1846). Jacob Katz Cogan and Lori D.

Ginzberg, "1846 Petition for Woman's Suffrage, New York State Constitutional Convention," *Signs* 22, no. 2 (1997): 427–439. See also chapter 2.

24. Part of this theory was based on the idea that the poor would be unduly influenced by those whom they depended on financially, or that they would sell their votes in times of financial need. Part was derived from the fear that that the poor would legislate to redistribute wealth, violating the property rights of others. Keyssar, *Right to Vote,* 5–6, 9–12. Independence was also understood to be a particularly gendered quality. Long associated with white manhood, it was defined in contrast to others in varying states of dependence, usually women, slaves, servants, and children. Joan R. Gundersen, "Independence, Citizenship, and the American Revolution," *Signs* 13, no. 1 (1987): 59–77; Carroll Smith-Rosenberg, "Captured Subjects/Savage Others: Violently Engendering the New American," *Gender and History* 5, no. 2, Summer 1993, 177–195.

25. William Blackstone, *Commentaries on the Laws of England,* vol. 1, *Of the Rights of Persons* (London: John Murray, 1862), 152.

26. New Hampshire had a property restriction in the colonial period. Its 1776 constitution did not discuss suffrage, but its 1784 constitution replaced the property requirement with payment of a poll tax. Williamson, *American Suffrage,* 12; Poore, *Federal and State Constitutions,* 2:1285. Vermont's 1777 constitution did not require either property or tax payment for enfranchisement. Poore, *Federal and State Constitutions,* 2:1861. Keyssar, *Right to Vote,* app. A.1, A.3.

27. Keyssar, *Right to Vote,* 20.

28. Charles H. Wesley, "Negro Suffrage in the Period of Constitution-Making, 1787–1865," *Journal of Negro History* 32, no. 2 (1947): 143–168. In 1831 a Quaker Philadelphian told French traveler Alexis de Tocqueville that although African Americans were legally entitled to the ballot, they did not vote because they would "be mistreated" if they attempted to do so. Tocqueville, *Journey to America*, trans. George Lawrence, ed. J. P. Mayer (New Haven: Yale University Press, 1960), 224–225, cited in Eric Ledell Smith, "The End of Black Voting Rights in Pennsylvania: African Americans and the Pennsylvania Constitutional Convention of 1837–1838," *Pennsylvania History* 65, no. 3 (1998): 279–299, 281.

29. In 1800 the Federalist victory was attributed to "the vote of a single Negro ward in the city of New York." Dixon Ryan Fox, "The Negro Vote in Old New York," *Political Science Quarterly,* vol. 32, no. 2 (1917): 252–256, cited in Wesley, "Negro Suffrage," 155. Graham Russell Hodges estimates that in the 1830s "perhaps a thousand [African Americans] could vote across New York State." Hodges, *Root and Branch: African Americans in New York and East Jersey, 1613–1863* (Chapel Hill: University of North Carolina Press, 1999), 253; Edward Price, "The Black Voting Rights Issue in Pennsylvania, 1780–1900," *Pennsylvania Magazine of History and Biography* 100, no. 3 (1976): 357.

30. Keyssar, *Right to Vote,* 6.

31. Poore, 2:1311.

32. Acts of the 15th New Jersey General Assembly, November 18, 1790, 670, Special Collections, University Archives, Rutgers University Library, http://www.njwomenshistory.org/Period_2/qualvoters.htm. On women's enfranchisement in New Jersey see I. N. Gertzog, "Female Suffrage in New Jersey, 1790–1807," *Women & Politics* 10, no. 2 (1990): 47–58; Edward R. Turner, "Women's

Suffrage in New Jersey: 1790–1807," *Smith College Studies in History* 1, no. 4 (1916): 165–187. On the deliberate nature of this language, see J. A. Klinghoffer and L. Elkis, "'The Petticoat Electors': Women's Suffrage in New Jersey, 1776–1807," *Journal of the Early Republic* 12, no. 2 (1992): 159–193.

33. Zagarri, *Revolutionary Backlash*, 30–37; Klinghoffer and Elkis, "'Petticoat Electors,'" 162.

34. Cited in Lewis, "Rethinking Women's Suffrage," 1030. Lewis notes that this percentage seems extremely unlikely as fewer than ten thousand women were legally qualified to vote. However, she also points out that lax inspections at the polls created a much broader franchise in New Jersey than the suffrage law would indicate, suggesting that perhaps even some married women without property may have voted (1030–1031).

35. Zagarri, *Revolutionary Backlash*, 31.

36. Keyssar, *Right to Vote*, 7. A man's autonomy took on greater importance after the Revolution, as the nation's new democratic political structure relied on an independent citizenry. Evelyn Nakano Glenn, *Unequal Freedom: How Race and Gender Shaped American Citizenship and Labor* (Cambridge, MA: Harvard University Press, 2002).

37. Keyssar, *Right to Vote*, 13–15, 35, 37–38.

38. Michael Kimmel, *Manhood in America: A Cultural History*, 3rd ed. (New York: Oxford University Press, 2002), 17–31.

39. Charles Sellers, *The Market Revolution: Jacksonian America, 1815–1846* (New York: Oxford University Press, 1992); Melvin Stokes and Stephen Conway, eds. *The Market Revolution in America: Social, Political and Religious Expressions, 1800–1880* (Charlottesville: University Press of Virginia, 1996). Although historians disagree about exactly when the transition from a subsistence- to capitalist-based economy took place in America, and about whether or not this change constituted a revolution, there seems to be little doubt that such a transformation did take place in early America. Richard Lyman Bushman, "Markets and Composite Farms in Early America," *William and Mary Quarterly* 55, no. 3 (1998): 351–347; Daniel Walker Howe, *What Hath God Wrought: The Transformation of America, 1815–1848* (Oxford: Oxford University Press, 2007).

40. Keyssar, *Right to Vote*, 34.

41. Wood, *Empire of Liberty*, 330.

42. Historian Sean Wilentz reports that this could be because "the legal complications of surveying western land and granting freehold titles often were too cumbersome to accommodate any propertied voting requirement." Wilentz, *The Rise of American Democracy: From Jefferson to Lincoln* (New York: Norton, 2005), 117.

43. Keyssar, *Right to Vote*, app. A.2. Louisiana, Maine, Mississippi, and Ohio all had tax or service requirements.

44. In most northern states, *very* gradually. See David N. Gellman, *Emancipating New York: The Politics of Slavery and Freedom, 1777–1827* (Baton Rouge: Louisiana State University Press, 2006); Richard S. Newman and James Mueller, *Antislavery and Abolition in Philadelphia: Emancipation and the Long Struggle for Racial Justice in the City of Brotherly Love* (Baton Rouge: Louisiana State University Press, 2011); Gary B. Nash and Jean R. Soderlund, *Freedom by Degrees: Emancipation in Pennsylvania and Its Aftermath* (New York: Oxford University Press, 1991); Joanne P. Melish, *Disowning*

Slavery: Gradual Emancipation and Race in New England, 1780–1860 (Ithaca, NY: Cornell University Press, 1998).

45. Keyssar, *Right to Vote,* 38. There is some evidence, however, that slaveholding politicians had to at least acknowledge the interests of the nonslaveholders, which served in some ways as a counterbalance to the slaveholding elite. See J. Mills Thornton, *Politics and Power in a Slave Society: Alabama, 1800–1860* (Baton Rouge: Louisiana State University Press, 1978); William G. Shade, *Democratizing the Old Dominion: Virginia and the Second Party System, 1824–1861* (Charlottesville: University Press of Virginia, 1996); Harry L. Watson, *Jacksonian Politics and Community Conflict: The Emergence of the Second American Party System in Cumberland County, North Carolina* (Baton Rouge: Louisiana State University Press, 1981).

46. Keyssar, *Right to Vote,* app. A.1, A.2.

47. Wood, *Empire of Liberty,* 712.

48. Kimmel, *Manhood in America,* 17–31.

49. Eric Foner, *Free Soil, Free Labor, Free Men: The Ideology of the Republican Party before the Civil War* (New York: Oxford University Press, 1995), xxiii.

50. These same trends were also making slavery seem more problematic. If a person's autonomy, independence, and therefore political fitness depended upon his labor, did not the enslaved, whose labor was appropriated by others, also possess independence and autonomy? Foner, *Free Soil.*

51. Carol Sheriff, *The Artificial River: The Erie Canal and the Paradox of Progress, 1817–1862* (New York: Hill and Wang, 1997).

52. The House of Representatives had open debates from its inception. Wood, *Empire of Liberty,* 58–60. In this period, some states began to open legislative debates. For example, Mississippi's 1832 constitution declared in article 3, section 21, that "the doors of each house shall be open except on such occasions of great emergency as, in the opinion of the house, may require secrecy." Poore, *Federal and State Constitutions,* 2:1071.

53. Howe, *What Hath God Wrought,* 228.

54. Howe, *What Hath God Wrought,* 226–232, 627.

55. Property restrictions and elite politics kept political participation consistently low in the early Republic; on average, only 20 percent of eligible voters voted between 1790 and 1800. By 1800, roughly 80 percent of eligible voters participated in elections. Wood, *Empire of Liberty,* 160, 302. However, some historians dispute whether interest translated into political action. Glenn C. Altschuler and Stuart M. Blumin, *Rude Republic: Americans and Their Politics in the Nineteenth Century* (Princeton, NJ.: Princeton University Press, 2000).

56. Joel H. Silbey, *The American Political Nation, 1838–1893* (Stanford, CA: Stanford University Press, 1991), 1.

57. On urban artisans' political engagement see Wilentz, *Chants Democratic.* On Democrats, Whigs, and the development of the second American party system, see Robert Vincent Remini, *The Election of Andrew Jackson* (Philadelphia: Lippincott, 1963); Richard Patrick McCormick, *The Second American Party System: Party Formation in the Jacksonian Era* (Chapel Hill: University of North Carolina Press, 1966); Joel H. Silbey, *The Partisan Imperative: The Dynamics of American Politics before the Civil War* (New York: Oxford University Press, 1985); Daniel Walker Howe, *The Political Culture of the American Whigs* (Chicago: University of Chicago Press, 1984); Michael

F. Holt, *The Rise and Fall of the American Whig Party: Jacksonian Politics and the Onset of the Civil War* (New York: Oxford University Press, 2003).

58. Jean H. Baker, *Affairs of Party: The Political Culture of Northern Democrats in the Mid-Nineteenth Century* (Ithaca, NY: Cornell University Press, 1983); David Waldstreicher, *In the Midst of Perpetual Fetes: The Making of American Nationalism, 1776–1820* (Chapel Hill: University of North Carolina Press, 1997); Mary P. Ryan, *Women in Public: Between Banners and Ballots, 1825–1880* (Baltimore: Johns Hopkins University Press, 1990); Mary P. Ryan, *Civic Wars: Democracy and Public Life in the American City during the Nineteenth Century* (Berkeley: University of California Press, 1997).

59. The seventeen were Connecticut, Delaware, Georgia, Louisiana, Maryland, Massachusetts, Mississippi, New Hampshire, New Jersey, New York, North Carolina, Ohio, Pennsylvania, Rhode Island, South Carolina, Tennessee, and Virginia. The first constitutions in Louisiana, Mississippi, Ohio, and South Carolina restricted the franchises to white males. Pennsylvania restricted the ballot to "freemen." Massachusetts, New Hampshire, and Rhode Island retained race-neutral language, but added "male" to their constitutions in 1780, 1784, and 1842, respectively. Massachusetts and New Hampshire added gender restrictions to their constitutions well before altering their property provisions (Massachusetts, 1821; New Hampshire, 1792). Georgia removed the terms "male" and "white" from its 1777 constitution in 1789. Virginia added "white" and "male" to its constitution in 1830 but retained a reduced property restriction for the franchise. The other fourteen states entered the union without property restrictions on the franchise in their original constitutions. Poore, *Federal and State Constitutions,* 2 vols. On a history of the term "freemen," which was applied exclusively to males, see B. Katherine Brown, "Freemanship in Puritan Massachusetts," *American Historical Review* 59, no. 4 (1954): 865–883; Richard C. Simmons, "Freemanship in Early Massachusetts: Some Suggestions and a Case Study," *William and Mary Quarterly* 19, no. 3 (1962): 422–428.

60. Maine did not use the word "white" in its constitution, but it did prohibit "Indians not taxed" from casting a ballot. Poore, *Federal and State Constitutions,* 1:790. In its constitution of 1845, Texas permitted all adult males to vote but excluded "Indians not taxed, Africans and descendants of Africans" from the franchise. Ibid., 2:1768.

61. Keyssar, *Right to Vote,* app. A.4, A.5. Although Georgia lacked a race restriction in its constitution, it is highly unlikely that free African American men were able to vote in this slaveholding state.

62. Nicholas Wood argues that in Pennsylvania free northern blacks were denied rights because of fears that their continued enfranchisement would escalate increasing sectional tensions. Wood, "'A Sacrifice on the Altar of Slavery': Doughface Politics and Black Disenfranchisement in Pennsylvania, 1837–1838," *Journal of the Early Republic* 31, no. 1 (2011): 75–106. See also Mia Bay, *The White Image in the Black Mind: African-American Ideas about White People, 1830–1925* (New York: Oxford University Press, 2000), 42–44; Stephen Kantrowitz, *More Than Freedom: Fighting for Black Citizenship in a White Republic, 1829–1889* (New York: Penguin Press, 2012), 16–17; Hugh Davis, *We Will Be Satisfied with Nothing Less: The African American Struggle for Equal Rights in the North during Reconstruction* (Ithaca, NY: Cornell University Press, 2011); and Gary B. Nash, *Forging Freedom: The Formation of Philadelphia's Black Community, 1720–1840* (Cambridge, MA: Harvard University Press, 1998). In the face

of this hostility, free African Americans instead relied on their own communities and over the course of the antebellum period built their own institutions for support.

63. Zagarri, *Revolutionary Backlash,* 164–180. Zagarri notes that outdoor public politics also were increasingly hostile spaces for free African Americans (171–173). On women's earlier political influence, see Mary Beth Norton, *Liberty's Daughters: The Revolutionary Experience of American Women, 1750–1800* (Ithaca, NY: Cornell University Press, 1996, 1980); Linda K. Kerber, *Women of the Republic: Intellect and Ideology in Revolutionary America* (New York: Norton, 1980); Catherine Allgor, *Parlor Politics: In Which the Ladies of Washington Help Build a City and a Government* (Charlottesville: University Press of Virginia, 2000); Susan Branson, *These Fiery Frenchified Dames: Women and Political Culture in Early National Philadelphia* (Philadelphia: University of Pennsylvania Press, 2001). However, women would find new ways to engage in party politics. Elizabeth R. Varon, *We Mean to Be Counted: White Women and Politics in Antebellum Virginia* (Chapel Hill: University of North Carolina Press, 1998); Ryan, *Women in Public.*

64. Although prompted by accusations of corruption in an intraparty struggle between Democratic-Republicans, women's disfranchisement in New Jersey also reflected the emerging trend away from property and toward identity as the legitimate marker of voting citizenship. Lewis, "Rethinking Women's Suffrage," 1031–1033; Judith Apter Klinghoffer and Lois Elkis, "'The Petticoat Electors,'" 186–189.

65. Poore, 1:35, 104, 196, 323, 442, 514, 538, 701, 790, 984; 2:1056, 1106, 1459, 1768, 2030.

66. On state constitutional amendment process in the 1820s–'50s, see Laura J. Scalia, *America's Jeffersonian Experiment: Remaking State Constitutions, 1820–1850* (DeKalb: Northern Illinois University Press, 1999).

67. Only Pennsylvania did not change its constitutional language about race as it replaced its property-holding provision with a taxation requirement in 1776. Wood, "'Sacrifice on the Altar of Slavery,'" 79.

68. States that did not extensively debate race restrictions in convention, such as Delaware and New Jersey, already had restrictions in place. Delaware's 1792 constitution restricted voters by race, and thus race and gender restrictions were passed without comment in its 1831 convention. M. M. Gouge William, *Debates of the Delaware Convention: For Revising the Constitution of the State; Or, Adopting a New One: Held at Dover, November, 1831* (Wilmington, DE: S. Harker, 1831), 186–189, 252. New Jersey disfranchised women and African Americans by statute in 1807 but did not revise its constitution until 1844, which readily incorporated the 1807 changes into the new constitution. New Jersey Constitutional Convention, *Journal of the Proceedings of the Convention to Form a Constitution for the Government of the State of New Jersey: Begun at Trenton on the Fourteenth Day of May, A.D. 1844, and Continued to the Twenty-ninth Day of June, A.D. 1844* (Trenton, NJ: Franklin S. Mills, 1844), 96–104.

69. New York held two conventions in this period in 1821 and 1846. North Carolina convened its convention in 1835 and Pennsylvania in 1837–38.

70. For the states altering their suffrage provisions between 1790 and 1820, the records of the actual speeches given in the legislatures or conventions are limited. Newspapers in this period rarely sent reporters to legislative proceedings, and when they did, what was recorded was often incomplete. For example, when faced with a lengthy debate about the franchise in the Connecticut convention the evening

of Wednesday, September 9, 1818, the *Connecticut Courant* reporter demurred from recording the speeches, saying only, "We would remark again, that, in the course of all these proceedings, there has been a great deal of desultory debate, which it is impossible, and would be improper to give: indeed, the whole business has been made a subject of conversation." *Connecticut Courant,* September 22, 1818, 2.

71. Each state altering its constitution was also doing so within partisan and political contexts that shaped convention debates in particular ways. For example, Republicans in Connecticut's 1818 convention advocated several reforms that could have helped them win elections, such as an independent judiciary, districted voting, and reapportionment, but these were defeated by a coalition of moderates and Federalists. Wilentz, *Rise of American Democracy*, 185. For the most part, I do not discuss these particulars because I am more concerned with broad themes and ideas articulated repeatedly in multiple contexts by diverse and distant speakers than with local partisan peculiarities.

72. Mentor, "Make Ready!!," *Connecticut Journal*, April 1, 1817, 3.

73. Nathaniel H. Carter, William L. Stone, and Marcus Tullius Cicero Gould, *Reports of the Proceedings and Debates of the Convention of 1821 Assembled for the Purpose of Amending the Constitution of the State of New York: Containing All the Official Documents Relating to the Subject, and Other Valuable Matter* (Albany: E. and E. Hosford, 1821), 237 (hereafter cited as *NY1821*).

74. At the end of 1821, Connecticut, Delaware, Georgia, Louisiana, Massachusetts, Mississippi, New Hampshire, New Jersey, New York, North Carolina, Ohio, and Pennsylvania all required voters to be taxpayers or have performed militia duty. Poore, *Federal and State Constitutions*, 2 vols.; Keyssar, *Right to Vote,* app. A.2.

75. *Columbian Register* (New Haven, CT), November 24, 1818, 2.

76. E. Guyer, *The Daily Chronicle and Convention Journal: Containing the Substance and Spirit of the Proceedings of the Convention Which Assembled at the State Capital in Harrisburg, May 2, 1837 to Alter and Amend the Constitution of the State of Pennsylvania* (Harrisburg: E. Guyer, 1837), 315.

77. Ibid., 321.

78. *Proceedings and Debates of the Convention of North Carolina Called to Amend the Constitution of the State, Which Assembled at Raleigh, June 4, 1835. To Which Are Subjoined the Convention Act and the Amendments to the Constitution* (Raleigh: Joseph Gales and Son, 1836), 61 (hereafter cited as *NC1835*).

79. *NC1835,* 61.

80. John Agg, *Proceedings and Debates of the Convention of the Commonwealth of Pennsylvania: To Propose Amendments to the Constitution, Commenced . . . at Harrisburg, on the Second Day of May, 1837* (Harrisburg: Packer, Barrett and Parke, 1837), 10:21 (hereafter cited as *PA1837*).

81. *PA1837,* 9:385.

82. *NC1835,* 80.

83. *NC1835,* 77–78.

84. Keyssar, *Right to Vote,* 14–15, 35–36.

85. The Pennsylvania delegate making this argument particularly was H. Gold Rogers, a twenty-five-year-old suffrage committee member from Allegheny. Rogers's

father, Edward, had served as a delegate to the New York Constitutional Convention in 1821. Harold D. Langley, "The Tragic Career of H. G. Rogers, Pennsylvania Politician and Jacksonian Diplomat," *Pennsylvania History* 31, no. 1 (1964): 30–61.

86. Guyer, *Daily Chronicle and Convention Journal,* 323.

87. *NY1821,* 185. Root is most likely referring to the national 1792 Militia Act, which restricted military duty to free white men. Robert Reinders, "Militia and Public Order in Nineteenth-Century America," *Journal of American Studies* 11, no. 1 (1977): 81–101.

88. *NY1821,* 180.

89. Ibid., 187–188. *NC1835,* 61.

90. *PA1837,* 10:49. The partisan politics here are particularly pointed since Jackson's fellow Democrats were some of the most vocal opponents of African Americans' voting rights in all the conventions. African American men also used Jackson's text to proclaim their own service to the state. See chapter 2.

91. *PA1837,* 10:82.

92. *NC1835,* 62.

93. *PA1837,* 9:327.

94. *NC1835,* 69. For further discussion of the application of familial metaphors to suffrage rights and the state, see chapter 3.

95. *PA1837,* 10:85.

96. In New York in 1821, women were discussed most extensively in relation to reforms to libel law, as supporters argued that the law was necessary to protect the "fairer sex" from libelous slanders. *NY1821.* In North Carolina, the longest discussion that included women was a debate about their presence in the viewing galleries at the convention. *NC1835.* On the other hand, New York's 1846 convention delegates spent a considerable amount of time discussing the rights of women as they debated extending property rights to married women. But the convention did not contemplate their enfranchisement. See Norma Basch, *In the Eyes of the Law: Women, Marriage, and Property in Nineteenth-Century New York* (Ithaca, NY: Cornell University Press, 1982).

97. *NY1821,* 248.

98. Ibid., 249.

99. *PA1837,* 9:378.

100. *NY1821,* 252. His fellow conservative delegate Colonel Young claimed that the ultimate logical conclusion to a franchise disconnected from property and applied equally to all people was the enfranchisement of black women: "On that principle, you must admit *negresses* as well as *negroes* to participate in the right of suffrage." Ibid., 191.

101. *PA1837,* 9:379.

102. Ibid.

103. Ibid., 9:389–390. Brown's comment about women's disfranchisement in New Jersey is interesting. Because he made it without offering any explanation or context, it seems to indicate that he believed his colleagues were familiar with the incident, even though it had taken place thirty years earlier.

104. Whereas we moderns understand gender and race to be merely socially meaningful rather than biologically determined, Americans in the nineteenth century believed those distinctions between persons to be grounded exclusively in biology.

105. *NC1835,* 78.

106. In New York State, African American voters, Wilentz notes, had been "overwhelmingly loyal to the Federalists. . . . In close elections, the black vote, although a small portion of the total, could swing key districts and even (or so it was alleged in 1813) decide the balance of power in the state assembly." Wilentz, *Rise of American Democracy,* 192. Partisan concerns over black voters' affiliation likely would also have factored into whether Pennsylvania and North Carolina's delegates supported or opposed their enfranchisement.

107. *NC1835,* 69.

108. Ibid.

109. There were race riots in Philadelphia in 1829, in 1834, and in 1838. Nash, *Forging Freedom,* 275–277.

110. *PA1837,* 9:393.

111. Ibid., 10:114.

112. Wood, "'Sacrifice on the Altar of Slavery.'"

113. *PA1837,* 9:393; 10:57–58.

114. They did not seem to have any trouble with a distinction based on sex, however.

115. Guyer, *Daily Chronicle and Convention Journal,* 312.

116. Guyer, *Daily Chronicle and Convention Journal,* 316. Earle, though a Democrat, was a member of the Pennsylvania's Abolition Society, as well as serving as the Liberty Party's vice presidential candidate in 1840. Wood, "'Sacrifice on the Altar of Slavery,'" 96.

117. *PA1837,* 10:84.

118. Ibid., 10:15.

119. William G. Bishop and William H. Attree, *Report of the Debates and Proceedings of the Convention for the Revision of the Constitution of the State of New York: 1846* (Albany: Office of the *Evening Atlas,* 1846), 1014–1015 (hereafter cited as *NY1846*).

120. Ibid., 1031.

121. Ibid.

122. Ibid., 1016.

123. Ibid., 1017.

124. Ibid., 1027–1028.

125. Ibid., 1030.

126. Ibid.

127. Gender, for them, so obviously disqualified women from political activity that it did not even merit consideration.

128. North Carolinians did not make arguments about the fluidity or instability of race in their suffrage convention. As a slave state, not only did North Carolina have legal means to define race, but its suffrage provision included a brief definition of race by referring to a voter's ancestry.

129. *NY1821,* 188.

130. Ibid.

131. *PA1837,* 10:64.

132. Ibid., 10:65.

133. *NY1821,* 365.

134. *PA1837,* 10:64.

135. Opponents pointed to legal precedents in which the word "white" had been used without confusion since the revolutionary era. See the arguments of Lycoming County, Pennsylvania, delegate Robert Fleming, ibid., 10:60, 62.

136. *NY1821,* 191.

137. Ibid., 365.

138. This comment conflates the Victorian ideal of white womanhood as fair-skinned with all women, handily ignoring all women of color. *PA1837,* 10:82.

139. *NY1846,* 1014.

140. *NY1821,* 191.

141. Ibid., 185.

142. *PA1837,* 10:57.

143. Ibid., 9:368.

144. *NY1846,* 1019.

145. *PA1837,* 10:114.

146. Evelyn Nakano Glenn's *Unequal Freedom* offers an excellent synthesis of the scholarship on the connections between gender, race, and the evolution of citizenship. See especially pages 18–55.

147. Dana D. Nelson, *National Manhood: Capitalist Citizenship and the Imagined Fraternity of White Men* (Durham, NC: Duke University Press, 1998).

2. Manhood and Citizenship

1. "New York State Convention," *Colored American,* August 29, October 31, 1840, January 2, 9, 1841, in *Proceedings of the Black State Conventions, 1840–1865,* ed. Philip S. and George E. Walker (Philadelphia: Temple University Press, 1979), 1:6, 8.

2. "Address of the New York State Convention to their Colored Fellow Citizens," *Colored American,* November 21, 1840, in Foner and Walker, *Proceedings,* 1:16.

3. "Address of the New York State Convention of Colored Citizens, to the People of the State," *Colored American,* December 19, 1840, in ibid., 1:22.

4. William G. Bishop and William H. Attree, *Report of the Debates and Proceedings of the Convention for the Revision of the Constitution of the State of New York: 1846* (Albany: Office of the *Evening Atlas,* 1846), 646 (hereafter cited as *NY1846).* The three other petitions were one presented on July 11 requesting "women and parsons to be voters and hold office," one presented on August 27 "in favor of women's rights," and one presented on September 21, "praying . . . that females be allowed to go to the polls and deposit their ballot." *NY1846,* 284, 763, 913. On the quoted petition's origins, see Lori D. Ginzberg, *Untidy Origins: A Story of Woman's Rights in Antebellum New York* (Chapel Hill: University of North Carolina Press, 2005); Jacob Katz Cogan and Lori D. Ginzberg, "1846 Petition for Woman's Suffrage, New York State Constitutional Convention," *Signs* 22, no. 2 (1997): 427–439. Roughly sixty-seven to sixty-eight petitions were presented to the convention (one batch of an unspecified number of petitions was presented "severally," making it difficult to know the precise number). Of these, only six others dealt with suffrage rights: two specifically sought black men's enfranchisement, and four referred to suffrage generally. *NY1846.*

5. *NY1846,* 646.

6. African Americans' claims for equality took many forms and appropriated varied rhetorical techniques, but I limit my analysis here to northern African American activists' public rhetoric about voting rights.

7. Martha S. Jones, *All Bound Up Together: The Woman Question in African American Public Culture, 1830–1900* (Chapel Hill: University of North Carolina Press, 2007).

8. Patrick Rael has argued that in this period black activists "appropriated the ideas of antebellum society, only to reformulate hostile notions into potent sources of empowerment and uplift." *Black Identity and Black Protest in the Antebellum North* (Chapel Hill: University of North Carolina Press, 2002), 3.

9. Black men's claim to manhood was essential beyond the political sphere, as one strain of white racist thinking sought to feminize black men, particularly the enslaved. Michael Kimmel notes that "American manhood . . . [was] grounded upon the exclusion of blacks and women, the nonnative-born (immigrants), and the genuinely native-born (Indians), each on the premise that they weren't 'real' Americans, and couldn't, by definition, be real men." He continues, "The perceived—or just as frequently, projected—effeminacy of nonwhite men was a standard racialist theme." Kimmel, *Manhood in America: A Cultural History*, 3rd ed. (New York: Oxford University Press, 2011), 67, 69.

10. "Proceedings of the National Convention of Colored Men held in the City of Syracuse, NY, October 4, 5, 6, and 7, 1864 with the Bill of Wrongs and Rights, and the Address to the American People," page 9, in *Minutes of the Proceedings of the National Negro Conventions, 1830–1864*, ed. Howard Holman Bell (New York: Arno Press, 1969) (hereafter cited as Bell, *Minutes*). Claiming the status of respectable men was also an essential strategy for black reformers in establishing independence for the African American community. Bruce Dorsey, *Reforming Men and Women: Gender in the Antebellum City* (Ithaca, NY: Cornell University Press, 2006).

11. The 1846 petition is just one indication that even before Seneca Falls, ideas about women's rights were certainly circulating, at least among northerners, radical Quakers, political abolitionists, and property-rights reformers. Ginzberg, *Untidy Origins*. See also Judith Wellman, *The Road to Seneca Falls: Elizabeth Cady Stanton and the First Woman's Rights Convention* (Urbana: University of Illinois Press, 2004). Martha Jones also traces women's rights ideas and arguments through the African American community as early as the 1830s. Jones, *All Bound Up Together.*

12. Elizabeth Cady Stanton and Susan B. Anthony, *The Selected Papers of Elizabeth Cady Stanton and Susan B. Anthony,* vol. 1, *In the School of Anti-Slavery,* ed. Ann D. Gordon (New Brunswick, NJ: Rutgers University Press, 1997), 78 (hereafter cited as *Papers: 1*).

13. "The Anniversaries, Thirty-Second Anniversary of the American Anti-Slavery Society," *New York Daily Tribune*, May 10, 1865, 8.

14. Though antislavery efforts were the central focus of much community activism, rejecting the colonization movement and ameliorating the condition of urban African Americans were also on the activists' agenda. Eric Burin, *Slavery and the Peculiar Solution: A History of the American Colonization Society* (Gainesville: University Press of Florida, 2008); Dorsey, *Reforming Men and Women,* 155–158; Richard S. Newman, Patrick Rael, and Phillip Lapsansky, *Pamphlets of Protest: An Anthology of Early African-American Protest Literature, 1790–1860* (New York: Routledge, 2000); Stephen Kantrowitz, *More Than Freedom: Fighting for Black Citizenship in a White*

Republic, 1829–1889 (New York: Penguin, 2012). On free black northern urban communities see Gary B. Nash, *Forging Freedom: The Formation of Philadelphia's Black Community, 1720–1840* (Cambridge, MA: Harvard University Press, 1991); Ira Berlin, *Slaves without Masters: The Free Negro in the Antebellum South* (New York: Oxford University Press, 1981); Julie Winch, *Philadelphia's Black Elite: Activism, Accommodation, and the Struggle for Autonomy, 1787–1848* (Philadelphia: Temple University Press, 1988); Shane White, *Somewhat More Independent: The End of Slavery in New York City, 1770–1810* (Athens: University of Georgia Press, 1991); Leslie M. Harris, *In the Shadow of Slavery: African Americans in New York City, 1626–1863* (Chicago: University of Chicago Press, 2003); and Graham Russell Hodges, *Root and Branch: African Americans in New York and East Jersey, 1613–1863* (Chapel Hill: University of North Carolina Press, 1999).

15. Nathaniel H. Carter, William Leete Stone, and Marchus Tulles Cicero Gould, *Reports of the Proceedings and Debates of the Convention of 1821 Assembled for the Purpose of Amending the Constitution of the State of New York: Containing All the Official Documents Relating to the Subject, and Other Valuable Matter* (Albany: E. and E. Hosford, 1821), 134; *NY1846,* 220, 424; John Agg, *Proceedings and Debates of the Convention of the Commonwealth of Pennsylvania: To Propose Amendments to the Constitution, Commenced . . . at Harrisburg, on the Second Day of May, 1837,* vols. 2, 9, 10 (Harrisburg: Packer, Barrett and Parke, 1837).

16. On the history of the black convention movement see W. H. Pease and J. H. Pease, "The Negro Convention Movement," in *Key Issues in the Afro-American Experience,* ed. Nathan I. Huggins, Martin Kilson, and Daniel M. Fox (New York: Harcourt Brace Jovanovich, 1971), 191–205; J. H. Pease and W. H. Pease, "Negro Conventions and the Problem of Black Leadership," *Journal of Black Studies* 2, no. 1 (1971): 29–44; Bella Gross, "The First National Negro Convention," *Journal of Negro History* 31, no. 4 (1946): 435–443; Howard H. Bell, "National Negro Conventions of the Middle 1840's: Moral Suasion vs. Political Action," *Journal of Negro History* 42, no. 4 (1957): 247–260.

17. Bell, *Minutes*; Foner and Walker, *Proceedings,* 2 vols.

18. Hugh Davis, "The Pennsylvania State Equal Rights League and the Northern Black Struggle for Legal Equality, 1864–1877," *Pennsylvania Magazine of History and Biography* 126, no. 4 (2002): 612; Gross, "First National Negro Convention," 440.

19. Pease and Pease, "Negro Conventions," 31–32.

20. Black activists in New York held two meetings, one in 1840 and another in 1841. Pennsylvania's African American activists met in 1841, Indiana's in 1842, and Michigan's in 1843. Foner and Walker, *Proceedings,* 1:5–30, 106–118, 173–175, 181–197.

21. The subjects of the conventions reflected this evolution: changing from conventions held "for the improvement of the people of color" to those held for "considering their moral and political condition as American Citizens." "Minutes of the Fourth Annual Convention for the Improvement of the Free People of Colour in the United States, held by adjournments, in the Asbury Church, New-York, from the 2d to the 12th of June inclusive, 1834," in Bell, *Minutes*; "Minutes of the National Convention of Colored Citizens: Held at Buffalo on the 15th, 16th 17th 18th and 19th of August, 1843, for the Purpose of Considering their Moral and Political Condition as American Citizens," in Bell, *Minutes.*

22. "Constitution of the American Society of Free Persons of Colour, for Improving Their Condition in the United States; for Purchasing Lands; and for the Establishment of a Settlement in Upper Canada, also the Proceedings of the Convention, with Their Address to the Free Persons of Colour in the United States," page 9, in Bell, *Minutes*.

23. "Minutes and Proceedings of the First Annual Convention of the People of Colour Held by Adjournments in the City of Philadelphia from the Sixth to the Eleventh of June, Inclusive, 1831," pages 4–5, in Bell, *Minutes*.

24. "Minutes of the State Convention, of the Colored Citizens of the State of Michigan, Held in the City of Detroit on the 26th & 27th of October, 1843, for the Purpose of Considering Their Moral and Political Condition, as Citizens of the State," in Foner and Walker, *Proceedings*, 1:181.

25. Conventions held in 1831 and 1832 advocated and gathered funding for a college in New Haven, Connecticut, but local resistance hindered this effort. By 1833 and 1834, the national conventions' focus had turned to manual labor schools. See Bell, *Minutes*.

26. "Proceedings of the State Convention of Colored People Held at Albany, New York, on the 22d, 23d, and 24th of July, 1851," in Foner and Walker, *Proceedings*, 1:73.

27. Ibid., 1:74.

28. "Proceedings of the State Convention of Colored Citizens of the State of Illinois, Held in the City of Alton, Nov. 13th, 14th, and 15th, 1856," in Foner and Walker, 2:73.

29. "Proceedings of the National Convention of Colored People, and Their Friends, held in Troy, NY, on the 6th, 7th, 8th, and 9th October, 1847," page 27 in Bell, *Minutes*.

30. "Proceedings of the State Convention of the Colored Freemen of Pennsylvania, Held in Pittsburgh, on the 23d, 24th, and 25th of August, 1841, for the Purpose of Considering Their condition, and the Means of Its Improvement," in Foner and Walker, *Proceedings*, 1:115.

31. "Address of the New York State Convention of Colored Citizens, to the People of the State," *Colored American,* December 19, 1840, in Foner and Walker, *Proceedings,* 1:20–21.

32. Ibid., 1:21.

33. Ibid., 1:20. Although the address listed these services to the state as reasons for black men's equal enfranchisement, it did not rest their claims upon service exclusively. Rather, it contended that suffrage was an inherent right of manhood.

34. "Minutes of the State Convention, of the Colored Citizens of the State of Michigan, Held in the City of Detroit on the 26th & 27th of October, 1843, for the Purpose of Considering Their Moral and Political Condition, as Citizens of the State," in Foner and Walker, *Proceedings,* 1:192. The Rochester national convention in 1853 included within its address to the people of the United States the full text of Andrew Jackson's 1814 proclamation of equality for black and white soldiers serving in New Orleans. "Proceedings of the National Convention, Held in Rochester on the 6th, 7th, and 8th of July, 1853, 'Address of the Colored National Convention, to the People of the United States,'" page 15, in Bell, *Minutes*.

35. "Report of the Proceedings of the Colored National Convention, Held at Cleveland, Ohio, on Wednesday September 6, 1848," page 16, in Bell, *Minutes.*

36. "Address of the Colored National Convention, to the People of the United States," Rochester, 1853, page 9, in Bell, *Minutes.*"

37. "Minutes of the State Convention of the Coloured Citizens of Pennsylvania, Convened at Harrisburg, December 12th and 13th, 1848," in Foner and Walker, *Proceedings,* 1:131.

38. Ibid., 1:131–132. This argument is similar to one made by John Hunt, a delegate to the New York 1846 constitutional revision convention, who stated that if African Americans could change their skin color they could be members of the political community. See chapter 1.

39. "Minutes of the State Convention of the Coloured Citizens of Pennsylvania," in Foner and Walker, *Proceedings,* 1:132.

40. "Constitution of the American Society of Free Persons of Colour, for Improving Their Condition in the United States; for Purchasing Lands; and for the Establishment of a Settlement in Upper Canada, Also the Proceedings of the Convention, with their Address to the Free Persons of Colour in the United States," page 11, Bell, *Minutes;* and "Minutes and Proceedings of the First Annual Convention of the People of Colour Held by adjournments in the City of Philadelphia from the Sixth to the Eleventh of June, Inclusive, 1831," page 5, in Bell, *Minutes.*

41. "Minutes and Proceedings of the Second Annual Convention for the Improvement of the Free People of Color in these United States, Held by Adjournments in the City of Philadelphia from the 4th to the 13th of June Inclusive, 1832," page 32, in Bell, *Minutes.*

42. The use of "panoply" here is gendered as well, adopting the meaning of the word as a complete set of armor, military gear typically worn by men. "New York State Free Suffrage Convention, September 8, 1845," in Foner and Walker, *Proceedings,* 1:39.

43. "Minutes of the State Convention of the Coloured Citizens of Pennsylvania," in Foner and Walker, *Proceedings,* 1:126.

44. Ibid., 1:131.

45. "Address of the New York State Convention to their Colored Fellow Citizens," *Colored American,* November 21, 1840, in Foner and Walker, *Proceedings,* 1:16.

46. Ibid., 1:17.

47. "Proceedings of the First Convention of the Colored Citizens of the State of Illinois, Convened at the City of Chicago, Thursday, Friday, and Saturday, October 6th, 7th, and 8th, 1853," in Foner and Walker, *Proceedings,* 2:64.

48. "Convention of the Colored Citizens of Massachusetts, August 1, 1858," in Foner and Walker, *Proceedings,* 2:101.

49. Julie Roy Jeffrey, *The Great Silent Army of Abolitionism: Ordinary Women in the Antislavery Movement* (Chapel Hill: University of North Carolina Press, 1998); Jones, *All Bound Up Together.*

50. Dorsey, *Reforming Men and Women,* 188–189; Faye E. Dudden, *Fighting Chance: The Struggle Over Woman Suffrage and Black Suffrage in Reconstruction America* (New York: Oxford University Press, 2011); Jones argues that this mode of activist engagement was essential given the vitriolic racist critique of African American women's public actions ubiquitous in the press in the period. Jones, *All Bound Up Together,* 23–58.

51. For example, *The Colored American* reported that there were "numerous" spectators "male and female" attending the 1840 convention in New York. *The Colored American*, August 29, 1840, in Foner and Walker, *Proceedings* 1:6.

52. "Report of the Proceedings of the Colored National Convention," held at Cleveland, Ohio, on Wednesday, September 6, 1848. In Bell, *Minutes*, 11–12.

53. Jeffrey, *Great Silent Army of Abolitionism*; Stacey M. Robertson, *Hearts Beating for Liberty: Women Abolitionists in the Old Northwest* (Chapel Hill: University of North Carolina Press, 2010); Beth A. Salerno, *Sister Societies: Women's Antislavery Organizations in Antebellum America* (Dekalb: Northern Illinois University Press, 2008).

54. On Garrisonian abolitionists and their approach to women's rights, see Aileen Kraditor, *Means and Ends in American Abolitionism: Garrison and His Critics on Strategy and Tactics, 1834–1850* (New York: Pantheon Books, 1969); Ellen Carol DuBois, *Feminism and Suffrage: The Emergence of An Independent Women's Movement in America, 1848–1869* (Ithaca, NY: Cornell University Press, 1978; with new preface, 1999).

55. Although Kraditor notes that the split in the movement was in part driven by divisions over women's participation in the society, she argues that this was in itself merely a reflection of a more fundamental division between conservative and radical abolitionists. Kraditor, *Means and Ends in American Abolitionism*, 10.

56. Dorsey, *Reforming Men and Women*, 185–186.

57. On the efforts of northern middle-class African Americans to preserve gender distinctions see James Oliver Horton, "Freedom's Yoke: Gender Conventions Among Antebellum Free Blacks," *Feminist Studies* 12, no. 1 (Spring 1986): 51–76; R. J. Young, *Antebellum Black Activists: Race, Gender, and Self* (New York: Garland, 1996).

58. "Suffrage Convention of the Colored Citizens of New York, Troy, September 14, 1858," in Foner and Walker, *Proceedings*, 1:99.

59. "Colored Men's State Convention of New York, Troy, September 4, 1855," in Foner and Walker, *Proceedings*, 1:91.

60. Jones, *All Bound Up Together*, 88.

61. Holly Berkley Fletcher, *Gender and the American Temperance Movement of the Nineteenth Century*, Studies in American Popular History and Culture (New York: Routledge, 2008); Scott C. Martin, *Devil of the Domestic Sphere: Temperance, Gender, and Middle-Class Ideology, 1800–1860* (Dekalb: Northern Illinois University Press, 2008); Ian R. Tyrrell, "Women and Temperance in Antebellum America, 1830–1860," *Civil War History* 28, no. 2 (1982): 128–152; Wellman, *Road to Seneca Falls*; Alisse Portnoy, *Their Right to Speak: Women's Activism in the Indian and Slave Debates* (Cambridge, MA: Harvard University Press, 2005). On northern women's partisan engagement in the antebellum period, see Ronald J. Zboray and Mary Saracino Zboray, *Voices without Votes: Women and Politics in Antebellum New England* (Lebanon: University of New Hampshire Press, 2010). Although very few southern women engaged in antebellum women's rights activism, they were politically engaged. See Elizabeth R. Varon, *We Mean to Be Counted: White Women and Politics in Antebellum Virginia*, Gender and American Culture (Chapel Hill: University of North Carolina Press, 1998).

62. Sally G. McMillen, *Seneca Falls and the Origins of the Women's Rights Movement* (New York: Oxford University Press, 2008), 104–148.

63. Wellman, *Road to Seneca Falls,* 193; Elizabeth Cady Stanton, *Elizabeth Cady Stanton as Revealed in Her Letters, Diary and Reminiscences,* ed. Theodore Stanton and Harriot Stanton Blatch, (New York: Arno, 1969), 1:146.

64. *Papers: 1,* 77.

65. Philip S. Foner, *Frederick Douglass on Women's Rights* (New York: Da Capo Press, 1976), 13–14.

66. McMillen, *Seneca Falls,* 126–127.

67. Judith Wellman sees a close comparison between the language used by New York convention delegates in 1821 and 1846 and that used by women's rights activists. She says that the arguments for voting expansion in 1821 "presaged every major theme that would emerge in the fight for woman's suffrage a generation later." I don't disagree, if the major themes are defined as suffrage as a natural vs. political right and the broad republican ideology that connected taxation with representation. However, my reading of the women's conventions documents finds that women gave little attention to the service/identity tropes being used in the constitutional conventions. Wellman, *Road to Seneca Falls,* 139–158. On women's service to the state, see Linda K. Kerber, *No Constitutional Right to Be Ladies: Women and the Obligations of Citizenship* (New York: Hill and Wang, 1998).

68. On the tensions over how activists interpreted the "proper" role of women in the abolition movement, see Jeffrey, *Great Silent Army of Abolitionism*; Robertson, *Hearts Beating for Liberty.*

69. A few of the many books that discuss the link between abolition and the early women's rights movement are DuBois, *Feminism and Suffrage*; Blanche Glassman Hersh, *The Slavery of Sex: Feminist-Abolitionists in America* (Urbana: University of Illinois Press, 1978); McMillen, *Seneca Falls;* and Carol Faulkner, *Lucretia Mott's Heresy: Abolition and Women's Rights in Nineteenth-Century America* (Philadelphia: University of Pennsylvania Press, 2011).

70. Women's Rights Committee, *The Proceedings of the Woman's Rights Convention Held at Worcester, October 23d & 24th, 1850* (Boston: Prentiss & Sawyer, 1851), 8 (hereafter cited as *Worcester1850*).

71. Women's Rights Committee, *The Proceedings of the Woman's Rights Convention, held at Worcester, October 15th and 16th, 1851* (New York: Fowler and Wells, 1852), 30 (hereafter cited as *Worcester1851*). Compared with those for Stanton and Anthony, the biographies of Lucy Stone are few. See Alice S. Blackwell, *Lucy Stone: Pioneer of Woman's Rights* (Charlottesville: University of Virginia Press, 1930); Elinor Rice Hays, *Morning Star: A Biography of Lucy Stone, 1818–1893* (New York: Harcourt, 1961); Andrea Moore Kerr, *Lucy Stone: Speaking Out for Equality* (New Brunswick, NJ: Rutgers University Press, 1992); Joelle Million, *Woman's Voice, Woman's Place: Lucy Stone and the Birth of the Woman's Rights Movement* (Praeger, 2003); Sally G. McMillen, *Lucy Stone: An Unapologetic Life* (New York: Oxford University Press, 2015).

72. Women's Rights Committee, *The Proceedings of the Woman's Rights Convention Held at Syracuse, September 8th, 9th, and 10th, 1852* (Syracuse: J. E. Masters, 1852), 7 (hereafter cited as *Syracuse1852*).

73. *Worcester1850,* 11–12.

74. Ibid., 20–21.

75. Wendell Phillips, *Shall Women Have the Right to Vote? Address by Wendell Phillips at Worcester, Mass, 1851* (Philadelphia: Equal Franchise Society of Pennsylvania, 1910), 8, National American Woman Suffrage Collection, Library of Congress.

76. *Syracuse1852*, 69.

77. Ibid., 15.

78. Ibid., 34.

79. Ibid., 30–34; Lori D. Ginzberg, *Elizabeth Cady Stanton: An American Life* (New York: Macmillan, 2010), 75.

80. *Syracuse1852*, 30.

81. Lucy Stone herself did refuse to pay taxes in 1857, after which her property was seized and auctioned off to cover the costs of her debt. McMillen reports that a "sympathetic neighbor purchased the items and allowed Lucy to buy them back." McMillen, *Seneca Falls*, 128. R. Richard Geddes and Sharon Tennyson, "Passage of the Married Women's Property Acts and Earnings Acts in the United States: 1850 to 1920," in *Research in Economic History*, vol. 29, ed. Christopher Hanes and Susan Wolcott (Bingley, UK: Emerald Group Publishing Limited, 2013), 153.

82. *Syracuse1852*, 46.

83. Ibid., 26.

84. Ibid.

85. On the evolution of republican motherhood see Linda K. Kerber, *Women of the Republic: Intellect and Ideology in Revolutionary America* (New York: Norton, 1980).

86. *Syracuse1852*, 26.

87. On Nichols's life and ideas see Marilyn S. Blackwell and Kristen Tegtmeier Oertel, *Frontier Feminist: Clarina Howard Nichols and the Politics of Motherhood* (Lawrence: University Press of Kansas, 2010).

88. *Worcester1851*, 64–65.

89. Ibid., 74.

90. On women's rights activists' critique and use of the family, see Nancy Isenberg, *Sex and Citizenship in Antebellum America* (Chapel Hill: University of North Carolina Press, 1998).

91. *Syracuse1852*, 31.

92. Ibid., 73.

93. Ibid., 47. Rhode Island held a convention to alter its constitution in 1842. See chapter 1.

94. *Worcester1850*, 15.

95. Congress passed the Militia Act on July 17, 1862, but recruitment of black soldiers began in earnest in 1863, after the Emancipation Proclamation announced the army's plan to accept African American men's service. John David Smith, ed., *Black Soldiers in Blue: African American Troops in the Civil War Era* (Chapel Hill: University of North Carolina Press, 2002), 1–2.

96. On the connection between black men's civil war military service and citizenship, see Christian G. Samito, *Becoming American under Fire: Irish Americans, African Americans, and the Politics of Citizenship during the Civil War Era* (Ithaca, NY: Cornell University Press, 2009).

97. During the Civil War, African American activists held only one national convention, in October 1864, but groups in Pennsylvania, Ohio, Kansas, and Louisiana

held state-level conventions between 1863 and April 1865. Bell, *Minutes*; Foner and Walker, *Proceedings*, 1:137–170, 342–353; 2:230–239, 242–256.

98. "Proceedings of the National Convention of Colored Men, Held in the City of Syracuse, N.Y., October 4, 5, 6 and 7, 1864; with the Bill of Wrongs and Rights, and the Address to the American People," page 24, in Bell, *Minutes*.

99. Ibid., 41–42.

100. *The Dred Scott Decision: Opinion of Chief Justice Taney, with an Introduction by J. H. Van Evrie. Also, an Appendix, Containing an Essay on the Natural history of the Prognathous Race of Mankind, Originally Written for the New York Day-Book by Dr. S.A. Cartwright* (New York: Van Evrie, Horton & Co., 1859), http://hdl.loc.gov/loc.law/llst.022.

101. "Proceedings of the State Equal Rights Convention, of the Colored People of Pennsylvania, Held in the city of Harrisburg, February 8th, 9th, and 10th, 1865, Together with a few of the Arguments Presented Suggesting the Necessity for Holding the Convention, and An Address of the Colored State Convention to the People of Pennsylvania," in Foner and Walker, *Proceedings*, 1:140.

102. "Proceedings of the National Convention of Colored Men, held in the City of Syracuse," pages 42–43, in Bell, *Minutes*.

103. "Proceedings of the State Equal Rights Convention, of the Colored People of Pennsylvania," in Foner and Walker, *Proceedings*, 1:163.

104. "Proceedings of the National Convention of Colored Men, held in the City of Syracuse," page 58, in Bell, *Minutes*.

105. Ibid., 24. To protest the unequal treatment of black soldiers, the convention passed a resolution asking Congress to ensure that there were no race-based distinctions among soldiers in assigning their pay, duties, and prospects for promotion.

106. Ibid., 33.

107. Ibid., 42.

108. Ibid., 60.

109. Although some women certainly did perform military service, they did so disguised as men. See Deanne Blanton and Lauren M. Cook, *They Fought Like Demons: Women Soldiers in the American Civil War* (Baton Rouge: Louisiana State University Press, 2002); Elizabeth D. Leonard, *All the Daring of the Soldier: Women of the Civil War Armies* (New York: Norton, 1999). Northern women's broad efforts to support the war in other ways were also later claimed by activists as state service. Nina Silber, *Daughters of the Union: Northern Women Fight the Civil War* (Cambridge, MA: Harvard University Press, 2005).

110. "Meeting of the Loyal Women of the Republic," *Papers: 1*, 487–493. Loyal Leagues founded by northern women appeared in Connecticut, Pennsylvania, Ohio, Illinois, and Wisconsin. Wendy Hamand Venet, *Neither Ballots nor Bullets: Women Abolitionists and the Civil War* (Charlottesville: University Press of Virginia, 1991), 102.

111. Editorial Note, *Papers: 1*, 480–481. Appeal by Elizabeth Cady Stanton, "To the Women of the Republic," in *Papers: 1*, 483.

112. Stanton, "To the Women of the Republic," in ibid., 483–486.

113. Susan B. Anthony to Amy Kirby Post, April 13, 1865, *Papers: 1*, 481. Venet notes that the composition of this group was mostly white, and that there is scant evidence that the Loyal League members actively recruited African American women and men. Venet, 110.

114. Susan B. Anthony, Address, "Meeting of the Loyal Women of the Republic," *Papers: 1*, 491.

115. William Lloyd Garrison, *The Letters of William Lloyd Garrison,* ed. Walter M. Merrill and Louis Ruchames, (Cambridge, MA: 1971–1981), 5:154, in *Papers: 1*, 488.

116. "Meeting of the Women's Loyal National League," *Papers: 1*, 498. The text of the petition that the league proposed to circulate was later attributed to the social reformer Robert Dale Owen, who would play a critical role in the drafting of the Fourteenth Amendment's text two years later. Ibid., 499n2.

117. Susan Zaeske, *Signatures of Citizenship: Petitioning, Antislavery, and Women's Political Identity* (Chapel Hill: University of North Carolina Press, 2003); Alisse Theodore Portnoy, "'Female Petitioners can Lawfully be Heard': Negotiating Female Decorum, United States Politics, and Political Agency, 1829–1831," *Journal of the Early Republic* 23, no. 4 (Winter 2003), 573–610.

118. Venet, *Neither Ballots nor Bullets,* 109–122.

119. Although the Senate never implemented an official gag rule, it did devise a complicated procedure by which it could avoid having to deal with antislavery petitions directly. When it received an antislavery petition, the Senate "would vote not on whether to receive the petition itself—this would dignify the petition—but on whether to accept the question of receiving the petition." Senate Historical Office, "Senate History, March 16, 1836, Gag Rule," https://www.senate.gov/artandhistory/history/minute/Gag_Rule.htm. Much to the relief of its organizers, the Loyal League's petition was dealt with directly. In a letter to Frances Miller Seward, the wife of Secretary of State William Seward, Stanton said, "Mr. Sumner presented the 'emancipation petition' last week, made a good little speech which called out some discussion & that the petition instead of being thrown under the table was referred." Elizabeth Cady Stanton to Frances Miller Seward, February 15, 1864, *Papers: 1*, 510.

120. At least Stanton and Anthony later recalled this to be true in their *History of Woman Suffrage.* Despite the biased nature of this source, there was a significant correspondence between Sumner and both Stanton and Anthony in this period, and it is possible that he would have expressed his support for their efforts. Elizabeth Cady Stanton, Susan B. Anthony, and Matilda Joslyn Gage, *History of Woman Suffrage,* vol. 2, *1861–1876* (New York: Fowler & Wells, 1882), 50–89.

121. While antislavery petitioning aligned women's rights activists with abolitionists in the pre-war period, the relationship was not easy. Venet notes, for example, that Stanton became quite angry when the American Anti-Slavery Society began a rival petition drive in 1863. Venet, 119–120.

122. Venet argues that the Loyal League helped shift women's rights activism away from moral reform and toward political action. Ibid., 148–149. Pennsylvania congressman William D. Kelley spoke to the league, and Massachusetts senator Henry Wilson credited the league's efforts as helping the antislavery cause in Congress. Ibid., 114, 122.

123. Ibid., 110; *Congressional Globe*, 38th Congress, 1st sess. 536 (February 9, 1864).

124. Elizabeth Cady Stanton to Caroline Healey Dall, May 7, 1864, *Papers: 1*, 519.

125. Elizabeth Cady Stanton, "Woman's One Political Right—Circulate The Petition!," *The Liberator,* December 18, 1863.

126. Elizabeth Cady Stanton, "Universal Suffrage," *National Anti-Slavery Standard*, July 29, 1865, *Papers: 1*, 550.

127. The documents are scarce between August and December of 1865. In this period, Anthony was visiting her brother in Kansas, participating in political activities there, and then engaging in a speaking tour along her route back to the East. Between August and September she visited relatives and then returned home to Rochester. By October, she was traveling and visiting friends. Her diary indicates, however, that in the fall she spent a lot of time at the New York offices of the *National Anti-Slavery Standard* and the American Anti-Slavery Society, for which she was a paid lecturer. By December, though, her correspondence begins to discuss the petition campaign and to urge her friends to support and participate in the drive for petition signatures. Elizabeth Cady Stanton and Susan B. Anthony, *Papers of Elizabeth Cady Stanton and Susan B. Anthony*, ed. Patricia G. Holland and Ann D. Gordon (Wilmington, DE: Scholarly Resources Inc., 1991), microfilm, ser. 3, reel 11 (hereafter cited as *Papers: Microfilm*).

128. By December of 1865, Anthony indicated in a letter to the well-respected Republican general Carl Schurz her belief that the only "right or safe basis of a republican government" was universal suffrage and implied that these ideas were held by others. In this letter Anthony asked Schurz to participate in a series of lectures she was organizing because "we believe you fully with us in the sentiment that the work of this hour is to establish a genuine republican government whose codes and constitutions shall be for persons, citizens, taxpayers, the governed—and not for race or color, sect or sex." Susan B. Anthony to Carl Schurz, December 30, 1865, ibid., ser. 3, reel 11.

129. "The Anniversaries," 8.

130. Wendell Phillips to Elizabeth Cady Stanton, January 14, 1866, *Papers: Microfilm*, ser. 3, reel 11.

131. Phillips, *Shall Women Have the Right to Vote?*, 14.

132. Lucy McKim married Wendell Phillips Garrison, the son of William Lloyd Garrison and the future editor of the *Nation* (1881–1906), on July 6, 1865. See "Across the Generations," Garrison Family Tree, http://www.smith.edu/libraries/libs/ssc/atg/popupgarrisontree.html; Elizabeth Cady Stanton to Martha Coffin Pelham Wright, January 20, 1866, *Papers: Microfilm*, ser. 3, reel 11.

133. Lucretia Coffin Mott to Martha Coffin Wright, November 2, 1865, *Papers: 1*, 558n1.

3. The Family Politic

1. U.S. Const. art. I, § 2. For discussion of the history of the Three-Fifths Compromise see Staughton Lynd, "Compromise of 1787," *Political Science Quarterly* 81, no. 2 (Jun., 1966), 225–250; Howard Ohline, "Republicanism and Slavery: Origins of the Three-Fifths Clause in the United States Constitution," *William and Mary Quarterly* 28, no. 4 (October 1971): 563–584; Jack N. Rakove, "The Great Compromise: Ideas, Interests, and the Politics of Constitution Making," *William and Mary Quarterly* 44, no. 3 (July 1987): 424–457; George William Van Cleve, *A Slaveholders' Union: Slavery, Politics, and the Constitution in the Early American Republic* (Chicago: University of Chicago Press, 2010).

2. *Congressional Globe*, 39th Cong., 1st sess. 356 (January 22, 1866) (hereafter cited as *CG*).

3. Congress's focus was on the metaphor of the political family of Americans. Historians have noted that the changes brought by the war and emancipation prompted many other Americans to reevaluate, re-create, or newly construct the idea of, legal meanings for, and lived experience of family. Some examples: Leslie A. Schwalm, *A Hard Fight for We: Women's Transition from Slavery to Freedom in South Carolina* (Urbana: University of Illinois Press, 1997); Peter W. Bardaglio, *Reconstructing the Household: Families, Sex, and the Law in the Nineteenth-Century South* (Chapel Hill: University of North Carolina Press, 1995); Noralee Frankel, *Freedom's Women: Black Women and Families in Civil War Era Mississippi* (Bloomington: Indiana University Press, 1999); Elizabeth Ann Regosin, *Freedom's Promise: Ex-Slave Families and Citizenship in the Age of Emancipation* (Charlottesville: University Press of Virginia, 2002); Amy Murrell Taylor, *The Divided Family in Civil War America* (Chapel Hill: University of North Carolina Press, 2005).

4. The Thirty-Eighth Congress ended on March 3, 1865, and the Thirty-Ninth Congress did not begin until December 4, 1865. See "Session Dates of Congress," http://history.house.gov/Institution/Session-Dates/30–39. Most states elected their representatives in even-numbered years, but congressional sessions in the Civil War era began in December of odd-numbered years. Those congressmen elected in 1864 were not seated in Congress until well over a year after their election. Congressional Directory, "Sessions of Congress Table," 2, http://www.senate. gov/reference/resources/pdf/congresses1.pdf. See also Congressional Quarterly, *Congressional Quarterly's Guide to United States Elections,* 3rd ed. (Washington, D.C.: Congressional Quarterly, 1994).

5. In initial meetings with the new president, radicals persuaded themselves that Johnson's goals were aligned with their own. See Joseph B. James, *The Framing of the Fourteenth Amendment* (Urbana: University of Illinois Press, 1956), 5–8; Eric Foner, *Reconstruction: America's Unfinished Revolution, 1863–1877* (New York: Harper & Row, 1988), 176–178, 180–185, 197; Eric L. McKitrick, *Andrew Johnson and Reconstruction* (Oxford: Oxford University Press, 1988), 61–67. Identifying and defining radicals, moderates, and conservatives among Republicans in the Civil War era have long occupied historians. See Eric Foner, *Free Soil, Free Labor, Free Men: The Ideology of the Republican Party before the Civil War* (New York: Oxford University Press, 1995); Allan G. Bogue, *The Earnest Men: Republicans of the Civil War Senate* (Ithaca, NY: Cornell University Press, 1981); Allan G. Bogue, *The Congressman's Civil War* (Cambridge: Cambridge University Press, 1989); Michael Les Benedict, *A Compromise of Principle: Congressional Republicans and Reconstruction, 1863–1869* (New York: Norton, 1974); Herman Belz, *A New Birth of Freedom: The Republican Party and Freedman's Rights, 1861 to 1866* (Westport, CT: Greenwood Press, 1976). I follow Eric Foner's definition of radicals as those Republicans who "shared the conviction that slavery and the rights of black Americans were the preeminent question facing nineteenth-century America." Foner, "The Ideology of the Republican Party," in *The Birth of the Grand Old Party: The Republicans' First Generation*, ed. Robert Francis Engs and Randall M. Miller (Philadelphia: University of Pennsylvania Press, 2002), 17.

6. For example, see Salmon P. Chase to Charles Sumner, June 25, 1865. "President Johnson makes a great mistake in refusing to recognize the colored citizens as

part of the people with which, in each state, he thinks himself not only authorized but bound to arrange the conditions of restoration. It is a moral, political, & financial mistake. . . . I am grievously disappointed." Salmon P. Chase, *The Salmon P. Chase Papers*, ed. John Niven (Kent, OH: Kent State University Press, 1998), 5:55–56. On Johnson's reconstruction plans see McKitrick, *Andrew Johnson and Reconstruction*, esp. chap. 6; Hans L. Trefousse, *Andrew Johnson: A Biography* (New York: Norton, 1989).

7. Charles Sumner to Francis Lieber, December 3, 1865, cited in James, *Framing of the Fourteenth Amendment,* 38.

8. James, *Framing of the Fourteenth Amendment,* 7–15.

9. Ibid., 37–38.

10. "From Washington," *New York Times,* December 3, 1865, 1.

11. The House and the Senate referred to this committee in different ways. For the sake of simplicity, I will refer to it either as the Joint Committee on Reconstruction (rather than the Senate's "Joint Committee to Enquire into the Condition of the States Which Formed the So-Called Federal States of America") or as the Joint Committee of Fifteen (as it was called in the House). James, *Framing of the Fourteenth Amendment,* 37–39.

12. Raoul Berger, *The Fourteenth Amendment and the Bill of Rights* (Norman: University of Oklahoma Press, 1989), 23–25; Robert J. Kaczorowski, "To Begin the Nation Anew: Congress, Citizenship, and Civil Rights after the Civil War," *American Historical Review* 92, no. 1 (February 1987): 55–58. See also the speech of Senator Lyman Trumbull, Republican from Illinois, *CG,* 39th Cong., 1st sess. 474–476 (January 29, 1866).

13. In Congress, constitutional amendments, bills, and resolutions were proposed by Representatives Thaddeus Stevens and John Bingham and by Massachusetts radical senators Charles Sumner and Henry Wilson. *CG,* 39th Cong., 1st sess. 10, 14, 18 (December 6, 11, 1866); *Journal of the Senate of the United States of America,* 39th Cong., 1st sess. 5–8, 38 (December 4, 13, 1865) (hereafter cited as Senate: *Journal*). For a discussion of Bingham's importance in the framing of the Fourteenth Amendment, see Erving E. Beauregard, *Bingham of the Hills: Politician and Diplomat Extraordinary* (New York: P. Lang, 1989).

14. For more on Trumbull, see Horace White, *The Life of Lyman Trumbull* (Boston: Houghton Mifflin, 1913); Mark M. Krug, *Lyman Trumbull: Conservative Radical* (New York: A.S. Barnes, 1965).

15. *CG,* 39th Cong., 1st sess. 211 (January 12, 1866).

16. Both the Senate bill and the Fugitive Slave Act had the same number of enforcement provisions organized in the same manner. Each explicitly declared that the courts and their officers were required by law to uphold the provisions of the act. Kaczorowski, "To Begin the Nation Anew," 59.

17. McKitrick, *Andrew Johnson and Reconstruction,* 277–278; Senate: *Journal,* 39th Cong., 1st sess. 72 (January 11, 1866).

18. Senate: *Journal,* 39th Cong., 1st sess. 132 (February 2, 1866); *Journal of the House of Representatives of the United States,* 39th Cong., 1st sess. 225, 232 (February 3, 5, 1866) (hereafter cited as House: *Journal*).

19. House: *Journal,* 39th Cong., 1st sess. 396–397 (March 13, 1866). On House procedure preceding the passage of Senate Bill 61, see Earl M. Maltz, *Civil Rights, the Constitution, and Congress, 1863–1869* (Lawrence: University Press of Kansas, 1990), 64–67.

20. Senate: *Journal,* 39th Cong., 1st sess. 235–237 (March 15, 1866).

21. Ibid., 270–289 (March 27, 1866). For a discussion of President Johnson's relationship with the radical and moderate Republicans, and of how central the Freedman's

Bureau and Civil Rights Act vetoes were to the alienation of Republicans who had originally sought good relations with Johnson, see McKitrick, *Andrew Johnson and Reconstruction*, 274–325.

22. Senate: *Journal*, 39th Cong., 1st sess. 317 (April 6, 1866); House: *Journal*, 39th Cong., 1st sess. 528 (April 9, 1866).

23. Constance McLaughlin Green, *The Secret City: A History of Race Relations in the Nation's Capital* (Princeton, NJ: Princeton University Press, 1969), 71–72; Kate Masur, *An Example for All the Land: Emancipation and the Struggle over Equality in Washington, D.C.* (Chapel Hill: University of North Carolina Press, 2010), esp. chaps. 2 and 4; Alfred Avins, *The Reconstruction Amendments' Debates: The Legislative History and Contemporary Debates in Congress on the 13th, 14th, and 15th Amendments* (Richmond: Virginia Commission on Constitutional Government, 1967), 70–74.

24. For example, a report in the *New York Tribune* of June 1865 stated, "[A] committee of negroes . . . recently called on [President Johnson] to petition the next Congress to grant them the right of franchise in this District, as preliminary to its concession elsewhere." Reprinted in *The Daily Journal* (Ogdensburg, New York), June 9, 1865.

25. *CG*, 37th Cong., 2nd sess. 1686 (April 16, 1862). On early Republican wartime emancipation efforts, see James Oakes, *Freedom National: The Destruction of Slavery in the United States, 1861–1865* (New York: Norton, 2013), 240–292.

26. See the arguments of Republicans Glenni Scofield of Pennsylvania on January 10 and of Burt Van Horn of New York on January 17, 1866. *CG*, 39th Cong., 1st sess. 179, 285 (January 10 and 17, 1866). For Washington, D.C., as a test case for radical Republican policies, see Robert Harrison, "An Experimental Station for Lawmaking: Congress and the District of Columbia, 1862–1878," *Civil War History* 53, no. 1 (March 2007): 29–53; and Masur, *An Example for All the Land*, 1.

27. Masur, *An Example for All the Land*, 131–133.

28. Petitions were received in favor of black suffrage in the District on December 11 and 21, 1865; January 16, 19, 22, and 23, 1866. All were presented by Henry Wilson, Charles Sumner of Massachusetts, and Benjamin Wade of Ohio. *CG*, 39th Cong., 1st sess. 16, 107, 242, 312, 337, 360 (1865–1866). The lead signature on the December 11 petition was that of John Francis Cook, a prominent minister and leader in black Washington. On the petition campaign see Lois E. Horton, "The Days of Jubilee: Black Migration during the Civil War and Reconstruction," and James Oliver Horton, "The Genesis of Washington's African American Community," in *Urban Odyssey: A Multicultural History of Washington, D.C.,* ed. Francine Curro Cary (Washington, D.C.: Smithsonian Institution Press, 1996), 20–41, 65–78. Also useful is Allan Johnston, *Surviving Freedom: The Black Community of Washington, D.C. 1860–1880* (New York: Garland, 1993). In addition to petitions, the African American community also used less official channels to pressure Congress to pass suffrage in Washington. The petition itself did not claim that manhood entitled African Americans to vote, but rather it relied on ideas of universal equality. Masur, *An Example for All the Land*, 133. It stated, "We, the Colored Citizens of the District of Columbia . . . are property holders . . . [and] pay no inconsiderable amount of taxes. . . . Our loyalty has never been questioned; our patriotism is unbounded. . . . Without the right of suffrage, we are without protection and liable to combinations of outrage. . . . These principles and considerations are the basis upon which we predicate our claim for suffrage, and civil equality before the law." Petition of Colored Citizens of the District of Columbia, Praying the Passage of an Act Allowing

them the Right of Suffrage, (endorsed December 11, 1865); Committee on the District of Columbia, Petitions—Memorials, (Sen39A-H4); 39th Congress; Records of the United States Senate, Record Group 46, National Archives, Washington D.C.

29. *New York Daily Tribune*, July 11, 1865, 4.

30. *Journals of the Council of the City of Washington*, 63rd council, 313–316, Washington, D.C., 1864–1871, cited in Green, *Secret City*, 76–78. In Georgetown, 812 people voted against black suffrage, 1 in favor. The mayor of Georgetown, in a letter to the president pro tempore of the Senate, stated, "I am . . . directed to state that the average vote at the four preceding annual elections for officers of our City Government was 541 being 270 less votes than were polled on the 28th." Henry Addison to Lafayette Foster, January 12, 1866 (endorsed January 13, 1866); Henry Addison to Lafayette Foster, January 12, 1866, (endorsed January 13, 1866); Committee on the District of Columbia, Petitions and Memorials Referred to Committees, (Sen39A-H4); 39th Congress; Records of the Senate; Record Group 46, National Archives, Washington D.C.

31. For example, see the argument of James F. Wilson, chair of the Judiciary Committee and original author of the text of the bill. *CG*, 39th Cong., 1st sess. 174–175 (January 10, 1865). See also Xi Wang, *The Trial of Democracy: Black Suffrage and Northern Republicans, 1860–1910* (Athens: University of Georgia Press, 1997), 317n91.

32. For exactly how little northern support there was for black suffrage, see Phyllis Field, *The Politics of Race in New York: The Struggle for Black Suffrage in the Civil War Era* (Ithaca, NY: Cornell University Press, 1982); and Emil Olbrich, *The Development of Sentiment on Negro Suffrage to 1860*, Bulletin of the University of Wisconsin No. 477, History Series, vol. 3, no. 1 (Madison: University of Wisconsin, 1912).

33. The 1857 Wisconsin referendum was problematic—it received not even one-third of the total votes of the number who voted for governor in the same election. Because the question was acted upon by fewer than ten thousand voters, it was challenged in court and not enforced until the state's supreme court decided in 1866 to allow it. Olbrich, *Development of Sentiment*, 77, 86, 89, 90, 98; Field, *Politics of Race*, 1–79; Wang, *Trial of Democracy*, 2–7; William Gillette, *The Right to Vote: Politics and the Passage of the Fifteenth Amendment* (Baltimore: Johns Hopkins University Press, 1965), 27; Robert R. Dykstra, *Bright Radical Star: Black Freedom and White Supremacy on the Hawkeye Frontier* (Cambridge, MA: Harvard University Press, 1993) 173–191.

34. Hanes Walton, Sherman C. Puckett, and Donald Richard Deskins, *The African American Electorate: A Statistical History* (Thousand Oaks, CA: CQ Press, 2012), 1:147, table 8.1; Wang, *Trial of Democracy*, 22. For a comprehensive discussion of the African American suffrage referenda between 1846 and 1870, see Walton, Puckett, and Deskins, *African American Electorate*, vol. 1, 145–160. Black suffrage garnered 44.83 percent of total votes in Connecticut, 46.72 percent of votes in Wisconsin, and 45.12 percent in Minnesota. Defeats in the District and in the territory of Colorado were a little more dramatic, with only 1.01 percent voting for black suffrage in Colorado and only 36 favorable out of 7,369 total votes in Washington and Georgetown. Gillette, *Right to Vote*, 25–26.

35. Senate: *Journal*, 39th Cong., 1st sess. 5 (December 4, 1865); House: *Journal*, 39th Cong., 1st sess. 32 (December 5, 1865).

36. Committee minutes, Committee on the Judiciary, 89–92, Docket Volume (39A–F13.13), 39th Congress, Records of the United States House of Representatives, Record Group 233, National Archives; *CG,* 39th Cong., 1st sess. 72 (December 18, 1865); 302–311 (January 18, 1865).

37. House: *Journal,* 39th Cong., 1st sess. 166–167 (January 18, 1866).

38. Senate: *Journal,* 39th Cong., 1st sess. 5, 70, 76, 82, 86, 180 (December 4, 1865; January 10, 12, 15–16, 1866; February 21, 1866).

39. Ibid., 582, 584 (June 27, 1866); Wang, *Trial of Democracy,* 28–33. African American men in Washington were not enfranchised until January 8, 1867, when the Congress overrode President Andrew Johnson's veto of the measure. Senate: *Journal,* 39th Cong., 2nd sess. 77 (January 8, 1867).

40. Enfranchising southern African American men was also attractive because it empowered the formerly enslaved population to pursue its own reconstruction and addressed the increasing demands emerging from the African American community for universal suffrage. On race, suffrage and reconstruction see Foner, *Reconstruction;* and *Free Soil, Free Labor, Free Men;* W. E. B. DuBois, *Black Reconstruction in America, 1860–1880* (New York: Simon & Schuster, 1998 [1935]); On Republican Party politics in the Civil War era, see Bogue, *Congressman's Civil War* and *Earnest Men;* Benedict, *Compromise of Principle;* David Montgomery, *Beyond Equality: Labor and the Radical Republicans, 1862–1872* (Urbana: University of Illinois Press, 1981); and Hans Trefousse, *The Radical Republicans: Lincoln's Vanguard for Racial Justice* (New York: Knopf, 1968).

41. James, *Framing of the Fourteenth Amendment,* 58–67.

42. *CG,* 39th Cong., 1st sess. 351 (January 22, 1866). A more detailed discussion of House Resolution 51 and representation appears in chapter 5.

43. Extensive debates among antislavery activists in the antebellum period about the nature of the Constitution as a proslavery or antislavery document did not resolve the paradoxical relationship between slavery, the Constitution, and the founding fathers. William Lloyd Garrison, "On the Constitution and the Union," *Liberator,* December 29, 1832, cited in William E. Cain, ed., *William Lloyd Garrison and the Fight against Slavery: Selections from The Liberator* (Boston: Bedford Books of St. Martin's Press, 1999), 87–88; Frederick Douglass, "The Constitution of the United States: Is it Pro-Slavery or Anti-Slavery? Speech Delivered in Glasgow, Scotland, March 26, 1860," in Douglass, *The Life and Writings of Frederick Douglass,* ed. Philip S. Foner (New York: International Publishers, 1950); Lysander Spooner, *Unconstitutionality of Slavery* (Boston: Bela Marsh, 1845); Wendell Phillips, "Address of the Executive Committee of the American Anti-Slavery Society to the Friends of Freedom and Emancipation in the United States," in *The Constitution: A Pro-Slavery Compact; or, Extracts from the Madison Papers, etc. Selected by Wendell Phillips,* 3rd ed., ed. Wendell Phillips (Boston: Andrews & Prentiss, 1856), courtesy of the Division of Rare and Manuscript Collections, Cornell University Library.

44. On nineteenth-century middle-class whites' definitions of masculinity see Anthony Rotundo, *American Manhood: Transformations in Masculinity from the Revolution to the Modern Era* (New York: Basic Books, 1993); Michael Kimmel, *Manhood in America: A Cultural History* (New York: Free Press, 1996); Mark C. Carnes, *Secret Ritual and Manhood in Victorian America* (New Haven, CT: Yale University Press, 1989); Mark C. Carnes and Clyde Griffen, *Meanings for Manhood: Constructions*

of Masculinity in Victorian America (Chicago: University of Chicago Press, 1990); Michael Kimmel, *The History of Men: Essays on the History of American and British Masculinities* (Albany: SUNY Press, 2005). For an interesting account of how gender enabled earlier politicians to create the American state, see Mark E. Kann, *A Republic of Men: The American Founders, Gendered Language, and Patriarchal Politics* (New York: NYU Press, 1998).

45. From Aristotle to the early modern European political philosophers, the organization of the family was envisioned as a model for the state. Mary Beth Norton argues that in colonial America, the family was "the real—not just metaphorical—foundation of the state." Norton, *Founding Mothers and Fathers: Gendered Power and the Forming of American Society* (New York: Knopf, 1996), 38. See also Carole Shammas, *A History of Household Government in America* (Charlottesville: University of Virginia Press, 2002), esp. 2–4. In the European context see Rachel Judith Weil, *Political Passions: Gender, the Family, and Political Argument in England, 1680–1714* (Manchester, UK: Manchester University Press, 1999); Lynn Hunt, *The Family Romance of the French Revolution* (Berkeley: University of California Press, 1992); Julia Adams, "The Rule of the Father: Patriarchy and Patrimonialism in Early Modern Europe," in *Max Weber's Economy and Society: A Critical Companion,* ed. Charles Camic, Philip S. Gorski, and David M. Trubek (Stanford, CA: Stanford University Press, 2005), 237–266; Su Fang Ng, *Literature and the Politics of Family in Seventeenth-Century England* (Cambridge: Cambridge University Press, 2007); Mary Lowenthal Felstiner, "Family Metaphors: The Language of an Independence Revolution," *Comparative Studies in Society and History* 25, no. 1 (1983): 154–180.

46. Masculinity is, of course, a mutable category being constantly re-created over time and endowed with multiple meanings at any given moment. Some of the many works that engage this fluidity are: Paul Smith, *Boys: Masculinities in Contemporary Culture* (New York: Harper Collins, 1998); Judith Halberstam, *Female Masculinity* (Durham, NC: Duke University Press, 1998). The problem of multiple masculinities was raised for me by Anne McClintock, "Masculinities and Other War Zones" (talk delivered at Crossing Boundaries/Shifting Boundaries, Graduate Student Conference, Department of French and Italian, University of Wisconsin, April 12, 2002).

47. Interpreting the founders' intent has been a central component of American constitutional law. See Leonard W. Levy, *Original Intent and the Framers' Constitution* (New York: Macmillan, 1988); Herman Belz, Ronald Hoffman, and Peter Albert, eds., *To Form a More Perfect Union: The Critical Ideas of the Constitution* (Charlottesville: University Press of Virginia, 1992); Jack N. Rakove, ed., *Interpreting the Constitution: The Debate over Original Intent* (Boston: Northeastern University Press, 1990); and Jack N. Rakove, *Original Meanings: Politics and Ideas in the Making of the Constitution* (New York: Knopf, 1996).

48. *CG,* 39th Cong., 1st sess. 765 (February 9, 1866).

49. Ibid., 353 (January 22, 1866).

50. Ibid., 458 (January 26, 1866)

51. Ibid., 1415 (March 15, 1866). Although Davis was elected as a Whig to fill the vacancy of John C. Breckenridge in 1861, in 1867 he was reelected as a Democrat. Given this fact, and the consistency of his language with racist Democratic Party rhetoric, I am grouping him with the Democrats for the purposes of this discussion. "Biographical Directory of Congress, 1774–present," *United States Congress,* http://bioguide.congress.gov/scripts/biodisplay.pl?index=D000099.

52. *CG*, 39th Cong., 1st sess. 458 (January 26, 1866). The 1860 edition of Webster's dictionary defined "patriarchal" as "belonging to patriarchs, possessed by patriarchs." It defined "patriarch" as "the father and ruler of a family; one who governs by paternal right." Noah Webster, *An American Dictionary of the English Language*, ed., rev., and enlarged Chauncy A. Goodrich (Springfield, MA: George and Charles Merriam, 1860).

53. *CG*, 39th Cong., 1st sess. 387 (January 23, 1866).

54. Ibid., 412 (January 24, 1866).

55. Ibid., 1112 (March 1, 1866).

56. Ibid., 387 (January 23, 1866)

57. Ibid., 355 (January 22, 1866).

58. Ibid., 459 (January 26, 1866).

59. Ibid., 882 (February 16, 1866).

60. Jean H. Baker, *Affairs of Party: The Political Culture of Northern Democrats in the Mid-Nineteenth Century* (Ithaca, NY: Cornell University Press, 1983). The Democratic Party relied most heavily on "ethnoreligious outsiders" and recent immigrant groups for its constituency and therefore reinforced the potency of race to unite its disparate members as Democrats through whiteness. See Joel H. Silbey, *The American Political Nation, 1838–1893* (Stanford, CA: Stanford University Press, 1991), 164. For a discussion of how immigrant groups and workers utilized whiteness to construct self-identity see David R. Roediger, *The Wages of Whiteness: Race and the Making of the American Working Class* (New York: Verso, 1991); Noel Ignatiev, *How the Irish Became White* (New York: Routledge, 1995); and Matthew Frye Jacobsen, *Whiteness of a Different Color: European Immigrants and the Alchemy of Race* (Cambridge, MA: Harvard University Press, 1998).

61. *CG*, 39th Cong., 1st sess. 575 (February 1, 1866).

62. Ibid.

63. Ibid., 176 (January 10, 1866).

64. Ibid., 118 (December 21, 1866).

65. Ibid., 880 (February 16, 1866).

66. See ibid., 178, 201 (January 10 and 11, 1866) and 246 (January 16, 1866). The black rapist was also a trope frequently adopted by Democrats to reject the enfranchisement of African American men, and its use undoubtedly contributed to the construction of the black rapist myth that emerged during Reconstruction. Diane Miller Sommerville argues that this myth gained legitimacy in the postwar period as a racist response to the political empowerment of black men. See Sommerville, "The Rape Myth in the Old South Reconsidered," in *A Question of Manhood: A Reader in U.S. Black Men's History and Masculinity*, vol. 1, ed. Darlene Clark Hine and Earnestine Jenkins (Bloomington: Indiana University Press, 1999), 438–472, and esp. 439–442. See also Diane Miller Sommerville, *Rape and Race in the Nineteenth-Century South* (Chapel Hill: University of North Carolina Press, 2004).

67. *CG*, 39th Cong., 1st sess. 448–449 (January 26, 1866).

68. Ibid., 355 (January 22, 1866).

69. Ibid., 766 (February 9, 1866).

70. Ibid., 769.

71. Ibid.

72. Ibid., 876 (February 16, 1866).

73. Ibid., 764 (February 9, 1866).

74. Ibid., 435 (January 25, 1866).

75. Quoted in James Brewer Stewart, *Holy Warriors: The Abolitionists and American Slavery* (New York: Hill and Wang, 1976), 98–99; Henry Mayer, *All on Fire: William Lloyd Garrison and the Abolition of Slavery* (New York: Norton, 1998), 326–327. On other abolitionists' more friendly perspective on the Constitution, see John Stauffer, *The Black Hearts of Men: Radical Abolitionists and the Transformation of Race* (Cambridge, MA: Harvard University Press, 2001).

76. *CG*, 39th Cong., 1st sess. 384 (January 23, 1866).

77. Ibid., 832 (February 14, 1866).

78. Ibid., 1181 (March 5, 1866).

79. Ibid., 682 (February 6, 1866).

80. Ibid., 536 (January 31, 1866).

81. Petition of Colored People in Georgia for the Elective Franchise, &c., (endorsed January 30, 1866); Committee on the Judiciary, Petitions—Civil Rights (HR 39A–H14.2); 39th Congress; Records of the U.S. House of Representatives, Record Group 233, National Archives, Washington D.C.

82. *CG*, 39th Cong., 1st sess. 180 (January 10, 1886).

83. Ibid., 684–685 (February 6, 1866).

84. To the Honorable Senate and House of Representatives of the United States, in Congress Assembled, from William Nesbit, Joseph C. Bustill, William D. Forten on Behalf of the Pennsylvania State Equal Rights League, February 20, 1866; Committee on the Judiciary, Petitions—Civil Rights (HR 39A–H14.2) 39th Congress; Records of the U.S. House of Representatives, Record Group 233, National Archives, Washington D.C.

85. *CG*, 39th Cong., 1st sess. 536 (January 31, 1866). Webster's 1860 dictionary defined "parricide" as "1. A person who murders his father or mother. 2. One who murders an ancestor, or anyone to whom he owes reverence." Webster, *American Dictionary of the English Language*.

86. *CG*, 39th Cong., 1st sess. 674 (February 6, 1866).

87. Ibid., 1226 (March 7, 1866).

88. To the Honorable Senate and House of Representatives of the United States, in Congress Assembled, from William Nesbit, Joseph C. Bustill, William D. Forten.

89. *CG*, 39th Cong., 1st sess. 410 (January 24, 1866).

90. Ibid., 1183 (March 5, 1866).

91. Ibid., 1231 (March 7, 1866).

92. Ibid., 1074 (February 28, 1866). Sumner's references to giving birth and nursing could also be read as maternal.

93. On the connections between the wartime service of African American men and post–Civil War rights policies see Mary Frances Berry, *Military Necessity and Civil Rights Policy: Black Citizenship and the Constitution, 1861–1868* (Port Washington, NY: Kennikat Press, 1977); Belz, *New Birth of Freedom*; and more recently Christian G. Samito, *Becoming American under Fire: Irish Americans, African Americans, and the Politics of Citizenship during the Civil War Era* (Ithaca, NY: Cornell University Press, 2009).

94. By emphasizing the military service of African American men during the Civil War, Republicans, like antebellum and wartime African American activists, drew on the history in America in which the disfranchised were granted voting rights in exchange

for their military service. Chilton Williamson, *American Suffrage: From Property to Democracy, 1760–1860* (Princeton, NJ: Princeton University Press, 1960), 79–82.

95. *CG*, 39th Cong., 1st sess. 310 (January 18, 1866).

96. Ibid., 259 (January 16, 1866).

97. Ibid., 175 (January 10, 1866).

98. Ibid., 1225 (March 7, 1866).

99. Petition of Colored Citizens of the District of Columbia, Praying the Passage of an Act Allowing Them the Right of Suffrage, (endorsed December 11, 1865); Committee on the District of Columbia, Petitions—Memorials, (Sen39A–H4); 39th Congress; Records of the United States Senate, Record Group 46, National Archives, Washington D.C.

100. Petition of Colored People in Georgia for the Elective Franchise.

101. To the Honorable Senate and House of Representatives of the United States, in Congress Assembled, from William Nesbit, Joseph C. Bustill, William D. Forten.

102. Ibid.

103. Petition of Colored Citizens of the District of Columbia.

4. The Rights of Men

1. Josiah Grinnell was a two-term Republican representative from Iowa. An unremarkable congressman, he later gained fame as the founder of Grinnell College and the town of Grinnell, Iowa. "Biographical Directory of Congress, 1774–present," *United States Congress*, http://bioguide.congress.gov/scripts/biodisplay.pl?index=G000478.

2. Neither Republican nor Democrat, Rousseau was elected as an Unconditional Unionist, but his extremely conservative opinions on race-based issues more frequently aligned with the Democratic members of the House than with Republicans. "Biographical Directory of Congress, *United States Congress*, 1774–1961, http://bioguide.congress.gov/scripts/biodisplay.pl?index=R000468.

3. *Congressional Globe*, 39th Cong., 1st sess. 3818–3819 (July 14 1866) (hereafter cited as *CG*); Josiah Bushnell Grinnell, *Men and Events of Forty Years: Autobiographical Reminiscences of an Active Career From 1850 to 1890* (Boston: D. Lothrop, 1891), 163–170.

4. For an analysis of the Sumner incident see David Herbert Donald, *Charles Sumner and the Coming of the Civil War* (New York: Knopf, 1960); more recently, Williamjames Hull Hoffer, *The Caning of Charles Sumner: Honor, Idealism, and the Origins of the Civil War* (Baltimore: Johns Hopkins University Press, 2010).

5. Gender was also a prominent element in Brooks's attack on Sumner and in the public's response to the incident. See Manisha Sinha, "The Caning of Charles Sumner: Slavery, Race, and Ideology in the Age of the Civil War," *Journal of the Early Republic* 23, no. 2 (2003): 251–252.

6. *CG*, 39th Cong., 1st sess. 3096 (June 11, 1866).

7. John Lyde Wilson, governor of South Carolina (1822–24), published a code duello in 1838 outlining the procedures for duels between southern gentlemen. In it he justified dueling as a natural defense of one's manhood and honor when no other mode of redress for an insult was available. "When one finds himself avoided in society, his friends shunning his approach, his substance wasting, his wife and children in want

around him, and traces all his misfortunes and misery to the slanderous tongue of the calumniator, who, by secret whisper or artful innuendo, has sapped and undermined his reputation, he must be more or less than man to submit in silence. . . . [Dueling] will be persisted in as long as a manly independence, and a lofty personal pride in all that dignifies and ennobles the human character, shall continue to exist." John Lyde Wilson, *The Code of Honor, (Or, Rules for the Government of Principles and Seconds in Dueling)* (Project Gutenberg, 1838, 2013), http://www.gutenberg.org/files/6085/6085-h/6085-h.htm. For a discussion of the relationship of violence, and especially dueling, to southern male culture see Bertram Wyatt-Brown, *Honor and Violence in the Old South* (New York: Oxford University Press, 1986). On the connections of physical violence to nineteenth-century constructions of masculinity see Elliott Gorn, *The Manly Art: Bare-Knuckle Prize Fighting in America* (Ithaca, NY: Cornell University Press, 1986). On the connections between gender roles and sectional conflict, see Catherine Clinton, "Sex and the Sectional Conflict," in *Taking Off the White Gloves: Southern Women and Women Historians,* ed. Michele K. Gillespie and Catherine Clinton (Columbia: University of Missouri Press, 1998), 46–63.

8. The Speaker of the House and the president of the Senate had signed House Resolution 127, enrolled the resolution as passed by both the House and Senate, and sent it to the secretary of state for distribution to the various states for ratification. *Journal of the Senate of the United States of America,* 39th Cong., 1st sess. 523, 527 (June 15, 1866); *Journal of the House of Representatives of the United States Congress,* 39th Cong., 1st sess. 841 (June 14, 1866).

9. Although the notion of separate spheres represented an ideal that many middle-class white families were told to expect, some historians' work has indicated that there were distinct limits to the public/private dichotomy. These are shown particularly clearly in the many works that focus on women's involvement in the public world of politics and those that explore men's involvement in the private world of the family. An excellent article critiquing the separate spheres model is Linda Kerber, "Separate Spheres, Female Worlds, Woman's Place: The Rhetoric of Women's History," *Journal of American History* 75, no. 1 (June 1988): 9–39.

10. On the development of interconnections between family and political community in American conceptualizations of power, see Mary Beth Norton, *Founding Mothers and Fathers: Gendered Power and the Forming of American Society,* (New York: Knopf, 1996).

11. Stephen M. Frank has found that until 1870 this shift in the focus of men's work lives did not necessarily translate into less time within the household, as many men worked from the home or quite near the home. However, he acknowledges that there was a cultural shift in the way that men's presence in the household was perceived. Frank, *Life with Father: Parenthood and Masculinity in the Nineteenth Century North* (Baltimore: Johns Hopkins University Press, 1998), 55–72.

12. Nancy Cott, "Marriage and Women's Citizenship in the United States, 1830–1934," *American Historical Review* 103, no. 5 (December 1998): 1452n33; Toby Ditz, "Ownership and Obligation: Inheritance and Patriarchal Households in Connecticut, 1750–1820," *William and Mary Quarterly* 47, no. 2 (April 1990): 235–265.

13. On the evolution of coverture in nineteenth-century marriage law, see Nancy Cott, *Public Vows: A History of Marriage and the Nation,* (Cambridge, MA: Harvard University Press, 2000), 2–55.

14. Cited in Anthony Rotundo, *American Manhood: Transformations in Masculinity From the Revolution to the Modern Era* (New York: Basic Books, 1993), 133.

15. On marriage and eighteenth-century politics see Mark E. Kann, *A Republic of Men: The American Founders, Gendered Language, and Patriarchal Politics* (New York: New York University Press, 1998), 79–104.

16. Rotundo, *American Manhood*, 115; Ruth H. Bloch, "Inside and Outside the Public Sphere," *William and Mary Quarterly* 62, no. 1 (January 2005): 99–106.

17. "Marriage and Divorce," *Southern Quarterly Review* 26 (1854): 351, cited in Cott, *Public Vows*, 7.

18. Kann, *Republic of Men*, 15–16. Dana Nelson argues in her book *National Manhood* that this fraternity, created with the advent of universal manhood suffrage, mitigated against other modes of alignment between men. She argues that this alignment was particularly detrimental to the possibility of alliances among men with common class and economic interests, to individual men's self-identification, and to the American democracy. Nelson, *National Manhood: Capitalist Citizenship and the Imagined Fraternity of White Men* (Durham, NC: Duke University Press, 1998).

19. Cited in Stephanie McCurry, *Masters of Small Worlds: Yeoman Households, Gender Relations, and the Political Culture of the Antebellum South Carolina Low Country* (New York: Oxford University Press, 1995), 260.

20. See chapter 1.

21. Michael Kimmel, *Manhood in America: A Cultural History* (New York: Oxford University Press, 2011), 11–42.

22. Ibid., 36–39.

23. Rotundo, *American Manhood*, 167–180.

24. Although women participated in electoral politics in the antebellum period, they did not cast ballots, rendering the ritual act of voting itself a gendered behavior. The relationship between manhood and American politics has been examined in the context of American expansionist policies in the antebellum period in Amy S. Greenberg, *Manifest Manhood and the Antebellum American Empire* (Cambridge: Cambridge University Press, 2005). For the link between manhood and expansion in the later nineteenth century, see Kristin L. Hoganson, *Fighting for American Manhood: How Gender Politics Provoked the Spanish-American and Philippine-American Wars* (New Haven, CT: Yale University Press, 1998).

25. See chapter 1.

26. *CG*, 39th Cong., 1st sess. 464 (January 27, 1866).

27. Ibid., 379 (January 23, 1866).

28. Ibid., 1181 (March 5, 1866).

29. Ibid., 570 (February 1, 1866). The term "negro" was not capitalized in the *Congressional Globe* in this period. Here I follow the capitalization practice of the original source.

30. Ibid., 682 (February 6, 1866).

31. Ibid., 356 (January 22, 1866).

32. Ibid.

33. Ibid.

34. Ibid.

35. Ibid., 430 (January 25, 1866).

36. Ibid., 1255 (March 8, 1866).

37. In the process, congressmen envisioned the default emancipated person as male, equating freedman with man and marginalizing African American women in their discussions of freedmen's rights.

38. *CG*, 39th Cong., 1st sess. 356 (January 22, 1866).

39. Ibid., 739 (February 8, 1866).

40. Ibid., 570 (February 1, 1866).

41. Ibid., 742 (February 8, 1866); 1182 (March 5, 1866).

42. Gender played a particularly important role in these definitions. See Rosemarie Zagarri, "The Rights of Man and Woman in Post-Revolutionary America," *William and Mary Quarterly* 55, no. 2 (1998): 203–230.

43. This did not mean, however, that enslaved people did not forge strong and meaningful familial relationships despite the numerous institutional barriers to those connections.

44. Kristin Hoganson, "Garrisonian Abolitionists and the Rhetoric of Gender, 1850–1860," *American Quarterly* 45, no. 4 (1993), 558–595.

45. *CG*, 39th Cong., 1st sess. 504 (January 30, 1866).

46. Ibid.

47. Ibid., 1266 (March 8, 1866).

48. Ibid., 1182 (March 5, 1866).

49. Senator Edgar Cowan of Pennsylvania argued that the Thirteenth Amendment did not offer justification for the Civil Rights Act because it did not disrupt all dependent relationships, only the very specific liberation of the slave from the master. He contended that it did not change the "involuntary servitude of my child to me, of my apprentice to me, or the quasi-servitude which the wife to some extent owes to her husband." Ibid., 499 (January 30, 1866).

50. Ibid., 505.

51. Although his approach was unusual, Johnson was not alone in identifying white men marrying black women as a potential source of racial intermarriage. In response to some of the Democrats' concerns, Lyman Trumbull mockingly declared that he "supposed that at his [Kentucky senator Davis's] time of life he would feel protected against [amalgamation] without any law to put him in the penitentiary if he should commit it." Davis then pointed to Illinois, Trumbull's home state, as a northern state with anti-interracial marriage laws. Trumbull replied that the presence of so many southerners in Illinois had required the law. This exchange indicated that some members of Congress were aware that historically the source of amalgamation, or miscegenation, in the South was white men's interaction with black women, not black men's connections with white women. Ibid., 600 (February 2, 1866).

52. Ibid., 604.

53. Ibid., 1679–1680 (March 27, 1866); 1757 (April 4, 1866).

54. Martha Elizabeth Hodes, *White Women, Black Men: Illicit Sex in the Nineteenth-Century South* (New Haven, CT: Yale University Press, 1997), 144–148.

55. Toby Ditz also situates control over women's sexuality at the heart of male power in "The New Men's History and the Peculiar Absence of Gendered Power: Some Remedies from Early American Gender History," *Gender and History* 16, no. 1 (2004): 1–35, 11.

56. *CG*, 39th Cong., 1st sess. 598 (February 2, 1866).

57. Ibid., 1155 (March 2, 1866).

58. Interestingly, in the next paragraph of his speech Eldridge infantilized African Americans, perhaps to appeal to the majority Republicans: "It is said that the negro race is weak and feeble; that they are mere children—'wards of the government'" (ibid.). He implied that therefore they might need a weaker punishment for some crimes until education shall equalize their situation. The juxtaposition of the violent black rapist and the childlike innocent in this speech seems incongruous to the modern reader, but it was typical of white racist rhetoric at the time.

59. On the very real rapes committed by white men on black women in the Reconstruction-era South and the connection between sexual violence, gender, and citizenship, see Hannah Rosen, *Terror in the Heart of Freedom: Citizenship, Sexual Violence, and the Meaning of Race in the Postemancipation South,* Gender and American Culture Series (Chapel Hill: University of North Carolina Press, 2009).

60. Amy Dru Stanley offers an excellent analysis of the relationship between marriage and contract for the emancipated in *From Bondage to Contract.* Although she carefully considers the ways that Congress, American culture, and the freedmen themselves conceptualized the marriage contract, she does not explicitly tie the right of contract to manhood. Stanley, *From Bondage to Contract: Wage Labor, Marriage, and the Market in the Age of Slave Emancipation* (Cambridge: Cambridge University Press, 1998).

61. *CG,* 39th Cong., 1st sess. 475 (January 29, 1866).

62. Ibid., 476.

63. Ibid., 1151–1152 (March 2, 1866).

64. Ibid., 263 (January 16, 1866).

65. Ibid., 1118 (March 1, 1866).

66. On the evolution of married women's property rights in the nineteenth century, see Marylynn Salmon, *Women and the Law of Property in Early America* (Chapel Hill: University of North Carolina Press, 1986); Richard H. Chused, "Married Women's Property Law: 1800–1850," *Georgetown Law Journal* 71 (1982): 1359–1425; Carole Shammas, "Re-Assessing the Married Women's Property Acts," *Journal of Women's History* 6, no. 1 (1994): 9–30; Joan Hoff, *Law, Gender, and Injustice: A Legal History of U.S. Women* (New York: NYU Press, 1991).

67. *CG,* 39th Cong., 1st sess. 1781–1782 (April 5, 1866).

68. Ibid., 1782.

69. Ibid., 506 (January 30, 1866).

70. Ibid., 1416 (March 15, 1866).

71. Ibid.

72. Ibid., 1271 (March 8, 1866).

73. Ibid., 382 (January 23, 1866).

74. Ibid.

75. See, for example, Pennsylvania Representative Benjamin Boyer's speech on January 10, 1866. Ibid., 178.

76. *CG,* 39th Cong., 1st sess. 478 (January 29, 1866).

77. Ibid., 606 (February 2, 1866).

78. Ibid., 1182 (March 5, 1866).

79. Ibid., 204 (January 11, 1866).

80. Ibid., 304 (January 18, 1866).

81. Ibid., 174 (January 10, 1866).

82. Ibid.

83. Ibid., 256 (January 16, 1866).

84. Ibid., 180 (January 10, 1866).

85. Ibid., 727 (February 7, 1866).

86. Ibid., 834 (February 14, 1866).

87. Ibid.

88. Ibid., 2462 (May 8, 1866).

89. Linda Kerber has argued that it is the right to serve the state that truly constitutes the differences in the legal status of men and women. Kerber, *No Constitutional Right to Be Ladies: Women and the Obligations of Citizenship* (New York: Hill and Wang, 1998); Kerber, "May All Our Citizens Be Soldiers and All Our Soldiers Citizens: The Ambiguities of Female Citizenship in the New Nation," in *Women, Militarism, and War: Essays in History, Politics, and Social Theory*, ed. Jean Bethke Elshtain and Sheila Tobias (Lanham, MD: Rowman & Littlefield, 1990), 89–104.

90. *CG*, 39th Cong., 1st sess. 832 (February 14, 1866).

91. Ibid., 685 (February 6, 1866).

92. Ibid., 833 (February 14, 1866).

93. Ibid., 1159 (March 2, 1866).

94. Ibid.

95. Ibid., 1256 (March 8, 1866).

96. Although most suffrage arguments sounded like this, Kansas representative Samuel Pomeroy offered a depiction of black southern men at odds with these portrayals. Arguing that southern states should not benefit from the representation of the emancipated, Pomeroy asked if the black man was denied the right to vote, "What kind of compensation is that for all his long years of fidelity to our old flag? What an answer to his earnest prayers for his freedom and our triumph! What a reward for his faithful nursing and kind treatment of our Union soldiers and prisoners!" Ibid., 1182 (March 5, 1866). This image of a faithful, submissive, religious African American was more consistent with proslavery rhetoric than with the emergent manhood language other prosuffrage Republicans were using. It emphasized a more nurturing and feminized kind of service to the political community. Pomeroy was not alone in making these kinds of arguments. Depictions of African American men as feminized, vulnerable, and in need of protection from the state were also a strain of argument more broadly present in public discourse about enfranchisement. But I have found that in the Thirty-Ninth Congress these arguments occurred less frequently than those emphasizing the manhood rights of emancipated men.

97. Ibid., 284 (January 17, 1866).

98. Ibid., 181 (January 10, 1866).

99. Ibid., 832 (February 14, 1866).

100. Ibid., 308 (January 18, 1866).

101. Ibid., 833 (February 14, 1866).

102. Ibid., 832

103. Ibid., 685 (February 6, 1866).

104. Ibid., 1231 (March 7, 1866).

105. Ibid., 833 (February 14, 1866).

106. Ibid., 205 (January 11, 1866).

107. Ibid., 256 (January 16, 1866).

5. That Word "Male"

1. Susan B. Anthony Diary, December 11–26, 1865, in Elizabeth Cady Stanton and Susan B. Anthony, *The Selected Papers of Elizabeth Cady Stanton and Susan B. Anthony,* vol. 1, *In the School of Anti-Slavery,* ed. Ann D. Gordon (New Brunswick, NJ: Rutgers University Press, 1997), 562 (hereafter cited as *Papers: 1*). Both the *New York Times* and the *Brooklyn Daily Eagle* reported cold and clear weather December 23–24 for New Yorkers heading to the area skating ponds. "The Holiday Season," *New York Times,* December 23, 1865; "Skating. The Ball Up. The Christmas Carnival," *Brooklyn Daily Eagle,* December 23, 1865.

2. Elizabeth Cady Stanton to Gerrit Smith, January 1, 1866, *Papers: 1,* 568–569.

3. See Chapter 2.

4. Petition of Fifty Women Asking for an Amendment to the Constitution that Shall Prohibit the Several States from Disfranchising any of their Citizens on the Grounds of Sex, (February 14, 1866); Committee on the Judiciary, Petitions and Memorials—Woman Suffrage, (HR 39A–H14.9); 39th Congress; Records of the U.S. House of Representatives, Record Group 233, National Archives, Washington DC.

5. Elizabeth Cady Stanton, "Legislation against Women," *Independent,* January 25, 1866; Elizabeth Cady Stanton, "Political Rights of Women," *Liberator,* December 29, 1865; Elizabeth Cady Stanton, Susan B. Anthony, and Lucy Stone, "A Petition for Universal Suffrage," *National Anti-Slavery Standard,* December 30, 1865, in Stanton and Anthony, *Papers of Elizabeth Cady Stanton and Susan B. Anthony,* ed. Patricia G. Holland and Ann D. Gordon (Wilmington, DE: Scholarly Resources Inc., 1991), microfilm, ser. 3, reel 11 (hereafter cited as *Papers: Microfilm*); Susan B. Anthony to Caroline Healey Dall, December 26, 1865, *Papers: 1,* 562–563.

6. Petition of 100 Ladies of Philadelphia, Jefferson County, NY, in Favor of a Constitutional Amd. Granting Suffrage to Women, (February 10, 1866). Committee on the Judiciary, Petitions and Memorials—Woman Suffrage, (HR 39A–H14.9); 39th Congress; Records of the U.S. House of Representatives, Record Group 233, National Archives, Washington DC.

7. Susan B. Anthony to Wendell Phillips, January 28, 1866, *Papers: 1,* 574.

8. It is difficult to label the advocates of woman suffrage at this time. Prior to the late 1860s, women engaged in gender-equity activism were understood to be "women's rights" activists. After the 1860s, as the movement's focus shifted from broader civil, property, and social equality to focus on achieving the franchise, its activists became known as "suffragists." Because 1866 was a transitional year, I will refer to the proponents of woman suffrage as woman suffrage activists or advocates as well as suffragists.

9. Editorial, *New York Tribune,* May 26, 1865. "Manhood suffrage" was the most accurate term used to describe what was also called "universal suffrage" or "negro suffrage," the expansion of the franchise to include all African American men.

10. "The President's Plan," *Harper's Weekly,* June 10, 1865. For a discussion of the political leanings of *Harper's Weekly,* see http://www.harpweek.com/02About/about.asp.

11. It is also interesting to note here that the editorial did not use the term "citizen," which the *Dred Scott* decision had deemed could not apply to African Americans. This would be remedied in the first section of the Fourteenth Amendment.

12. "The Great Struggle," *Harper's Weekly,* August 19, 1865.

13. Anthony Diary, August 4, 1865, *Papers: 1*, 552.

14. Wendell Phillips to Elizabeth Cady Stanton, between January 9 and 12, 1866, in *Papers: Microfilm*, ser. 3, reel 11.

15. See Stanton, *Universal Suffrage National Anti-Slavery Standard,* July 29, 1865, *Papers: 1*, 550–551. Prior to the start of the congressional session, the suffragists' correspondence reveals that they had not necessarily formed any particular plan for getting women's rights included in the Republican congressional agenda. More frequently they mentioned continuing the state-level activism that had characterized their prewar work. On Friday, October 13, 1865, Anthony wrote in her diary that she and Lucretia Mott had met with a New York politician, Democrat Andrew J. Colvin, to discuss the "work for Women's Right to suffrage in N.Y." and to strategize for the forthcoming state legislative session. *Papers: 1*, 557.

16. Both proposals were referred to the Committee on the Judiciary. Schenck's resolution was discussed and postponed, perhaps in favor of other plans being considered by the Joint Committee on Reconstruction. The committee asked to be discharged from considering Broomall's proposal on January 23, 1866. Schenck's resolution is confusingly numbered, as it is identified in the *Journal of the House of Representatives* as H. R. No. 1, which indicates it is a bill rather than a resolution. However, the surrounding text clearly identifies it as a joint resolution: "Mr. Schenck, by unanimous consent, introduced a joint resolution (H. R. 1) proposing an amendment to the Constitution of the United States to apportion representatives according to the number of voters in the several States; which was read a first and second time." *Journal of the House of Representatives*, 39th Cong., 1st sess. 16, 32, 38 (December 5, 11, 1865) (hereafter cited as House: *Journal*). House of Representatives, Committee on the Judiciary, Docket Volume, 39th Cong. (HR21), Record Group 233, National Archives (hereafter cited as House Judiciary: Docket); House of Representatives, Committee on the Judiciary, Minutes, 39th Cong. (HR 1863), Record Group 233, National Archives (hereafter cited as House Judiciary: Minutes).

17. *New York Daily Tribune*, December 14, 1865, *Papers: 1*, 563n3. Many moderate-to-conservative Republicans in Congress seemed willing to expand the franchise to include only "literate" voters, thereby excluding many lower-class African Americans but also immigrants. Restricting the franchise to the literate seemed to be a way to support Republican policy on African Americans and yet at the same time prevent a wholesale enfranchisement of the emancipated. This support for a literate franchise foreshadowed some of the means used to disfranchise African Americans after Reconstruction ended. Jenckes's resolution was referred to the Judiciary Committee, which rejected it. *Congressional Globe,* 39th Cong., 1st sess. 18 (December 11, 1865) (hereafter cited as *CG*); House Judiciary: Docket; House Judiciary: Minutes.

18. Elizabeth Cady Stanton to Ann Terry Greene Phillips, undated, before January 9, 1866, *Papers: Microfilm,* ser. 3, reel 11.

19. Elizabeth Cady Stanton to Gerrit Smith, New York, January 1, 1866, *Papers: 1*, 568.

20. Susan B. Anthony to Caroline Healey Dall, December 26, 1865, *Papers: 1*, 562–563.

21. Ibid., 563.

22. Elizabeth Cady Stanton to the editor, *National Anti-Slavery Standard*, December 26, 1865, *Papers: 1,* 564.

23. Ibid., 565. Stanton's use of African American women in this argument is typical of the woman suffrage arguments she made at this time. Although there were a significant number of African American women involved in the suffrage movement, many of whom were allies of Stanton and Anthony in 1866, in this period Stanton seems to have been more interested in using the idea of black women's disfranchisement than in truly assisting black women to achieve equal rights in a way consistent with their needs, worldview, and gender identities. For more on how white women suffragists disregarded the goals of African American suffragists see Rosalyn Terborg-Penn, *African American Women in the Struggle for the Vote, 1850–1920* (Bloomington: Indiana University Press, 1998); and Louise Michele Newman, *White Women's Rights: The Racial Origins of Feminism in the United States* (New York: Oxford University Press, 1999).

24. Petitions and Memorials—Woman Suffrage. The other rights-related petitions submitted to Congress during this session that used the "will pray" language did not consistently include either the words "justice" or "equality" in their concluding sentence.

25. U.S. Const., art. IV, § 4.

26. Petitions and Memorials—Woman Suffrage.

27. Ibid.

28. Elizabeth Cady Stanton, Susan B. Anthony, and Matilda Joslyn Gage, eds., *History of Woman Suffrage,* vol. 2, *1861–1876* (New York: Fowler & Wells, 1882), 91.

29. Stevens was long vilified in early Reconstruction histories as a heartless congressional dictator and biased author of unjust and corrupt policies imposed on the South. In the past fifty years, however, historians have come to admire his passion for his cause, as well as his political skill. See, for example, Fawn Brodie, *Thaddeus Stevens, Scourge of the South* (New York: Norton, 1966); and Hans Louis Trefousse, *Thaddeus Stevens: Nineteenth-Century Egalitarian* (Chapel Hill: University of North Carolina Press, 1997).

30. On Fessenden, see Charles A. Jellison, *Fessenden of Maine, Civil War Senator* (Syracuse, NY: Syracuse University Press, 1962), and more recently Robert Cook, *Civil War Senator William Pitt Fessenden and the Fight to Save the American Republic* (Baton Rouge: Louisiana State University Press, 2011).

31. Michael Les Benedict, *A Compromise of Principle: Congressional Republicans and Reconstruction, 1863–1869* (New York: Norton, 1974), 38–39; Cook, *Civil War Senator,* 196.

32. Michael Les Benedict reports that Grimes was an early opponent of black suffrage, even before it became clear that President Johnson opposed it as well. Benedict, *Compromise of Principle,* 144, 353. Grimes has not benefited from a contemporary biography, but there is some good information in William Salter, *James W. Grimes, Governor of Iowa, & U.S. Senator, 1854–1869* (New York: D. Appleton, 1870). See also Joseph B. James, *The Framing of the Fourteenth Amendment* (Urbana: University of Illinois Press), 44–45. There is no published biography of Howard, but Earl Maltz offers a rich description of his relationship to Reconstruction policy in a 2006 article, contending that Howard had a greater concern with constitutional limitations than did the radicals. Maltz, "Radical Politics and Constitutional Theory: Senator Jacob M. Howard of Michigan and the Problem of Reconstruction," *Michigan Historical Review* 32, no. 1 (2006): 19–32.

33. There were two biographies produced on Williams in the mid-twentieth century, but nothing more recent has been published. Oscar Christensen, *The Grand Old Man of Oregon; The Life of George H. Williams* (Eugene, OR: University of Oregon, 1939); Sidney Teiser, "Life of George Williams: Almost Chief-Justice," *Oregon Historical Quarterly* 47, no. 3 (1946): 255–280; 47, no. 4 (1946): 417–440.

34. Note of interest: Ira Harris's daughter Clara and her fiancé, Harris's stepson Henry Rathbone, were the couple who accompanied Abraham and Mary Lincoln to Ford's theater the night Lincoln was assassinated. Rathbone was injured in the attack. Elizabeth D. Leonard, *Lincoln's Avengers: Justice, Revenge, and Reunion after the Civil War* (New York: Norton, 2004), 4–5.

35. Johnson's primary claim to legal fame was that he had been one of two attorneys hired to defend John A. Sanford and to argue against Dred Scott's citizenship before the Supreme Court in *Dred Scott v. Sanford*. Don Fehrenbacher notes that even after the decision had become controversial, Johnson remained a staunch defender of the Court and of Chief Justice Taney. Fehrenbacher, *The Dred Scott Case: Its Significance in American Law and Politics* (New York: Oxford University Press, 1978), 282, 578, 580. Benedict, *Compromise of Principle*, 352; James, *Framing of the Fourteenth Amendment*, 45. On Johnson, see Bernard Christian Steiner, *Life of Reverdy Johnson* (Baltimore: Norman, Remington, 1914).

36. On Conkling, see David M. Jordan, *Roscoe Conkling of New York: Voice in the Senate* (Ithaca, NY: Cornell University Press, 1971). On Bingham, see Erving E. Beauregard, *Bingham of the Hills: Politician and Diplomat Extraordinary* (New York: P. Lang, 1989). There seem to be no biographies written about Blow. However, his family is well represented in the historical record—Dred Scott had been born into slavery in the possession of Henry Blow's parents, who sold him in 1830. Don E. Fehrenbacher, *Slavery, Law and Politics: The Dred Scott Case in Historical Perspective* (Oxford: Oxford University Press, 1981), 121–122. Henry Taylor Blow fully supported Scott's legal efforts, testifying in Scott's case in Missouri. Ultimately, Henry's brother, Taylor Blow, purchased and then emancipated Scott and his family. "Missouri's Dred Scott Case, 1846–1857," Missouri State Archives, http://www.sos.mo.gov/archives/resources/africanamerican/scott/scott.asp. Also of note, Blow's daughter, Susan Elizabeth, organized the first successful public kindergarten in the United States. "Susan Blow," State Historical Society of Missouri, Historic Missourians, http://shs.umsystem.edu/historicmissourians/name/b/blow/index.html.

37. James, *Framing of the Fourteenth Amendment*, 44; Gaillard Hunt, *Israel, Elihu and Cadwallader Washburn; A Chapter in American Biography* (New York: Macmillan Company, 1925).

38. It appears that neither Grider nor Rogers was eminent enough to merit scholarly attention. Grider was elected to the House as a Whig in 1843 and served until 1847. He was reelected in 1861 and '63 as a Unionist. He ran for the Thirty-Ninth Congress as a Democrat, serving until his death in September of 1866. Andrew Rogers was elected as a Democrat to the Thirty-Eighth Congress in 1863, reelected for the Thirty-Ninth, but defeated in 1866. "Biographical Directory of Congress, 1774–present," *United States Congress*, http://bioguide.congress.gov/scripts/biodisplay.pl?index=G000455 and http://bioguide.congress.gov/scripts/biodisplay.pl?index=R000387.

39. James, *Framing of the Fourteenth Amendment*, 42–43; Benedict, *Compromise of Principle*, 348–353. On Boutwell see Thomas Domer, "The Role of George S.

Boutwell in the Impeachment and Trial of Andrew Johnson," *New England Quarterly* 49, no. 4 (1976): 596–617; Thomas H. Brown, *George Sewall Boutwell, Human Rights Advocate* (Groton, MA: Groton Historical Society, 1989). Morrill is best known for his role in establishing the land-grant colleges. On Morrill see William Belmont Parker, *The Life and Public Services of Justin Smith Morrill* (Boston: Houghton Mifflin, 1924). Coy F. Cross, *Justin Smith Morrill: Father of the Land-Grant Colleges* (East Lansing: Michigan State University Press, 1999).

40. Although we know a fair bit about the political backgrounds and alignments of the committee's members, their motivations remain opaque. At the committee's first substantive meeting on January 9, the members passed a resolution to treat all committee activities, the ideas shared in its discussions, and the votes taken therein "as of a strictly confidential character, until otherwise ordered." The one record that remains, the journal of the Joint Committee's proceedings, reveals the process through which legislation was developed in the committee, but it did not record debates among the members. Benjamin B. Kendrick, ed., *The Journal of the Joint Committee of Fifteen on Reconstruction*, The Faculty of Political Science of Columbia University, Studies in History, Economics and Public Law (New York: Columbia University, 1914), 40.

41. Earl Maltz offers a comprehensive and informative analysis of the partisan, ideological, and personal divisions among the members of the Thirty-Ninth Congress in *Civil Rights, the Constitution, and Congress, 1863–1869* (Lawrence: University Press of Kansas, 1990).

42. Kendrick, *Journal of the Joint Committee*, 41.

43. Alexander Keyssar, *The Right to Vote: The Contested History of Democracy in the United States* (New York: Basic Books, 2000). See chapter 1.

44. Stevens, although never taking any positive action on women's enfranchisement, acknowledged the roadblock that gendered constitutional language would create. In his January 31, 1866, speech advocating the committee's first version of the Fourteenth Amendment, he declared that he objected to Representative Schenck's representation proposal because it used the word "male." That word, Stevens said, "was never in the Constitution of the United States before. Why make a crusade against women in the Constitution of the nation?" The *Congressional Globe* reported that this comment was met with laughter. *CG*, 39th Cong., 1st sess. 536–537 (January 31, 1866). Stevens went on to declare, "I certainly shall never vote to insert the word 'male' or the word 'white' in the national Constitution. Let these things be attended by the states." Stevens, *The Selected Papers of Thaddeus Stevens*, ed. Beverly Wilson Palmer and Holly Byers Ochoa (Pittsburgh: University of Pittsburgh Press, 1998), 73–74. The committee members' private positions on women's voting rights were difficult to trace. For the months during which the Fourteenth Amendment was drafted, I was unable to find in the published correspondence of the members or in papers held at the Library of Congress any evidence of the committee members' (or other prominent radicals') perspective on women's voting rights. Correspondence consulted: Palmer and Ochoa, *Selected Papers of Thaddeus Stevens, April 1865–August 1868*, vol. 2, 3–36; Thaddeus Stevens Papers, 1865, box 3, folder 1, Library of Congress; Sumner, *The Selected Letters of Charles Sumner*, vol. 2, ed. Beverly Wilson Palmer (Boston: Northeastern University Press, 1990), 301–346; George Boutwell Papers, microfilm, Ohio Historical Society, Columbus, Ohio; Roscoe Conkling Papers, 1769–1895, microfilm, Library of Congress; Elihu

B. Washburne Papers, 1816–1887, 31.4 linear feet, Manuscript Division, Library of Congress; William Pitt Fessenden Papers, 1832–1878, microfilm, Library of Congress; Justin Smith Morrill Papers, microfilm, Library of Congress.

45. Kendrick, *Journal of the Joint Committee of Fifteen*, 41. The *Chicago Republican's* entire report on the committee stated, "The Reconstruction Committee held another meeting this morning, but the proceedings were not public." "News from Washington . . . The Reconstruction Committee," *Chicago Republican*, January 9, 1866, 4, col. 5.

46. Kendrick, *Journal of the Joint Committee of Fifteen*, 43.

47. Note that the lack of gendered language in this proposal implied that any state that disfranchised African American women would require the reduction of the state's representation.

48. Kendrick, *Journal of the Joint Committee of Fifteen*, 53. The language in this plan repaired the gender problem of Morrill's proposal: only when the ballot was denied because of race would representation be reduced.

49. House: *Journal*, 39th Cong., 1st sess. 179 (January 22, 1866).

50. *CG*, 39th Cong., 1st sess. 141 (January 8, 1866).

51. Ibid.

52. Ibid.

53. Ibid., 357 (January 22, 1866).

54. Ibid., 358.

55. Ibid., 357.

56. Ibid.

57. Ibid., 378 (January 23, 1866).

58. Ibid., 404 (January 24, 1866).

59. Ibid., 405.

60. Ibid., 433 (January 25, 1866).

61. Like Lawrence, Brooks conveniently overlooked the fact that women were represented under the current system.

62. Although Anthony had helped design her petition to appeal to Republicans by adopting their language, she was certainly not above playing politics by sending copies of the petition to Democrats like Brooks in the hope that they would push the Republicans in the right direction—a strategy she and Stanton would wield further in the later years of the 1860s. See chapter 6 below.

63. Because Brooks made his argument on January 23, 1866, he brought Stanton and Anthony's petition to the attention of Congress a full day before Benjamin Gratz Brown officially presented it to the Senate.

64. Susan B. Anthony to James Brooks, January 20, 1866, printed in *CG*, 39th Cong., 1st sess. 380 (January 23, 1866).

65. Ibid., 379–380.

66. Ibid.

67. Ibid., 380.

68. House: *Journal*, 39th Cong., 1st sess.

69. The first petition presented was not referred to the Joint Committee on Reconstruction as the Senate had not yet passed the resolution establishing it. Of the other suffrage petitions that were not sent to the committee, three dealing with the constitution of Colorado were tabled, one was referred to the Committee on the

Territories, and the final petition was specific to suffrage in the District of Columbia and was referred to that committee. Senate: *Journal,* 39th Cong., 1st sess.

70. *CG,* 39th Cong., 1st sess. 390 (January 24, 1866). Brown was elected as an Unconditional Unionist (UU), but by the 1870s he had returned to the Democratic Party, running for vice president on the Democratic ticket with Horace Greeley in 1872. "Biographical Directory of Congress, 1774–present," *United States Congress,* http://bioguide.congress.gov/scripts/biodisplay.pl?index=B000905.

71. House petitions followed a different trajectory. Most of the black male enfranchisement petitions sent to the House were referred to the Joint Committee. Fourteen of the nineteen woman suffrage petitions introduced in the House, however, were referred to the Judiciary Committee. Committee on the Judiciary, Petitions—Woman Suffrage, (HR 39A–H14.9), 39th Congress, Records of the U.S. House of Representatives, Record Group 233, National Archives, Washington DC.

72. Each body of Congress established its own set of rules, regulated by a committee on the rules. Given the large number of representatives compared with the relatively few senators, it seems reasonable that the House did not permit discussion over routine matters such as petitions.

73. *CG,* 39th Cong., 1st sess. 829 (February 14, 1866).

74. Ibid., 951.

75. Ibid., 952.

76. Ibid.

77. Most other petitions supporting black men's suffrage rights were presented to the House and Senate as universal suffrage petitions.

78. Petitions acknowledged as woman suffrage petitions are filed in the National Archives in Petitions and Memorials—Woman Suffrage. Those petitions italicized in table 2 were submitted as universal suffrage petitions but turned up in this folder. Their texts were identical to the other petitions requesting women's enfranchisement. A few other woman suffrage petitions were filed with other "civil rights" petitions in Committee on the Judiciary, Petitions—Civil Rights, (HR39A–H14.2), 39th Congress, Records of the U.S. House of Representatives, Record Group 233, National Archives, Washington DC.

79. *CG,* 39th Cong., 1st sess. 518 (January 31, 1866). It is questionable whether Lane knew that the petitioners were beautiful, but by claiming this he legitimated their position as respectable, feminine ladies rather than strong-minded masculine women and at the same time positioned himself and his fellow senators as their manly protectors.

80. Ibid., 518–519 (January 31, 1866).

81. See, for example, Sumner's extensive speech opposing House Resolution 51 on February 6, 1866, ibid., 673–687.

82. *CG,* 39th Cong., 1st sess. 704 (February 7, 1866).

83. Ibid., 705.

84. Senate: *Journal,* 39th Cong., 1st sess. 221–222 (March 9, 1866).

85. Bolstered by the growing schism between the president and the radicals in Congress caused by the president's veto of the Freedman's Bureau bill and Civil Rights bill, the radicals who earlier in the year might have compromised by agreeing to House Resolution 51 in order to avoid a party schism instead voted against it. Ibid., 221; James, *Framing of the Fourteenth Amendment,* 55–91; Eric L. McKitrick, *Andrew Johnson and Reconstruction* (Chicago: University of Chicago Press, 1960).

86. *CG,* 39th Cong., 1st sess. 1320 (March 12, 1866).

87. Stevens's omnibus proposal was modeled after one suggested to him by social reformer Robert Dale Owen. James, *Framing of the Fourteenth Amendment,* 100–101; Kendrick, *Journal of the Joint Committee of Fifteen,* 83–84.

88. Kendrick, *Journal of the Joint Committee of Fifteen,* 102.

89. James, *Framing of the Fourteenth Amendment,* 112.

90. Robert Dale Owen, "Political Results from the Varioloid," *Atlantic Monthly,* June 1875, 665.

91. *CG,* 39th Cong., 1st sess. 2459 (May 8, 1866).

92. Ibid., 2511 (May 9, 1866); House: *Journal,* 685–687 (May 10, 1866).

93. *CG,* 39th Congress, 1st sess. 2766 (May 23, 1866).

94. Ibid.

95. Madison's collected writings had been published in 1865. James Madison, *Letters and Other Writings of James Madison: Fourth President of the United States* (Philadelphia, PA: J.B. Lippincott), 1865; *CG,* 39th Cong., 1st sess. 2767 (May 23, 1866).

96. *CG,* 39th Cong., 1st sess. 2767 (May 23, 1866).

97. Senate: *Journal,* 39th Cong., 1st sess. 504–505 (June 8, 1866).

98. House: *Journal,* 39th Cong., 1st sess. 834 (June 13, 1866); Senate: *Journal,* 39th Cong., 1st sess. 527 (June 15, 1866).

99. Senate: *Journal,* 39th Cong., 1st sess. 501 (June 8, 1866).

100. James, *Framing of the Fourteenth Amendment,* 73, 93, 97; Ohio senator John Sherman received a letter from the editor of the Cincinnati *Gazette,* suggesting that it did not particularly matter whether House Resolution 127 could pass, so long as it offered "a scheme,—upon which we can go into the election." E. D. Mansfield to John Sherman, May 2, 1866, John Sherman Papers, Library of Congress, cited in James, *Framing of the Fourteenth Amendment,* 122. On a solely pragmatic level, Republicans could have preferred the gender-based amendment language because it more closely reflected the language states used to define their voting populations. (See chapter 1.)

101. Some evidence for this comes from congressional correspondence. Senator Lyman Trumbull, Republican of Illinois, received a letter from a Chicago constituent, E. Larned, who objected to the use of the word "male" in any representation provision but acknowledged that "the omission of 'male' might reduce the amendment's chances of ratification." E. Larned to Lyman Trumbull, March 10, 1866, Lyman Trumbull Papers, Library of Congress, cited in and paraphrased by James, *Framing of the Fourteenth Amendment,* 91.

102. *CG,* 39th Cong., 1st sess. 2987 (June 6, 1866).

6. White Women's Rights

1. Elizabeth Cady Stanton, Susan B. Anthony, Matilda Joslyn Gage, eds., *History of Woman Suffrage,* vol. 2, *1861–1876* (New York: Fowler & Wells 1882), 171 (hereafter cited as *HWS: 2*).

2. *HWS: 2,* 170. The convention received Anthony's letter to Congress, the *New York Times* reported, "with tumultuous clappings of kidded hands." "The May Anniversaries," *New York Times,* May 11, 1866, 8.

3. "Eleventh National Woman's Rights Convention," in Elizabeth Cady Stanton and Susan B. Anthony, *The Selected Papers of Elizabeth Cady Stanton and Susan B.*

Anthony, vol. 1, *In the School of Anti-Slavery,* ed. Ann D. Gordon (New Brunswick, NJ: Rutgers University Press, 1997), 587 (hereafter cited as *Papers: 1*). Equal suffrage faced an uphill battle in New York State. The legislature had repeatedly opted to keep property restrictions for African American male voters. In 1846 and 1860, the state's voters rejected referenda that would have allowed black men to vote without restriction. Phyllis Field, *The Politics of Race in New York: The Struggle for Black Suffrage in the Civil War Era* (Ithaca, NY: Cornell University Press, 1982).

4. *Papers: 1,* 585. Although Stanton appeared at most of these meetings, Anthony was almost always present. She was often joined by prominent African American activist Charles Remond; young equality activist Bessie Bisbee; well-known radical newspaper editor Parker Pillsbury; America's first ordained female minister, Olympia Brown; and Louisa Jacobs, daughter of the self-emancipated author and abolitionist Harriet Jacobs. The lecture schedule was so tight, however, that the speakers had to "stagger their arrivals and departures" and so may not have shared the stage at any given meeting. "Itinerary of ECS and SBA Indicating Events Documented on Film," in Elizabeth Cady Stanton and Susan B. Anthony, *Papers of Elizabeth Cady Stanton and Susan B. Anthony,* ed. Patricia G. Holland and Ann D. Gordon (Wilmington, DE: Scholarly Resources Inc., 1991), microfilm, ser. 3, reel 11 (hereafter cited as *Papers: Microfilm*). Editorial note, in Elizabeth Cady Stanton and Susan B. Anthony, *The Selected Papers of Elizabeth Cady Stanton and Susan B. Anthony,* vol. 2, *Against an Aristocracy of Sex,* ed. Ann D. Gordon (New Brunswick, NJ: Rutgers University Press, 2000), 23 (hereafter cited as *Papers: 2*); Faye E. Dudden, *Fighting Chance: The Struggle over Woman Suffrage and Black Suffrage in Reconstruction America* (New York: Oxford University Press, 2011), 92.

5. Petition, New York State Equal Rights Convention, November 21, 1866, *Papers: 1,* 603.

6. Dudden notes that given the conservative turn the state Republican Party leadership was taking in 1867, getting outsiders elected to the convention was the suffrage advocates' best strategy for expanding the franchise in New York. Thus the AERA had additional motivation to advocate universal suffrage in the election of convention delegates. Dudden, *Fighting Chance,* 101.

7. Susan B. Anthony, speech to the Equal Rights Convention meeting, December 6, 1866, *Papers: 2,* 2.

8. Resolutions of the Equal Rights Convention in Syracuse, New York, December 14, 1866, *Papers: 2,* 8.

9. *Auburn Daily Advocate,* January 7, 1866, 3.

10. Speech by Susan B. Anthony to the Equal Rights Convention in Troy, New York, February 18, 1867, *Papers: 2,* 24.

11. The meeting held in Rochester attracted a larger crowd, at six hundred. Editorial note, *Papers: 2,* 6. However, the Syracuse meeting had low turnout. Ibid., 8.

12. *Yates County Chronicle,* December 20, 1866, 2.

13. *Yates County Chronicle,* December 27, 1866, 2.

14. Elizabeth Cady Stanton, *Address in Favor of Universal Suffrage: For the Election of Delegates to the Constitutional Convention. Before the Judiciary Committees of the Legislature of New York, in the Assembly Chamber, January 23, 1867, in Behalf of the American Equal Rights Association* (Albany: Weed, Parsons, 1867), 6.

15. Ibid.

16. Ibid.

17. Ibid., 7.

18. Ibid., 9.

19. Ibid.

20. Stanton's correspondence indicates that sarcasm was a deliberate rhetorical strategy. Writing to Frederick Douglass about the speech, she said, "I hope if it is possible you will be in Albany for both our claims should be set off in the strongest way & you can attack the property qualification with all the force of your sarcasm far better than I could, who am a long stride behind even that." Stanton to Frederick Douglass, January 8, 1867, *Papers: 2,* 11–12.

21. Stanton, *Address in Favor of Universal Suffrage,* 11. Article 2, section 3 of the constitution declared that no person should lose their voting residency requirements "while kept at any alms house or other asylum, at public expense; nor while confined in any public prison." Benjamin P. Poore, *The Federal and State Constitutions, Colonial Charters, and Other Organic Laws of the United States, Part II* (Washington, DC: U.S. Government Printing Office, 1878), 1353.

22. Stanton, *Address in Favor of Universal Suffrage,* 11.

23. Ibid.

24. The activists' hope that partisan outsiders would dominate the convention was thwarted by the method by which delegates at large were selected, which Dudden notes, ensured that "a corps of party hacks would be scrutinizing every convention proposal for partisan risk and advantage." Dudden, *Fighting Chance,* 102.

25. *HWS: 2,* 286. Dudden contends that at the conclusion of their campaign "the AERA leaders had to regard the 1867 New York Constitutional Convention as principally an occasion for propagandizing their cause." Dudden, *Fighting Chance,* 102. I agree that the suffragists knew there was virtually no chance that New York would enfranchise women. However, I do believe that the convention was more to them than a propaganda showcase. They had sufficient faith in this particular political moment to risk a new rhetorical strategy that challenged the Republican/abolitionist alliance that had proven so dissatisfactory in Congress.

26. Edward F. Underhill, ed., *Proceedings and Debates of the Constitutional Convention of the State of New York, Held in 1867 and 1868, in the City of Albany* (Albany: Weed, Parsons, 1868), 38 (June 11, 1867) (hereafter cited as *NY1868*). The AERA opposed this move, and Stanton wrote a letter to the *New York Tribune* rejecting it as "a work of supererogation." Graves's motion was subsequently tabled. Elizabeth Cady Stanton, "Female Suffrage Committee," *New York Tribune,* June 19, 1867, *Papers: 2,* 72.

27. *NY1868,* 96 (June 19, 1867). Curtis was a friend and colleague of the American transcendentalists, contributor and political editor to *Harper's Monthly,* a founding figure in the Republican Party, and a delegate at large to the convention. Mabel Abbott and Gail Schneider, Biographical Note, Finding Aid, George William Curtis Papers, Special Collection in the Archives and Library of the Staten Island Museum, http://www.state nislandmuseum.org/images/uploads/collections/Curtis_(George_William)_Papers_ Finding_Aids.pdf. Curtis had long supported women's enfranchisement, and in July he made a lengthy and erudite speech urging the convention to enfranchise New York's women. It was reprinted later by the AERA as a pamphlet: George William Curtis, *Equal Rights for Woman* (American Equal Rights Association, 1867). For copies of the petition sent to the New York State Constitutional Convention, see *Papers: Microfilm,* ser. 3, reel 12.

28. As late as its annual meeting in May 10, the AERA considered a resolution praising Greeley for supporting woman suffrage in his newspaper. "Meeting of the American Equal Rights Association in New York," May 9–10, 1867, *Papers: 2,* 62.

29. The *New York Times,* in a lengthy critical editorial, called Greeley's support of Davis repulsive and inexpedient, "simply detestable," and speculated that it derived from a growing "love of notoriety." *New York Times,* May 28, 1867.

30. Stanton began the meeting, giving a version of her February speech to the legislature. Editorial note, "Hearing Before the Committee on Suffrage, New York Constitutional Convention, in Albany," *Papers: 2, 75.*

31. *New York Daily Tribune,* Friday, June 28, 1867, 5, col. 2.

32. *New York Herald,* no date. From DLC, Rare Books Division, S. B. Anthony Scrapbook no. 2, in *Papers: Microfilm,* ser. 3, reel 12. The *New York Tribune* reported that the audience applauded this remark. "Hearing before the Committee on Suffrage, New York Constitutional Convention, in Albany," *New York Tribune,* June 27, 1867, *Papers: 2,* 76.

33. *Albany Evening Journal,* June 28, 1867, *HWS: 2,* 284.

34. Elizabeth Cady Stanton to Martha C. Wright in *Elizabeth Cady Stanton as Revealed in Her Letters, Diary and Reminiscences,* ed. Theodore Stanton and Harriot Stanton Blatch (New York: Arno, 1969), 2:116.

35. Ibid.

36. Given the timing of its presentation, it is likely this report was prepared before Stanton and Anthony appeared before the Suffrage Committee.

37. *NY1868,* 176–179 (June 28, 1867).

38. Ibid., 178–179.

39. Ibid., 178.

40. Beginning with the American Revolution, the argument that military service bestowed voting privileges had long enabled the disfranchised to acquire the right to vote. Chilton Williamson, *American Suffrage: From Property to Democracy.* See chapter 1.

41. *NY1868,* 270 (July 13, 1867).

42. Ibid.

43. For a discussion of the term "manly" see Gail Bederman, *Manliness and Civilization: A Cultural History of Gender and Race in the United States, 1880–1917,* (Chicago: University of Chicago Press, 1995), 16–23; Elliott Gorn, *The Manly Art: Bare-Knuckle Prize Fighting in America* (Ithaca, NY: Cornell University Press, 1986), 140–147; and Anthony Rotundo, *American Manhood: Transformations in Masculinity from the Revolution to the Modern Era* (New York: Basic Books, 1993), 10–30. At least one contemporary source indicates that the term "manhood" did not refer to all persons. At the first annual meeting of the AERA on May 9, 1867, Parker Pillsbury stated, "Manhood or malehood suffrage is not a remedy for evils such as we wish to remove." *HWS: 2,* 205.

44. *NY1868,* 207 (July 9, 1867).

45. Ibid., 213.

46. Ibid., 331 (July 17, 1867).

47. *Papers: 2,* 75n5.

48. "Mass Convention in Westchester Co., New York," *National Anti-Slavery Standard* (New York), July 20, 1867, *Papers: Microfilm,* ser. 3, reel 12. On July 12, Stanton sent a letter to the editor of the *New York Tribune* (Horace Greeley) that began, "Sir: Allow me through your column to ask the pardon of Gens. Merritt and Morris, Cols. Duganne, Seaver, and Axtell, for ignorantly robbing them of

the glory and honorable scars won in the second revolution. But, Mr. Editor, if the 'bullet and ballot' do go together, remember women fought in the late war; some fought and died on the battlefield. If they did not do as much as man to prosecute the war, they did far more to mitigate its horrors." Here she backed away from her assertive tactics and adopted Anthony's more subtle argument about women's military service. *New York Tribune,* July 12, 1867, 2, col. 3.

49. There is some evidence that the $300 fee for sending a substitute was actually accessible to many, regardless of social class. Societies were formed to help poorer men pay the fee, and a fairly affordable draft insurance was sold that would pay it if a man was drafted. So despite the reputation of the war as a "poor man's fight," this was not necessarily exclusively due to commutation fees. See James McPherson and James K. Hogue, *Ordeal by Fire: The Civil War and Reconstruction,* 4th ed. (New York: McGraw-Hill, 2010), 385. However, it was certainly easier for the wealthy to pay substitutes.

50. Anthony wrote to Anna Elizabeth Dickinson on July 12, 1867, that Curtis "is very earnest & true, it seems to me." *Papers: 2,* 79.

51. *NY1868,* 283 (July 16, 1867). On September 1, Stanton wrote to Emily Howland that Curtis had presented the petition "by our engineering." Elizabeth Cady Stanton to Emily Howland, September 1, 1867, in Stanton, *Elizabeth Cady Stanton as Revealed,* 2:117. Mary Greeley's suffrage activism continued after the New York convention, when she became an executive officer of the AERA during 1868 and petitioned Congress in 1868 during the Fifteenth Amendment debates. *Papers: 2,* 189–190n6.

52. *New York Times,* July 18, 1867, 1, col. 6; *HWS: 2,* 287.

53. The suffragists later suggested that the presentation of Curtis's petition was a deliberate strategy specifically designed to draw attention to Greeley in the press. *HWS: 2,* 286–287.

54. *World* (New York), July 18, 1867, 1, col. 4.

55. *New York Herald,* July 18, 1867, 6, col. 5.

56. Petitions from women were presented to the convention in many different ways. On June 26, Curtis submitted a petition headed by the signature of Elizabeth Cady Stanton's mother, who was listed as "Mrs. Daniel Cady," perhaps because Daniel Cady was a well-known lawyer in the state. But on June 28, there were multiple petitions sent from women. These all used the honorific "Mrs." and the woman's own first and last names (Mrs. Eliza Osborn, Mrs. Lina Vandenberg) or under her own name or initials, Lucretia Sutton, A. H. Sabin. *NY1868,* 176–177 (June 28, 1867).

57. In her biography of Victoria Woodhull, Barbara Goldsmith depicts Mary Cheney Greeley as a deeply unhappy, depressed, manic woman who probably killed one of her children through neglect. Further, she argues that the Greeleys' marriage was extremely troubled. Stanton and Anthony may have been aware of this and thus taken advantage of the rift in the family. Goldsmith, *Other Powers: The Age of Suffrage, Spiritualism, and the Scandalous Victoria Woodhull* (New York: Knopf, 1998), 55–62, 132–133. Stanton claimed that Greeley's anger resulted in immediate retaliation. When they met at a party a few weeks after the petition was presented, he reportedly told Stanton that he had "given

strict orders at the Tribune office that you and your cause are to be tabooed in the future, and if it is necessary to mention your name, you will be referred to as 'Mrs. Henry B. Stanton.'" Stanton to Emily Howland, in *Papers: Microfilm*, ser. 3, reel 12. However, the editors of *The Selected Papers of Elizabeth Cady Stanton and Susan B. Anthony* have found that Greeley did not begin referring to Stanton as Mrs. Henry Stanton until after her National Woman Suffrage Association passed a resolution criticizing Greeley and his paper on July 7, 1869. *Papers: 2*, 77n3.

58. *NY1868*, 364–372 (July 18, 1867). Dudden notes, however, that none of the major New York papers carried Curtis's speech, and so woman suffrage did not appear to the public to be a major issue in the convention. Dudden, *Fighting Chance*, 103.

59. *NY1868*, 416–444, 453–470, 537–540 (July 22, 23, 25, 1867).

60. Bickford went on to say, "Small chance then will gentlemen have to 'catch the speaker's eye,' especially if the speaker be a ladies' man, as he will be if any man at all." *NY1868*, 443 (July 22, 1867).

61. *NY1868*, 540 (July 25, 1867).

62. Ibid., 428 (July 22, 1867).

63. Ibid., 428–430.

64. Ibid., 430.

65. Ibid., 456 (July 23, 1867).

66. Ibid., 442 (July 22, 1867).

67. Ibid., 441. On July 10, 1867, Lucy Stone and Henry Blackwell spoke at the capitol, arguing that even if woman suffrage was not made part of the constitution, it should be submitted to the voters as a referendum. *Papers: 2*, 80n1.

68. *NY1868*, 538, 540.

69. Ibid., 537.

70. In New York, no expansion of the franchise ever took place as a result of the constitutional convention. In 1869, the state's voters defeated the convention's proposed constitutional changes. Ernest Henry Breuer, ed., *Constitutional Developments in New York, 1777–1958: A Bibliography of Conventions and Constitutions with Selected References for Constitutional Research* (Albany, NY: State Education Department, 1958), 33–35. But New York was not alone: in July Michigan's constitutional convention considered but defeated woman suffrage, as did the Connecticut Legislature. *Papers: 2*, 86–87nn1–2.

71. *Papers: 2*, 88–89. Wood's position on black suffrage was consistent with the position that Stanton and Anthony were evolving—he repeatedly refused to support the expansion of the franchise to include black men if it did not also include women. Ibid., 49–50n2. Historian Rosalyn Terborg-Penn has argued that Wood never supported black male suffrage. Terborg-Penn, *African American Women in the Struggle for the Vote, 1850–1920* (Bloomington: Indiana University Press, 1998), 30. Kansas African American activist Charles Langston reported that an "impartial suffrage" convention Wood had convened in early April was less friendly to black suffrage than to woman suffrage. Lucy Stone to Elizabeth Cady Stanton, April 10, 1867, *Papers: 2*, 48–49, 51n6. Dudden notes that Wood had "alienated supporters of black suffrage by persistently amending black suffrage measures to include women,

and voting against them when they did not." Further, she reports that Wood and Langston had frequently clashed in the past and continued to do so throughout the Kansas suffrage referenda campaigns. Dudden, *Fighting Chance,* 109, 111–113, 120–122.

72. *HWS: 2,* 232. On women's rights politics in Kansas, see Michael L. Goldberg, *An Army of Women: Gender and Politics in Gilded Age Kansas* (Baltimore: Johns Hopkins University Press, 1997), and Marilyn S. Blackwell and Kristen Tegtmeier Oertel, *Frontier Feminist: Clarina Howard Nichols and the Politics of Motherhood* (Lawrence: University Press of Kansas, 2010). The best account of the 1867 Kansas campaign can be found in Faye Dudden's book *Fighting Chance.*

73. Dudden, *Fighting Chance,* 140.

74. Henry Blackwell returned to Kansas in October, and Olympia Brown continued her activism through the November elections, joining Stanton and Anthony for a few of their early meetings. *Papers: 2,* 88–89nn2, 4. Other local Kansan suffragists organized and agitated to support the woman suffrage referendum. Ellen Carol DuBois, *Feminism and Suffrage: The Emergence of an Independent Women's Movement in America, 1848–1869* (Ithaca, NY: Cornell University Press, 1978), 84–85.

75. DuBois, *Feminism and Suffrage,* 91; Susan B. Anthony to Anna E. Dickinson, September 23, 1867, *Papers: 2,* 92, 94n6. Notably absent from this statement of support was Greeley himself.

76. Susan B. Anthony to Anna E. Dickinson, September 23, 1867, *Papers: 2,* 92.

77. *HWS: 2,* 931. Olympia Brown recalled that these speakers "were sent out under the auspices of the Republican Party to blackguard and abuse the advocates of woman's cause while professedly speaking upon 'manhood suffrage.'" *HWS: 2,* 260–261.

78. *Papers: 2,* 93n5.

79. *HWS: 2,* 250.

80. Cited in Dudden, *Fighting Chance,* 118. Dudden notes that the suicide of Kansas Republican Senator and leader James Lane had left the state party in disarray, creating openings for intraparty conflict and maneuvering to gain control of Kansas's Republican machine. Ibid., 110, 131.

81. Ibid., 118.

82. Ibid., 124. Dudden finds that the members of this organization seemed to have effectively taken control of the Kansas Republican Party. She also reports that Kansas's Republicans neglected to campaign for black men's voting rights. In particular, they snubbed Charles Langston, the most prominent African American leader in the state, which in turn created a degree of animosity between Langston and the women's rights leaders in the state. Ibid., 111, 121–123.

83. Some suffragists later reported that they faced hostility from local African American leaders. See, for example, Olympia Brown's contribution to the chapter on Kansas in *HWS: 2,* 261.

84. There were earlier indications that the suffragists could use Democrats for their own purposes. In the petition campaign of 1866, Elizabeth Cady Stanton had written to Martha Coffin Wright that "we have had a thousand petitions printed, and when they are filled they will be sent to Democratic members who will

present them to the House. But if they come back to us empty, Susan and I will sign every one, so that every Democratic member may have one with which to shame those hypocritical Republicans." Elizabeth Cady Stanton to Martha Coffin Pelham Wright, New York, January 6, 1866, *Papers: Microfilm*, ser. 3, reel 11.

85. *Papers: 2*, 51 n10. Dudden notes that Robinson had cooperated with Democrats as early as 1864, a fact that made other Republicans suspect his loyalty. She suggests that Robinson was less interested in what Democrats could do for women's voting rights than in what they could do for his own electoral prospects. Dudden, *Fighting Chance*, 110–112.

86. *HWS: 2*, 234. Two weeks later, Stone's husband, Henry Blackwell, used almost the same language in a letter to Stanton and Anthony, saying that "if the Republicans came out against us the Democrats will take us up." H. B. Blackwell to Elizabeth Cady Stanton and Susan B. Anthony, April 21, 1867, *Papers: 2*, 51n10.

87. Ellen Carol DuBois reports that Lawrence County Democrats collaborated with woman suffrage Republicans to oppose the standard Republican party line, and that in Leavenworth, Democrats added woman suffrage to their printed ballots. DuBois, *Feminism and Suffrage*, 92.

88. Ibid., 93.

89. Dudden, *Fighting Chance*, 127–128.

90. In a speech recorded in his published account of the Kansas campaign, Train described himself as "that wonderful eccentric, independent, extraordinary genius, and political reformer of America." George Francis Train, *The Great Epigram Campaign of Kansas: Championship of Woman, Thirty Speeches in Two Weeks in All Parts of Kansas*, (Leavenworth, KS: Prescott & Hume, 1867), 40. For more on Train's background, see Dudden, *Fighting Chance*, 127–129, 136.

91. Anthony wrote to Anna Dickinson about Train: "But, how funny; that Geo. Francis Train is coming into the state for a month—to talk for woman—what sort of a furor he will make." *Papers: 2*, 93.

92. Historians have debated Train's impact on both the success of the referendum in Kansas and the suffragists' racism. Some situate him at the center of the move to seek Democratic approval, essentially blaming his influence for the suffragists' use of racist rhetoric. This deemphasizes the active role woman suffrage supporters took in creating their own partisan political strategy and shifts the focus of historical analyses away from the political context that constrained their actions. For example, Ellen DuBois asserts that Stanton and Anthony abandoned their own abolitionist traditions and turned to "Train's racism." DuBois, *Feminism and Suffrage*, 96.

93. Henry Blackwell, "What the South Can Do: How the Southern States Can Make Themselves Masters of the Situation," New York, January 15, 1867, in Printed Ephemera Collection, portfolio 127, folder 11, Library of Congress, http://hdl.loc.gov/loc.rbc/rbpe.12701100.

94. Train, *Great Epigram Campaign*, 32.

95. Ibid., 8–9.

96. *HWS: 2*, 244.

97. Dudden, *Fighting Chance*, 121–124.

98. Ibid., 130.

99. Elizabeth Cady Stanton, *Eighty Years and More: Reminiscences 1815–1897* (Boston: Northeastern University Press, 1993), 247.

100. William Lloyd Garrison to Susan B. Anthony, January 4, 1868, *Papers: 2*, 125.

101. Dudden, *Fighting Chance,* 133–135.

102. *Congressional Globe,* 39th Cong., 1st sess. 219 (January 12, 1866) (hereafter cited as *CG*).

103. Ibid., 218.

104. Historian Jean Baker has argued that racism and racist cultural productions such as minstrel shows and songs provided the means by which Democrats could construct party unity through an emphasis on the collective whiteness of its members. Baker, *Affairs of Party: The Political Culture of Northern Democrats in the Mid-Nineteenth Century* (Ithaca, NY: Cornell University Press, 1983).

105. *CG,* 39th Cong., 1st sess. 3214 (June 16, 1866).

106. *CG,* 39th Cong., 2nd sess. 84 (December 12, 1866). At this point, Doolittle was a Republican; however, he supported President Johnson and in 1868 joined the Democratic Party. In light of his later defection, and given the nature of his comments, I considered them Democratic rhetoric. See "Biographical Directory of Congress, 1774–present," *United States Congress,* http://bioguide.congress.gov/scripts/biodisplay.pl?index=D000428.

107. House of Representatives, Report No. 2 on Suffrage in the District of Columbia, 39th Cong., 1st sess. 1–2 (December 19, 1865), *The Reports of the Committees of the House of Representatives made during the First Session Thirty-Ninth Congress, 1865–66* (Washington, D.C.: Government Printing Office, 1866).

108. *CG,* 39th Cong., 1st sess. 1268 (March 8, 1866).

109. Ibid., 246 (January 16, 1866).

110. See Diane Miller Sommerville, *Rape and Race in the Nineteenth-Century South* (Chapel Hill: University of North Carolina Press, 2004); Diane Miller Sommerville, "The Rape Myth in the Old South Reconsidered," in *A Question of Manhood: A Reader in U.S. Black Men's History and Masculinity,* vol. 1, ed. Darlene Clark Hine and Earnestine Jenkins (Bloomington: Indiana University Press, 1999); Crystal Nicole Feimster, *Southern Horrors: Women and the Politics of Rape and Lynching* (Cambridge, MA: Harvard University Press, 2009); Martha Hodes, "The Sexualization of Reconstruction Politics: White Women and Black Men in the South after the Civil War," *Journal of the History of Sexuality* 3, no. 3 (1993): 402–417.

111. *CG,* 39th Cong., 1st sess. app. 133 (February 26, 1866).

112. Ibid., app. 182 (April 6, 1866).

113. Sommerville, "Rape Myth in the Old South," 438–472, esp. 439–442. See also George M. Frederickson, *The Black Image in the White Mind: The Debate on Afro-American Character and Destiny, 1817–1914,* 2nd ed. (Middletown, CT: Wesleyan University Press, 1971, 1987); and Joel Williamson, *The Crucible of Race: Black-White Relations in the American South since Emancipation* (New York: Oxford University Press, 1984).

114. *CG,* 39th Cong., 1st sess. 196 (January 11, 1866).

115. Ibid., 177 (January 10, 1866).

116. Although Cowan was a conservative Republican, he disagreed with the party's Reconstruction policy, and his arguments nearly always adopted Democratic Party rhetoric to oppose that policy; therefore, I believe it justified to consider his rhetoric within the context of the Democratic Party. See Eric Foner, *Reconstruction:*

America's Unfinished Revolution, 1863–1877 (New York: Harper & Row, 1988), 237; and "Biographical Directory of Congress, 1774–present," *United States Congress,* http://bioguide.congress.gov/scripts/biodisplay.pl?index=C000819.

117. *CG,* 39th Cong., 2nd sess. 62 (December 11, 1866).

118. *CG,* 39th Cong., 1st sess. 203 (January 11, 1866).

119. DuBois, *Feminism and Suffrage,* 103–104.

120. Elizabeth Cady Stanton, "Who Are Our Friends," *Revolution,* vol. 1, no. 2, January 15, 1868, 24. Unless otherwise cited, all *Revolution* articles are from *Papers: Microfilm,* series 1, reels 1–3.

121. Stanton, "Who Are Our Friends," 24.

122. Elizabeth Cady Stanton, "To Our Radical Friends," *Revolution,* vol. 1, no. 19, May 14, 1868, 296.

123. Elizabeth Cady Stanton, "Mrs. Stanton before the District Committee," *Revolution,* vol. 3, no. 5, February 4, 1869, 88.

124. Susan B. Anthony, "Susan B. Anthony in Tammany Hall," *Revolution,* vol. 2, no. 1, July 9, 1868, 1.

125. Elizabeth Cady Stanton, "William Lloyd Garrison Crucifies Democrats, Train, and the Women of 'The Revolution,'" *Revolution,* vol. 1, no. 4, January 29, 1868, 50.

126. Elizabeth Cady Stanton, "Sharp Points," *Revolution,* vol. 1, no. 14, April 9, 1868, 212–213.

127. Stanton, "William Lloyd Garrison Crucifies Democrats."

128. Stanton, "Mrs. Stanton before the District Committee."

129. Noah Webster and Chauncy A. Goodrich, *An American Dictionary of the English Language,* rev. ed. (Springfield, MA: George and Charles Merriam, 1860), 1100.

130. Elizabeth Cady Stanton, "Women and Black Men," *Revolution,* vol. 3, no. 5, February 4, 1869, 88.

131. Dudden, *Fighting Chance,* 155–160. Blair joined the Republican Party to reject slavery's expansion and had served in Congress as a conservative Republican in the 1850s. But after the war his virulent racism and opposition to Reconstruction pushed him to the Democrats, who nominated him for the vice presidency in 1868. "Biographical Directory of Congress, 1774–present," *United States Congress,* http:// bioguide.congress.gov/scripts/biodisplay.pl?index=B000523. For more on Blair, see William Earl Parrish, *Frank Blair: Lincoln's Conservative* (Columbia: University of Missouri Press, 1998).

132. "Grand Democratic Demonstration at Indianapolis; Gen. Blair's Speech," *New Orleans Times,* September 29, 1868, 1.

133. Ibid.

134. Ibid., 2.

135. Ibid., 1.

136. Elizabeth Cady Stanton, "Frank Blair on Woman's Suffrage," *Revolution,* vol. 2, no. 13, October 1, 1868, 200. Note here that in addressing her argument to "women of the republic," Stanton assumes a white female readership, in typical fashion completely ignoring the perspective of African American women.

137. Dudden, *Fighting Chance,* 159.

138. Neither Stanton nor Anthony self-identified as a Democrat. Stanton was more comfortable with, and had family connections to, the party, but never, as far as we know, declared herself a Democrat. However, this did not stop the two women in a time of political flux and in the midst of the search for allies from turning to the Democrats as a possible source of support for their particular cause. It is also well documented that the suffragists also sought connections with working women's associations and labor organizations in this same period. See DuBois, *Feminism and Suffrage,* 105–162.

139. Elizabeth Cady Stanton, "Gerrit Smith on Petitions," *Revolution,* vol. 3, no. 2, January 14, 1869, 24.

140. Ibid., 130.

141. On the evolution of racism and feminism in the post-Reconstruction women's rights movement, see Lisa Tetrault, *The Myth of Seneca Falls: Memory and the Women's Suffrage Movement, 1848–1898* (Chapel Hill: University of North Carolina Press, 2014); Louise Michele Newman, *White Women's Rights: The Racial Origins of Feminism in the United States* (New York: Oxford University Press, 1999).

Conclusion

1. *Congressional Globe,* 40th Cong., 3rd sess. 286 (January 11 1869) (hereafter cited as *CG*). Its language would be slightly altered through the amendment process so that the final Fifteenth Amendment would read: "The right of citizens to vote shall not be denied by the United States or by any State on account of race, color, or previous condition of servitude." U.S. Congress, *Statutes at Large,* 40th Congress, 3rd sess., no. 14, 346. On the politics behind and evolution of the Fifteenth Amendment see William Gillette, *The Right to Vote: Politics and the Passage of the Fifteenth Amendment* (Baltimore: Johns Hopkins University Press, 1965); and Xi Wang, *The Trial of Democracy: Black Suffrage and Northern Republicans, 1860–1910* (Athens: University of Georgia Press, 1997).

2. Although this proposed Fifteenth Amendment tacitly permitted states to disfranchise people on the basis of their sex, it did not specify the gender of the protected citizens.

3. *CG*, 40th Cong., 3rd sess. 561 (January 23, 1869).

4. Ibid., 1013 (February 8, 1869).

5. Ibid., 1001 app., 289–290 (February 8, 1869).

6. Ibid., app., 169 (February 6, 1869).

7. Ibid. Bayard's position is interesting given his family connections. Bayard's brother, Edward Bayard, was married to Tryphena Cady, Elizabeth Cady Stanton's sister. Egbert Cleave, *Cleave's Biographical Cyclopaedia of Homoeopathic Physicians and Surgeons* (Philadelphia: Galaxy, 1873), 51; "Biographical Directory of Congress, 1774–present," *United States Congress,* http://bioguide.congress.gov/scripts/biodisplay.pl?index=B000248.

8. *CG*, 40th Cong., 3rd sess. 1239 (February 15, 1869).

9. Bingham presented his version on January 29, 1869. It declared, "No state shall make or enforce any law which shall abridge or deny to any male citizen of the United States of sound mind and twenty-one years of age or upward the equal exercise, subject to such registration laws as the State may establish, of the elective

franchise at all elections in the State wherein he shall have actually resided for a period of one year preceding such election, except such of said citizens as shall engage in rebellion or insurrection, or who may have been, or shall be, duly convicted of treason or other infamous crime." Ibid., 728 (January 29, 1869). Bingham's amendment only received twenty-four votes. Senate: *Journal,* 40th Cong., 3rd sess. 235 (January 30, 1869).

10. Bingham's colleague Samuel Shellabarger, a moderate Republican from Ohio, proposed a similar amendment. His was likewise defeated 122–61. *CG,* 40th Cong., 3rd sess. 744 (January 30, 1869).

11. Ibid., 1317 (February 17, 1869). While the other amendments Conkling referred to were most likely those like the ones proposed by Bingham and Shellabarger, it is not inconceivable that he could have also been thinking of the Fourteenth Amendment.

12. Historian Glenda Gilmore argues that this is exactly what happened in North Carolina, as white men sought to redefine black men as rapists and therefore dangerous to white women if empowered with the franchise. Gilmore, *Gender and Jim Crow: Women and the Politics of White Supremacy in North Carolina, 1896–1920* (Chapel Hill: University of North Carolina Press, 1996).

13. Elizabeth Cady Stanton to Gerrit Smith, January 1, 1866, in Elizabeth Cady Stanton and Susan B. Anthony, *The Selected Papers of Elizabeth Cady Stanton and Susan B. Anthony,* vol. 1, *In the School of Anti-Slavery,* ed. Ann D. Gordon et al. (New Brunswick, NJ: Rutgers University Press, 1997), 569.

INDEX

abolitionists, 36, 51–52, 53, 109; debates about slavery in Constitution, 198n43; political manhood, 42; rejection of woman suffrage, 107–108; women as, 48; women's rights and, 35

activists. *See* African American activists; women's rights activists

"Address to the Free Colored Inhabitants of these United States," 40

"Address to the People of New York," 41

AERA. *See* American Equal Rights Association

African American activists, 8, 60, 72; in Kansas, 190n97, 221nn82–83; manhood arguments, 33–41, 49–54, 80–81; political conventions, 33–41, 49; protests against disfranchisement, 3, 7, 34–36, 38, 41; and women's rights movement, 35, 41–42, 51–54, 134, 150. *See also* specific activists

African American men: brotherhood, 71, 75; as feminized, 184n9, 207n96; gender identity, 101–103, 109, 145, 165–166; head-of-household status, 87–92; participatory citizenship, 85–87, 96–103; rights of manhood, 79–92; right to self-protection, 97–99; and sexual control over white women, 80, 88–92, 90–91, 153–154, 158–159, 226n12

African Americans: citizenship, 4–5, 49, 60, 85–87, 208n11 (see also *Dred Scott v. Sanford*); civil rights, 59–60; communities, 178n62; economic independence, 37–38; education, 37, 152; emancipation, 3–4, 35, 36, 60, 85–86, 190n95; families, 87–92; social "elevation" or "racial uplift," 36–42; temperance, 36–37. *See also* racism; slavery

African Americans' enfranchisement, 2, 12, 53–54, 131, 135–136, 197n34; dangerous voter arguments, 10–11, 23–25; disfranchisement, 11–12, 15, 20, 22–27, 32, 36, 125, 209n17; in District of Columbia, 60–61, 158, 198n39; Kansas

referendum, 147–151; military service arguments, 19–23, 34, 38–39, 49–50, 75–76, 99–101, 141–142, 155; opponents of, 23–26, 30, 63–71, 96–97; petitions for, 35, 60, 71–73, 75–77, 120, 124, 214n71; state constitutional convention debates over, 19–23; supporters of, 25–27, 70–71, 96–103, 133–134, 142; and taxation, 18–19, 23, 38–39, 138

African American women: activism by, 41–42; disfranchisement of, 213n47; marginalization of, 183n138, 205n37, 210n23, 224n136; in patriarchal family structures, 89; sexual exploitation of, 91

Allen, Richard, 36

Amar, Akhil Reed, 169n2

American Anti-Slavery Society, 35, 42, 53–54, 193n127

American Colonization Society (ACS), 35–36

American Equal Rights Association (AERA), 133–144, 146–149, 161, 217n26

American Revolution: African Americans, military service, 20–21, 38–39; democratic logic, 10; electoral population, 13; white men, military service, 69–70

Anthony, Susan B., 5–6, 136, 193nn127–128; and African American activism, 53–54; and congressional politics, 52; on Fourteenth Amendment, 133; Kansas woman suffrage campaign, 147–151; leadership in Loyal League, 51–52, 105; at meetings in New York, 216n4; meetings with Republicans and abolitionists, 107–108; partisan political strategies, 213n62; petitions, 104–106, 109–111, 119–125; racist suffrage arguments, 6–7, 135, 149–151, 156–157, 160–161, 165, 222n92; on republicanism rhetoric, 109; rhetorical attacks on manhood, 134–135, 140–142; support for abolition, 51–52; women's military service arguments, 140–141, 219n48

CPSIA information can be obtained
at www.ICGtesting.com
Printed in the USA
LVHW092052040321
680610LV00008B/432